BALL BUSTER?
TRUE CONFESSIONS OF A
MARXIST BUSINESSMAN
BERTELL OLLMAN

NEWSDAY— "DELIGHTFUL book ... quite often HILARIOUS, [Ollman's] madcap adventure humanizes the left. Here is a revolutionary tract that will make you smile."

NEW YORK VILLAGER— "a fun book ... sometimes horrifying ... sometimes HILARIOUS ... a mad merry-go-round that gets wilder and crazier as the story unfolds."

THE BUSINESS JOURNAL— "one of the FUNNIEST BOOKS OF THE YEAR ... Ollman has a fine wit, an eye for the ludicrous and a lovable ability to laugh at himself. Both the humor and the compelling narrative make the book difficult to put down."

MICHAEL PARENTI (author and lecturer)— "Ollman's book will have you laughing, groaning (in empathy) and thinking ... Here's the best kind of entertainment—it instructs while it DELIGHTS."

NATION— "[Ollman] has a GIFT FOR THE RIDICULOUS and has certainly written an amusing book ... There is even some discussion of humor and its place in radical politics"

BALTIMORE CITY PAPER— "one of the FUNNIEST documents to come out of the American left ... It is a great story, funny and sad and undeniably significant. HIGHEST MARX."

SAN FRANCISCO CHRONICLE— "the story related in Ollman's book is absurd, moving and thought provoking ... [also] fascinating ... and even a little FRIGHTENING."

FINANCIAL WORLD— "This MADCAP ADVENTURE ... owes more to the Marx Brothers than to Karl Marx ... and will be read with enjoyment even by those who find Ollman's perception of reality at odds with their own."

VERMONT VANGUARD PRESS— "Not laughing? You will when you read this book ... an exciting, HILARIOUS and instructive plunge into the world of business."

LOS ANGELES TIMES— "a candid and cautionary book ... Ollman comes across as likable, WITTY and undogmatic."

HOWARD SHERMAN (Professor of Economics, University of California, Riverside)— "I haven't laughed so hard in many years. Yet is was also so moving that I even cried in places. And all the while I felt I was really learning something about the painful paths of small business."

THE FLINT JOURNAL— "[it's] a giant leap for a Marxist to start up a small business. In this book. Bertell Ollman describes with clarity, grace and HUMOR his adventures in mid-air ... If he had been a novelist he couldn't have come up with a better sub-plot than his concurrent battle to save his chairmanship at the University of Maryland."

LIBRARY JOURNAL— "Λ ΙΙUMOROUS and intriguing account."

BOOKLIST— "The story brims with ironies ... A HUMOROUS, offbeat, cautionary tale."

BALTIMORE SUN— "Perhaps the most riotous business venture in recent history ... The ironies of mixing Marxism with Christianity are nothing compared to the ironies of mixing Marxism and capitalism ... *Ball Buster?* attains Biblical proportions."

NATIONAL GUARDIAN— "For the account of his adventures in trying to market his board game Class Struggle, the ORDER OF MARX, with Groucho, Harpo, and Chico ribbons goes to Bertell Ollman, Marxist professor and activist, who keeps trying to make the left laugh."

BALTIMORE
The Evening Sun
"What's This? A Marxist in Business?"

The New York Times
"NYU Prof., Marxist Game Inventor, Finds Art Imitates Life"

The New York Times
"College Post for Marxist Scholar Stirs Maryland Dispute"

LOUISVILLE
The Courier-Journal
"Class Struggle Deserves Highest Marx"

Publishers Weekly
"New Marxist Board Game Finds a Niche in Book Stores"

The Washington Post
"Marxist Scholar Becomes Issue in Md. Gubernatorial Race"

Star
"Prof. Planning Dangerous Monopoly Game with Our Kids"

L'EXPRESS (PARIS)
"The Star of the Frankfurt International Book Fair This Year Was Not a Book But a Game, Class Struggle"

THE CHRONICLE
of Higher Education
"AAUP Censures Univ. of Md. for Refusal to Appoint Marxist Dept. Chairman"

The New York Times
"A Marxist-Turned-Capitalist Finds Bottom Line Too Low"

The New York Times
"Marxist Movie Hero?"

The News American
Baltimore • Maryland
"A Marxist Prof.'s Class Struggles: Court Hears his $300,000 Suit, as Hollywood Plans Film on the Businessman"

THE CLASS STRUGGLE STORY IN HEADLINES: 1978-1982

BALL BUSTER?
TRUE CONFESSIONS OF A MARXIST BUSINESSMAN
BERTELL OLLMAN

SOFT SKULL PRESS
BROOKLYN, NEW YORK
2002

BALL BUSTER?
TRUE CONFESSIONS OF A MARXIST BUSINESSMAN
BERTELL OLLMAN
ISBN: 1-887128-92-1
Copyright © 1983, 2002 by Bertell Ollman

First Paperback Edition

Cover Design by Raoul Ollman

Soft Skull Press is distributed to the book trade by Publishers Group West, 1 800 788 3123, www.pgw.com. Visit www.softskull.com for more information about this and other Soft Skull titles.

SOFT SKULL PRESS
71 BOND STREET
BROOKLYN, NY 11217

To the 10 million small business people in America, to the 20 million who were in business and went bust,
and to the more than 50 million people who dream of one day owning their own businesses

—A CAUTIONARY TALE.

ACKNOWLEDGMENTS

For services to these *Confessions* over and beyond the call of duty and the hourly rate of wages—one red star, plus a freight reduction of 10 percent, are awarded to Marilyn LaPorte, Alan Orling, Sol Yurick, Bob Carroll, Emile de Antonio, John Toll, John Birnbaum, and Barry Schwartz.

Two red stars, plus a premium tie-in, a two-for-one advertising allowance, and a rebate on all group sales of more than $500, go to Ira Shor, Bill Livant, Nick Bakalar, Margaret Nell, and Marie and Michael Brown.

Three red stars, plus shipping and mailing costs and a profit-sharing plan (no returns), go to the brothers Polsky (Howard and Milton), Ed Nell, Isidore Silver, and Paul and Jo Ann Gullen.

Four red stars, plus a 21-gun salute and my undying devotion, go to Paule Ollman, who also takes the cake.

Whatever errors, distortions, and exaggerations have crept into this work are also their fault. They should have seen them (what did they think I was paying them for?).

—Bertell Ollman
President, Class Struggle, Inc.

Contents

Contents

INTRODUCTION:
CHAMBER OF COMMERCE SEES RED

"Sixty-five Liberty Street, please." Whether it fell out of a fortune cookie or came with the American dream, the address was an inspired act of naming. The cab took no more than 10 minutes to get from New York University, which is at the southern end of Greenwich Village, to Wall Street, but my inner journey from professor to corporation president about to attend his first meeting of the New York Chamber of Commerce had taken just over a year.

I held out my membership card just in case my best suit and tie did not cancel out a full growth of scraggly reddish beard and an academic haircut. Once past the guard, I ran up the white marble stairs, not wanting to keep the business community waiting.

In a large hall whose illuminated stained-glass ceiling reminded me of a Venetian palace, I found over 200 oversized faces looking down at me from the walls, but only a few living people. As I discovered later, the unsmiling portraits belong to past presidents of the Chamber, Alexander Hamilton and a couple of Rockefellers among them. Of the 18, perhaps 20, warm bodies present, all but two were men, and the average age was well over 50. The hall may have looked like an aristocratic palace, but it functioned as a capitalist mausoleum.

The chairman, a touch more distinguished than the rest—though it might have been the raised dais or the crossed American flags that separated us, or his black female stenographer (the only black in the room)—had just begun his annual report. Choosing one of the well-padded black leather chairs, I sat down and began to scribble: "The new logo for the Chamber ... ads to promote New York City ... succeeded in getting rid of unnecessary governmental regulations ... This year, 60 foreign banks have joined the Chamber as compared to only ten last year. We must be doing something right."

"Are there any questions?" the chairman asked. "If not, this year's meeting will come to a close." It was all happening a little too fast. Familiar with lengthy scholarly meetings, I found it hard to believe that a 20-minute report was all that happened at the annual meeting of the Chamber of Commerce.

Just as the gavel was about to come down, someone in the back of the room raised his hand. "Are there members of the board of directors of the Chamber present? I would like to ask them ..." It seemed to me that the fellow had asked a reasonable question, but the chairman thought otherwise. "No," he responded, "they are very busy people." Maybe he considered an audience of 20 too large and was trying to make sure that attendance at next year's meeting would be less.

My turn, my time, had come. The chairman recognized me, and I stood up, a little unsure about how to begin. As the only person in the room whose image did not come off the front cover of *Business Week*, some words of introduction were necessary. "Mr. Chairman, permit me to preface my question with a few introductory remarks. I am a new member of the Chamber. My name is Bertell Ollman, and for a little over a year I have been president of a game company. My 10 years as a Professor of Politics at New York University did little to prepare me for the rigors and frustrations of life as a businessman. How was I to know that banks only lend money to businesses that can prove they don't really need it? Finding suppliers who know how to keep a deadline, tracking down lost goods, the tax swamp—these are all problems I was ill prepared to solve." The smiles and nodding heads showed I had struck a responsive chord.

"Most troubling of all has been the endless search for customers. What began as a search for people who might be interested in our product soon became a way of viewing everybody. Friends, relatives, casual contacts could all be sold if only they were approached right. Smiling became something I did to sell games. I think I've become a good salesman, but people I know are beginning to avoid me. Bankruptcy is always around the corner. My work and worry go on seven days a week. I'd get an ulcer if I had the time for one." More nods, fewer smiles.

"Mr. Chairman," I continued, "I shall soon emerge from this

nightmare, scarred, somewhat dulled and brutalized, but what of the poor souls I leave behind? Though I have long known that a democratically planned society would mean a better life for workers, through my experience in business I have come to understand that we capitalists, as human beings, would also benefit from a rejection of the profit system." At this, my listeners began to shuffle uncomfortably. "So the question I would like to ask is this: What is the Chamber of Commerce doing to look into the possibility that what is commonly called 'socialism,' instead of being the enemy, may be the means to our common salvation?"

None of the gilt-framed portraits fell off the wall, but it did seem as if Alexander Hamilton lost some of his rosy glow, and John D. Rockefeller's notoriously thin lips disappeared altogether. The New York Chamber of Commerce had just heard its first socialist speech. Would the chairman pick up my gauntlet, and if he did, what impassioned script would he write with it? The lords of Gotham City waited for the wit and wisdom of their leader to put everything right.

"Thank you for your interesting suggestion ... (ahem), but the Chamber is wedded to the idea of private enterprise, which has given us the richest society in the world ... (pause) and the best health care [sic]. I don't think the Chamber views socialism as a solution to any problem."

The collection of saints along the wall may have been satisfied, but I couldn't resist coming back one more time. "As a member of the Chamber, I would like to pursue the matter. What can I do to promote such an inquiry?"

The answer this time came quick, and was meant to be final. "There is nothing." And polite. "Of course, you could seek out one of our committees, but they are all busy doing something else."

During our exchange, some members of the audience had become visibly agitated. Believing that the discussion required another kind of conclusion, one elderly gentleman could hold himself back no longer. "No, no," he insisted, "we don't need socialism. The Chamber of Commerce has better ways to solve

America's problems ... like giving money to the Boy Scouts. Just last night I went to a meeting of the Boy Scouts as representative of the Chamber. At the end of the meeting, everyone stood up and sang 'The Star-Spangled Banner.'" Then, pointing to me as if for emphasis, he added, "You would have been as proud as I was, young man, if you had heard how well those boys sang our national anthem." And he sat down, fixing me with a triumphant glare.

Having settled all important matters of the day and turned back the threatened barbarian invasion from Greenwich Village, the meeting was officially adjourned. I waited in my seat to see if anyone would come over. The last speaker averted his eyes. The chairman quickly descended from the dais and marched out of the room. It was then that two younger businessmen, including the man who had asked the first question, approached me.

"We liked what you said. They really needed to hear it." They held out their hands and introduced themselves. The taller, balding one went on: "That's democracy for you. How do these guys even know what the members want?"

Given a receptive listener, their anger began to build: "It's old money which dominates this organization. That and the banks ... Our interests are not the same as theirs ... All those guys on the wall intimidate me. I guess that's what they're up there for." Still, there might be something we could do, if we stood together, "No?" Within minutes, a caucus, the first socialist caucus in the New York Chamber of Commerce, was born.

"We'll give them a run for their money," they assured me. And I couldn't help adding, "Today, the Chamber of Commerce. Tomorrow, the world." What business are my new comrades in? They are partners in a small collection agency, "squeezing blood out of turnips." I run a company that produces one socialist game. The struggle to take over the New York Chamber of Commerce will not be an easy one.

One more contradiction (or is it absurdity?) in my life, but by this time such contradictions had ceased to bother me, or so I told anyone who asked. Having traveled so far down this twisted path, I was determined to explore the rest. Still, I could not keep from asking, once again, what am I doing here? How did a Marxist professor get lost in the jungle of capitalist business? Am I winning or losing, and by which set of rules? What are the chances that I will ever emerge alive, my socialist principles intact, my family and friends still talking to me? It was in order to find answers to these questions, to satisfy myself as much as anyone else, that I decided to set down my true confessions as a Marxist businessman.

"The American system of ours, call it Americanism, call it capitalism, call it what you like, gives each and every one of us a great opportunity if we only seize it with both hands and make the most of it."

—Al Capone (1929)

"All legislators suppose that an alteration to children's games really is just a 'game' ... They don't appreciate that if children introduce novelties into their games, they'll inevitably turn out to be quite different people from the previous generation; being different, they'll demand a different kind of life, and that will then make them want new institutions and laws ... In fact, it's no exaggeration to say that this fellow [the game inventor] is the biggest menace that can ever afflict a state."

—Plato, *The Laws*

FAUST

On first reading Goethe's Faust, my strongest reaction was that the good doctor had given away too much. His soul was too high a price to pay for youth. I was quite young at the time and didn't believe that anything was worth such a sacrifice. As an older and wiser man, I developed an obsession about breaking out of the ghetto in which capitalist justice has placed people with radical political ideas. We are usually tolerated, but segregated behind high walls of media indifference. How often have I wondered what it would be like to climb these walls, to reach out to "ordinary people" over breakfast from the pages of their daily newspaper, or to surprise them on their favorite talk show while they are driving to work, or to join in an evening's family pastime.

What wouldn't I give for a chance to help bring socialist ideas to the American people, to poke a few holes in the corporate Attica that imprisons our free and democratic future? Faust gave his soul for less. My opportunity came when I invented Class Struggle, the world's first Marxist board game. It was then that my own devil awoke and said he would help me get into every home in the land. He would help find investors, stir up favorable publicity in the press, and even make me a movie star (something I never believed), and in return he only wanted my soul.

"No ..." I said. "Yes," he answered. "I want you to make and sell this goddam game yourself. From cloistered professor, you'll become a Marxist businessman."

"What kind of animal is that?" I asked.

"You'll find out," he smiled.

ONE:
IN SEARCH OF CRITICAL GAMES

Sol Yurick writes radical novels, good ones, and loves to speculate on how culture gets inside people's bones. In the early 1970s, Sol and I spent a lot of time musing over Monopoly, a game many Leftists love to hate, others hate to love, and practically everybody plays. According to Shelly Berman, the comedian, "Monopoly evokes a unique emotion, the surge of thrill you get when you know you've wiped out a friend." But what else is going on as we accumulate property and scheme how to beggar our neighbors? Are we simply expressing some atavistic urge for power, or tuning in, consciously or unconsciously, to the attitudes that are most highly prized in our business-oriented society?

As in most games, people play Monopoly as individuals and take individual credit or blame for the result. Where skill counts, it is personal decisions that determine who wins. Where chance dominates, you win if you are lucky. Skill and luck are each considered personal qualities. In neither case can anyone else be blamed if you lose.

After playing a few games, one is ready to go into the marketplace and make a million. Except for a few minor difficulties: No one hands you $500 at the start, or rewards you for passing "Go." Properties are far more expensive than even Boardwalk, and everywhere you go you must pay. Surprise! All the properties have been given out before you arrived. There is a real monopoly game going on, but you haven't been invited to play. More than likely, you could not afford the stakes.

With over 80 million games sold since 1935, Monopoly was always cast as the leading villain in our cultural discussions, but Sol and I soon discovered that the scene contained much worse. At least Monopoly never openly extolled the negative human qualities that it fostered. On the contrary, part of its success lies in the aura of objectivity that surrounds it: "Just the facts, folks

1

... this is how it is ... no tears, but no hallelujahs either." ˙

Several more recent board games, on the other hand, positively exalt all that is vile. Their credos are clearly revealed in their names: Easy Money; Ratrace; Lie, Cheat, and Steal. Counterstrike, another of this genre, boasts on its cover that it "brings out the worst instincts in you, from avarice through downright treachery." What does it mean when Little Red Riding Hood's wolf no longer has to hide his fangs behind Grandma's shawl? Is it the board game, selling at a rate of over a billion dollars' worth per year, that has come of age, or capitalism?

Appalled by our findings, Sol and I began to seek out the opposition. Where were the critical, and especially the socialist, games? There just had to be games that use the inequalities of our society to criticize greed rather than to exacerbate it. We knew that capitalist culture would not take kindly to such games, but if they existed, we should be able to find them. I visited department stores, perused books and journals, put ads in game magazines, and queried friends from around the world.

Only half-realizing it, I had entered into a fairyland where fun is king and everybody his subject. I soon discovered that there is nothing new about the "message" board game, but that the pro-business propaganda which had seemed co-determinate with the board-game form is of relatively recent origin. Games of one kind or another have been around as long as people have. Some scholars have even defined man as the game-playing animal. Long before our species left the caves, we entered into contests that had agreed-upon rules and goals, lasted for a limited period, and produced pleasure rather than material goods. These contests were always accompanied by a conception of who one is, who one's opponents are, and what is important that diverged drastically from the conception of reality that ordered people's daily lives.

The board game, where markers take the place of people and a decorated board serves as the field of play, first made its appearance in ancient Sumer over 4,000 years ago. Excavations among the tombs of ancient Egypt and Palestine show that they, too, had board games. Dice, which were first used in magical ceremonies, became a staple of board games by Greek and Roman times. While facilitating gaming, the early association of dice with gambling led more virtuous members of the community to reject all pastimes in which dice were used. Once the Christian Era had begun, the story of Roman soldiers throwing dice to dispose of Jesus' newly crucified garments added the spice of sacrilege to their already unsavory reputation. The connection of gaming with gambling, magic, and un-Christian dissatisfaction with God's plan for mankind led to several attempts by both Church and State to ban games. To no avail. With a lot of time on their hands, the aristocracy in particular enjoyed playing games, the most popular of which were early versions of chess and checkers.

Starting in the sixteenth century with the Game of Goose (an Italian reworking of an ancient Greek idea) and picking up steam by the late eighteenth century, a host of new board games became available. In keeping with the pedagogical concerns of the period, many were unabashedly didactic. The Fortification Game (1712) expounded Vauban's then-revolutionary ideas on fortifying a city. A Journey Through Europe, or the Play of Geography (1759) speaks for itself. Other games taught history, math, and quite soon—though not immediately—moral behavior. Such was the New Game of Virtue Rewarded and Vice Punished (1818), marking the return of the old order after the decades of disruption caused by the French Revolution.

America's entry into the board-game derby came toward the middle of the nineteenth century with Mansions of Happiness. In this game, one tries to land on squares called "Justice and Piety," and to avoid others called "Cruelty," "Immodesty," and "Ingratitude." No doubt sticking to a subject that we Americans knew best, other similar games followed: the Checkered Game of Life and the Game of Christian Endeavor, where players get rewarded for such niceties as "Taking flowers to the sick" and "Stopping man from beating horse."

It wasn't until the Great Depression of the 1930s, and particularly with the appearance of Monopoly, that business values began to replace Christian virtues as the core message of the industry. At the moment, there are 15 to 20 successful business-oriented games on toy shelves throughout the country, and not a single well-known game extolling Christian virtues. The current craze in the industry is for fantasy (Dungeons and Dragons) and war games (Stalingrad, Battle of the Bulge, Waterloo). Though Monopoly-style games continue to sell, more and more games are aimed at redirecting people's frustrated power drives onto other, more imaginative, and less restrictive spaces.

Like other elements of culture, games are shaped by the same dominant values that they in turn help shape, and as such reflect what a society is and wants from its people, what it would have them believe and learn, and what it would help them to forget. Insofar as they teach anything, raise socially useful expectations, substitute a make-believe equality for real inequality, allow people to let off steam and to dream while keeping them amused and occupied, games—overall—serve the social order. Marx once referred to religion as the opium of the people, but this applies equally well today to games—as, indeed, to TV, mass spectator sports, pornography, and pot. America has blessed its citizens with many opiums.

Yet this is not the whole story, for games can also serve a critical purpose, introducing uncomfortable facts, unmasking social foibles, encouraging opposition, and even presenting alternative futures. This, too, emerges from their history. Games, like science fiction, often provide the cover for fundamental criticism and even revolt. Is it only a coincidence that in chess, the medieval game *par excellence*, a knight or a bishop can corner a king? Card games originating in the same period made the jack, again representing a knight, the highest trump card. Among the early board games, the Game of Good Children (eighteenth-century France) offers a mocking view of marriage and the family—marrying the first woman you meet leads to getting cuckolded—and Roarem Castle (nineteenth-century England) satirizes the lives of the still-powerful aristocracy.

In America today, I found but one game mildly critical of the status quo, but I did find that one. This was Anti-Monopoly (1973). In this game, true to the world in which we live, monopolies exist at the start, and—less true or possible, I'm afraid—players representing antitrust attorneys move around the board and break them up. It is a liberal game, focusing on the size of power concentrations rather than on the question of who holds power, and argues for the breakup of these concentrations rather than for a transfer of power from the few owners of property to the large majority who are now without.

Though I uncovered a few critical games, and some critical angles in traditional games, my search for a socialist game had proven futile. One respondent to an ad I placed in a game magazine said that he had invented a socialist game. Its name: Police State. Its purpose was to show ... well, need I say? I originally expected to find socialist games in the "socialist" countries, but I discovered that board games are not very popular there. The few board games in the Soviet Union deal with sports or getting to the moon before the Americans. In Hungary, there is a game in which players circle the board picking up furniture for their summer *dachas*. And Poland has a game called Director, in which players compete to make their factories rich. If there are socialist board games in these countries, I have still to hear of them.

Though there were no socialist games, I discovered quite late in my research one board game that came very close to what I was looking for. It was from Ralph Anspach, the inventor of Anti-Monopoly, that I learned that Monopoly itself had begun as a critique of the very system it has done so much to promote. The official history of Monopoly, recorded in endless *Reader's Digest*-like articles, holds that Charles Darrow, an unemployed Philadelphia worker, invented the game in 1933, and sold it to Parker Brothers, who in turn have sold Darrow's pro-business inspiration to the world. Anspach's research shows that the real inventor of Monopoly was Elizabeth Magie, a Quaker follower of the Single Tax economist Henry George. She invented the game in 1903 and called it the Landlord Game. Its squares carried such inspired names as "Lord Blueblood's Estate" and "The Soakum Lighting Co."

A 1925 version of her game, by now called Monopoly, which was made by Louis Thun, states in its Introduction, "Monopoly is designed to show the evil resulting from the institution of private property. At the start of the game, every player is provided with the same chance of success as every other player. The game ends with one person in possession of all the money. What accounts for the failure of the rest, and what one factor can be singled out to explain the obviously ill adjusted distribution of the community's wealth which this situation represents? Those who win will answer 'skill.' Those who lose will answer 'luck.' But maybe there will be some, and these, while admitting the element of skill and luck, will answer with Scott Nearing [a socialist writer of the time] 'private property.'"

Compare this with the Introduction to the rules in Monopoly sets that are now being sold: "The idea of the game is to buy and rent or sell property so profitably that one becomes the wealthiest player and eventually monopolist." Obviously, something has gone amiss. The lopsided accumulation of wealth, which Magie had denounced, has become the goal of the whole exercise. David has come out of the locker room looking like Goliath. What had begun as the only serious attempt to question the foundations of our social system has ended up as its most effective defender. Why?

Not long after I began my investigation into games, I developed the nagging doubt that maybe I really didn't know what I was looking for. What were socialist games, anyway? The frightening story of the metamorphosis of the Landlord's Game into Monopoly gave new urgency to this question. I had been content to think of socialist games as simply the opposite of Monopoly and other business-oriented games. They would not promote greed or present American society as a battleground where everyone had the same chance to win. But if everyone did not have the same chance to win, what kind of game could that be? I began to suspect that maybe there were no socialist games because there could be none. For a game to play well, all the players must begin with the same advantages and disadvantages. They must have an equal chance of winning. No one would want to play a game where the other fellow starts with all the chips and you start broke, where his connections (Daddy) and special knowledge of the rules (schooling) permit him to advance to the choice squares, where he has a half-dozen throws of the dice to your one, and where if he wins often enough, he gets to play with his own board dice. Not much of a game, but it happens to be life in our society. To make a game of life did not seem to hold many possibilities for gaming.

On the other hand, to make a fair game, to give each player the same chance of winning, meant the distortion of real life. The defection of Monopoly to the camp of the enemy was only partly the result of changing the labels and introductions. More fundamentally, it came from making everyone an equal participant from the start in the struggle to amass property. Whatever her game's progressive trimmings and her own intentions, Elizabeth Magie had invented a capitalist game, and it was only a matter of time and a little business razzle-dazzle (which in America always comes in time) before its internal dynamic asserted itself.

My conclusion left me with a head-splitting dilemma: For a game to meet the elementary requirements of gaming, it could not be socialist. If it were socialist, focusing on the inequalities in our society and showing what could be done about them, it could not be a game. Unless ... And it is with this "unless" that I struggled for a long time. I hated to accept such a bleak conclusion. A socialist game, I was convinced, could break through mountains, establish beachheads on the furthest shore. It could sing to people in a voice they would understand. And yet, if such a game didn't already exist, it must mean ... No, too negative. I would try. The discussions with Sol and others went on ... as if ... if only. And then, a huge breakthrough.

What if the players are not individuals, but classes? What if they represent classes? In *The Ragged Trousered Philanthropists*, my favorite socialist novel, Robert Tressell has his working-class hero adopt such a ploy in a charade he plays with his fellow workers in order to explain the labor theory of value. I had restaged this scene many times in my NYU classes. Would it work here, in the game? One could make capitalists and workers roughly equal in power, though of course the sources of their power are very different. The game could even explore these different sources of power, and when and how they are used. The game could deal with the class struggle. The game would *be* Class Struggle. The main pieces fell quickly into place. Until one morning I tumbled out of bed to be greeted by the world's first Marxist board game. Class Struggle, anyone?

TWO:
RETURN TO THE CITY IN MCCARTHY'S HEARSE: THE MAKING OF A MARXIST PROFESSOR

Why was I so disturbed by the lack of critical games, when most other people simply take it for granted? I was born and raised in Milwaukee, heartland, U.S.A., I played baseball for the American Legion, took inspiration from Memorial Day, earnestly desired that "we" (sic) annex Canada when I first learned about the War of 1812, and viewed Communists as agents of a foreign power. At 15, I entered a Quaker Oats contest on "What Makes America Great?," sure that I would win first prize. My answer was that it is the unique mixture of Europeans, Africans, Asians, Indians, Christians, and Jews, all cooperating together, that made America the great country it is today. (The judges, who must have been Commie simps, didn't even award me an honorable mention.) Where, then, did I "go wrong"? How does a kid who stood up straight as a board when he pledged allegiance to the flag grow up to become a Marxist professor and inventor of a socialist board game?

I can hear Cy and Mary Ollman, my parents, assure you that the fault is not theirs. Didn't they give me everything I wanted? What other mother would buy her 6-year-old two trayloads of foods on his first visit to a cafeteria ... because he wanted it? All their lives, they worked at thankless and repetitive jobs—my father in breweries and printing plants, my mother in clothing factories—worked and sweated, and saved every nickel for their only child, Bertell, so he could become—why not?—a doctor. "America ... what a wonderful country ... all you have to do is want to work." And want to work they did, 50 and 60 hours a week, ever since arriving in America before World War I, my mother as a teenager from Russia and my father as an 8-year-old from England.

They wanted to work so much that there was little time for schooling, either in the ways of the New World or in the Jewish faith of the Old. "Work earns money and respect." "Work makes

9

life sweet." This is the only catechism I ever learned at home.

Union newspapers came before every election and told my parents how to vote. Roosevelt and Hitler provided the two poles for measuring good and bad. Cy and Mary also envied the bosses their stately homes but hated them for being so stingy, and believed that whether one was rich or poor was all a matter of luck. Radical politics seems to have bypassed their lives altogether. My mother remembers seeing Communist agitators on the stump in the '30s. I say "seeing" rather than "hearing," because she was so appalled by their bearded, "dirt around the collar" appearance that she refused to listen.

Not a little fear enters into my parents' thinking on this subject. To this day, my father warns me, "America is the greatest country in the world. Stop criticizing it so much, or they'll lock you up." No, my loving, self-sacrificing parents are not at fault if I went wrong. They did their best. On the other hand, as I got older, I began to wonder—what had all their work brought them?

From my earlier years, too, I remember believing that things had to make sense, that problems have solutions, and that authorities of all sorts should be able to give reasons for what they do. And try as hard as I could, war, poverty and racism made no sense to me whatsoever. Teachers who treated me unfairly generally got a lecture for their trouble: "Miss Zinns, it isn't right to give me a zero for looking out the window ... on such a beautiful spring day." When my parents said over and again, "That's just the way it is," "You can't change the world," "It's all a matter of luck," this struck me as so obviously wrong that I frequently got angry. There had to be better answers. Without quite knowing what they were, the kind of questions I was asking ever more persistently were turning me into a rebel.

After a year and a half of college in Milwaukee, I came in the fall of 1954 to the University of Wisconsin in Madison, then as now, an oasis of cosmopolitan culture in the vast desert of the Middle West. My response to all this stimulation was to join every foreign-student organization on campus. I think I was the only person to be a member of both the Arab Student Association and the Israel Club.

When the Student League for Industrial Democracy, a small national alliance of liberals and social democrats, advertised an organizing meeting, I was the only one with enough interest to trudge through a heavy snow to attend. Waiting for me there was Gabriel Kolko, then an organizer for SLID and a graduate student in the UW history department. I'm afraid Gaby didn't have much of a choice. By a unanimous vote, I was elected president of the new SLID chapter at the University of Wisconsin. "SLID Slides" ran the headline in next morning's *Daily Cardinal*, but my serious education in socialist ideas had begun.

With all the world's problems to choose from, SLID decided to challenge the Communist youth group on campus, the Labor Youth League (LYL), to a series of public debates on Marxism. I was clearly in over my head, but with Kolko—already a considerable scholar who has since become one of America's leading revisionist historians—as my tutor, I was able to hold my own. Two years later, I debated the LYL again on the topic, "Marxism Has More Holes in It Than Swiss Cheese" (the title was my idea). Luckily, they knew even less about Marx than I did.

Not all of SLID's activities were directed at the mini-Communist menace. Operating in the mid-50s in Joe McCarthy's home state, we conducted a campaign against an attempt by the American Legion to set itself up as judge of what books should go into the university library and another against Senator McCarthy himself. When McCarthy died later that year, I went to Appleton, Wisconsin, for his funeral, intending to write something on it for a student magazine. In the confusion at the cemetery, I lost my ride back to town and put out my hitchhiking thumb just as the hearse was passing. The driver stopped and I got in, the first person to enter the hearse since McCarthy's body had left it. The symbolism was too much: to the soil goes the old, reactionary politician, and from the soil and into the City of Man (beaming from ear to ear) comes a young radical to stake his claim on the future. In my youthful enthusiasm, I felt sure that the trip back to Appleton in McCarthy's hearse was a sign, a promise, and a foreboding.

At the University of Wisconsin, my developing socialist ideas had a distinctly moralistic bent. Erich Fromm's *Sane Society*, with its emphasis on imagining more humane utopias, satisfied me completely. The appeal was to all men of good will. Though I became increasingly sensitive to social inequalities and knew something about the power of money to make hypocrites of those who have it, the idea of classes and class struggle remained foreign to my thinking, at least about the United States. Marxism was a doctrine I associated with the Soviet Union and its American defenders. Yet the scope and ambition of Marxism, its complexity and rhetorical power, and even the internecine squabbles of its adherents, began to exercise a strange fascination over me.

I stayed on at Wisconsin to do a master's degree and wrote my thesis on the history of hostile criticisms of Marxism from 1880 to 1930. This work left me something of an expert on anti-Marxism, but I still hadn't read much of what Marx himself wrote. I was left in the intellectually awkward position of knowing Marx was wrong—the critics had convinced me of that—but not being quite sure of what he had said, since interpretations of this differed. Clearly, something had to give.

It was at Oxford, where I arrived in 1957, that I took on the forbidding task of reading Marx's and Engels's own works, first in order to respond to embarrassing questions raised by my new British friends and later as part of the research for the doctor of philosophy degree. *Universities and Left Review* (now *New Left Review*), then as now Britain's leading socialist theoretical journal, had begun publishing the year before. The editors, all Oxford students or recent graduates of Oxford, started a study group on alienation theory, which I promptly joined. Possessing more confidence than good sense, I offered to read the first paper—the subject, Erich Fromm's theory of alienation. They tore it to shreds.

Never before or since have I been so harshly and minutely and correctly picked to pieces. "Noble socialist sentiments divorced from class analysis," they argued, "are so much hot air. Whether uplifting or not, they explain nothing and convince no one who is not already convinced. The place to begin any appeal for change is with an analysis of what is wrong and why, an analysis that focuses on the material conditions of life and how different classes of people, particularly workers and owners, both affect and are affected by these conditions. The thinker who supplies the framework for this analysis and shows us best how to carry it off is Karl Marx."

The teacher who most influenced my thinking while I was in England was Isaiah Berlin, who held the Chichele Chair of Political Theory at Oxford. Talking half again as fast as anyone else but introducing twice or three times as many insights from a dozen different fields, Isaiah Berlin has the justifiable reputation of being the most exciting teacher of his time. This disciple of John Stuart Mill's lectures on liberalism has made socialists by the score. For someone who says he is opposed to Marxism, Berlin was simply too rational, too critical, too honest, too intelligent, too skeptical, too full of a love for life that capitalism denies to the great majority, too respectful of Marx (presented as a wise and wily old fox) to do much more than whet our appetite for the forbidden fruit.

Berlin overwhelmed me and delighted me and frustrated me and stimulated me to do my best work, chiefly in opposition to his own ideas. I recall how after a conference with him I used to sit on the stairs outside his office writing furiously for up to an hour, taking down what he had said, responding to his provocations, capturing related insights that he had jolted and teased into consciousness, and trying once again to reformulate my position. Berlin not only invited such a reaction but helped build it, fuel it, point it in a half-dozen directions and even nudge it along with the warm respect he showed for all serious opposition.

I wrote my doctoral thesis on Marx's conception of human nature under Berlin's humanly supportive but academically demanding supervision. Here, at last, was a chance to make my peace with Marx ... and Berlin. The battle for my political soul was hard fought. Pulling in one direction were Berlin's probing questions and the enormous baggage of critical works I had digested while doing my M.A. thesis at Wisconsin. Tugging the other way was Marx himself, slowly, painstakingly putting together the complex tapestry that is capitalist society.

While it would be an exaggeration to say I had to be dragged, kicking and screaming each step of the way, into the Marxist camp, it is true that I came to every chapter in Marx with a half-dozen reasons, gleaned from the critics, for believing what he was about to say was wrong. Except he never quite said that. I finally concluded that the best-known criticisms of Marxism were simply off the point, that is off the point that Marx was trying to make and against which these criticisms were supposedly directed. What Marx *did* say began to make more and better sense out of my world than the partial and disconnected ways in which I had formerly understood it. About halfway through writing my thesis, I began to think of myself—still tentatively at first—as a Marxist.

It was while at Oxford that I met Paule, the lovely, sensuous warrior who has struggled at my side ever since, inspiring, tempering, prodding me to live up to the French Revolution reflected in her eyes. As uncompromising as Mount St. Helens in full explosion, Paule has no toleration for injustice of any kind, or for those who tolerate it. She is a part of this story because she is a part of me, of what her tenderness, natural dialectic, keen critical judgment, and commitment have helped me to become.

Paule had come to London from Paris to work as an *au pair* girl in a family while learning English. It took one short punting (boating) trip up the Cherwell—short because her pole stuck in the mud and she fell in the water—to know that we would get married. Like mine, Paule's parents were factory workers. The same overwork, insults, and insecurities had left similar marks on their offspring. We suffer at the same indignities; our anger and compassion flow along the same grooves, are directed toward the same people and events. The power of class to unite us despite all cultural differences has never ceased to amaze us. Paule has helped to soften and to steel me, to make me feel at home in an emotional world that I had known only as a tourist, and to give me the strength and the joy to do battle—if necessary, for a lifetime.

To recruit talent for their fledgling universities, England's ex-colonies often repair to the mother country, especially to Oxford and Cambridge. It must seem like the safe thing to do. With my thesis unfinished, I was in no hurry to return to the United States. There was a whole world still to explore, imperial dragons to slay, and some small contribution to make, alleviating ignorance if not hunger. So, in 1963, when I was offered a job to teach political theory at the University of the West Indies in Jamaica, I gladly accepted.

Jamaica's politics were more intense, more personal, closer to the edge of disaster than any I had known. The stakes were life or continuing despair, a gnawing, debilitating hopelessness that only visitors' eyes could avoid. My chance to help came when Michael Manley—then head of a trade union and later prime minister—asked me to join the Policy Planning Committee of the People's National Party (PNP), the major opposition party in Jamaica.

Over the next two years, I served on this committee, headed up the party's research bureau, and worked with radical factions in and out of the party to move its mildly socialist policies further left. In 1965, we actually got a conference majority committed to a program of public ownership that was more extensive than anything that then existed in Cuba, only to lose control of the party executive to a conservative faction that proceeded to scotch the whole program. So close. Few even in Jamaica know how close we came to giving the Western Hemisphere its first democratically elected radically socialist government. I might be in Jamaica today if the government hadn't finally prevailed upon the president of the university to dismiss me, only a few months after my three-year teaching contract had been renewed. The battle over renewing my contract had pitted the university administration against the teaching faculty, with the president of the university admitting to a confidant that the government wanted me out. Although I had not broken any law, I was more involved in opposition politics than the clique in power considered prudent or acceptable for a foreigner. Also, my frequent public criticisms of American aggression in Vietnam and the Dominican Republic must have embarrassed the regime in the eyes of its dominant northern neighbor and friend. Jamaican politics being what it is, I can't rule out either the widespread hostility provoked by my TV debate with a clergyman in the middle of a prolonged drought on whether it pays to pray for rain.

The opportunity to settle old scores against me finally came when I was ordered out of the only bookstore on campus by its owner (an uncle of the prime minister) while conducting an inquiry into overpricing. I was a member of the All-University Bookstore Committee, and a similar investigation two years earlier had resulted in substantially reduced prices. This time, after a comic-opera interlude of threat and counterthreat, the president simply dismissed me without either listing charges or giving me a chance to defend myself as called for in the university's own charter.

Faculty and students were equally incensed, but while the faculty debated and debated and finally produced a weak resolution criticizing the president, the students went on strike, the very first strike in the history of the West Indian student movement. As a group, West Indian students are exceptionally respectful of established authority, and no one—not I or anyone else—expected them to risk their academic careers on behalf of a white, American, Marxist professor. Their action, when it came, put a lump in my throat that I can still feel.

The student strike vote was 756 to 2, the minority proposing to "send Ollman back to China." The next morning, the students, colorfully dressed in their red graduation robes, marched to the Administration Building and locked the president in his office "until Ollman obtains justice." Like any frustrated administrator, his first reaction was to call the police, but they refused to come. The solicitor general of Jamaica, whose son was leading the strike, found an old regulation that no one had ever heard of that forbade police involvement until substantial damage had been done to property. Some smooth words of compromise eventually secured the president his liberty and me another three weeks on campus, during which our differences were all but committeed to death. With the students leaving campus for the summer, the president pressed his advantage and I was forced to leave the university and the country. My Jamaican love affair had come to an end.

From Jamaica, I went to Paris, where I spent a year finishing my thesis, and in the summer of 1967 I received a Doctor of Philosophy degree from Oxford University. That fall, after almost a decade of self-imposed exile, I returned to America with Paule and our young son, Raoul, and began teaching at New York University. On hearing my clipped accent, many people asked me what country I was from. But I was still the boy from Milwaukee, a little smoother (or was it rougher?) at the edges from all the travel, except that I was no longer a reformer but a confirmed or, as the media like to say, an "avowed" Marxist. I had become who I am today, which is to say someone who views capitalist society predominantly in terms of class struggle. And it is this outlook that informs all my teaching, writing, and political activities, from my involvement as a foot soldier in the antiwar movement to the content of the book that was born out of my thesis, *Alienation: Marx's Conception of Man in Capitalist Society.*

When *Alienation* appeared in 1971, most critics were enthusiastic. My department at NYU was sufficiently impressed to give me tenure. The public at large began to think of me as a scholar. But at home, in Milwaukee, my parents were embarrassed to show the book to relatives—because it has Karl Marx's picture on the cover!

THREE:
CLASS STRUGGLE IS THE NAME OF THE GAME

Class struggle is a more serious topic than death, which, for all its somber allusions, continues to serve as a rich mine of comedy. Nobody laughs at class struggle. Few mention its name, certainly not in polite company. For the most part, class struggle is disguised, denied, disemboweled. Worse than dangerous, it is in bad taste, and the very terms needed to think about it have been erased from the vocabulary. Hence, the shock at meeting it in a game. "A game called Class Struggle?"

Since biblical times, Western civilization has known the power of the word to break through logjams in the mind, to permit people to see the ordinary in extraordinary ways, to turn around notions of "right" and "wrong" and reorder thinking along a new axis. "Jahweh," the unpronounceable name of God, was one such word. In our era, "class struggle" is another. It is a question and an answer, an analysis, a threat and a vision, all wrapped into one. And even people who don't know what it means sense that this is so. Becoming aware of "class struggle" administers a jolt from which one's thinking never wholly recovers. The entire social map is rearranged, and one can never look at bosses or workers in quite the same way. No other idea in Marxism packs such a wallop. From the beginning, I never doubted that my socialist game would be called Class Struggle.

It was Plato, not Marx, who first said, "A city is always composed of at least two parts, which are at war with one another—the rich and the poor." In this war, the poor have numbers while the rich have money, money to buy instruments of force but also means to influence the thinking of the poor. For the longest time, this was the popular wisdom. Even today, people who study slave societies have no difficulty grasping the decisive role played by the division between slaves and slave owners. Feudalism, too, is generally interpreted along lines of the cleavage between serfs and feudal lords. In both cases, it is the conflict (actual and potential) between those who produce food, clothing, etc., and those who control the means by which production occurs that conditions major political and cultural developments in these societies.

Then, in capitalism, something happens, not to society, but to the ability and/or willingness of most people to view society in the above manner. Capitalism, too, has people—now called "workers"—who produce the goods we all use; and there is another, much smaller group who own and control the means, now chiefly machines, factories, and offices, that are used in the production of these goods. These are the capitalists. The clash of these two classes over jobs, wages, conditions of work, etc.—and the institutionalized power to decide on such matters (see Reagan's budget, for example)—is at the core of what is meant by "class struggle."

The main advantage of organizing thinking around the notion of "class struggle" is that it avoids the oversimplification of identifying history with its consequences (and victors), enabling us to grasp capitalism (and slavery and feudalism before it) as a society pregnant with different possible outcomes. In the case of the workers, "class struggle" also helps them link up what they are suffering from with who is responsible for it, what groups have an interest in change, and how these groups can be brought together. The capitalists' entire power and all their privileges depend on keeping the more numerous workers from making these connections, which is why the media and schools controlled by the wealthy have put a virtual embargo on the notion of "class struggle" and which accounts for the outlaw status of this idea in our culture.

Could I reproduce the main elements of this struggle in a game and at the same time create a game that would be fun to play? I refused to sacrifice either amusement or education for the other, but how to combine them? Marx said, one must "force the frozen circumstances to dance by singing to them their own melody." Yes, this is what I wanted to do. I wanted to make capitalism dance by teaching people its secret melody, the class struggle.

Singing and dancing are fun. For capitalism, they would now become dangerous.

I began by listing the main strengths and weaknesses of each class on board squares drawn up for this purpose, so that the Workers, for example, improve their positions when trade unions or a Workers' political party are formed and lose strength when their unions are taken over by bureaucrats or when there is an increase of unemployment. The Capitalists, on the other hand, benefit from the spread of the market overseas and their control over Congress and the courts, but suffer setbacks from such events as a stock-market crash and the Watergate scandal. A currency made up of "Assets" and "Debits," representing strengths and weaknesses, made it possible to weight each square in function of its importance in the overall class struggle. In the game, players throw the dice and move around the board gathering their forces for periodic confrontations labeled "Election," "General Strike," and "Revolution."

To deal with the problem of strategy, I hit on the idea of class alliances. Players could enter into alliances with one another and these alliances would help determine the outcome of the different confrontations. But what classes other than Workers and Capitalists should I include? What should their relationship be to the two major classes whose struggle clearly predominates in our society? Why should any class want to join an alliance? And, above all, how complex could I afford to be—what was the age group for which I was preparing this game?

•••

The search for answers to these and related questions began in 1971, very much as a part-time activity. Friends, to whom I mentioned what I was doing, found the idea amusing, but didn't take it very seriously. "Nice if it could work, but ..." And I doubt if anyone thought that I would ever finish. As the years turned over, even Paule and Raoul began to think of my hobby as something extra to be carted around during vacations and as sure evidence of my growing eccentricity. Yet the elements of a socialist game were slowly coming together like the pieces of a giant puzzle whose picture I was also painting and constantly retouching. In May 1975, Class Struggle was ready to be tested.

I worked hard all day finishing enough Chance Cards. The bulky cardboard playing surface was lined and ready. Monopoly money and player pieces and an ordinary pair of dice filled out the essentials. I had kept Sol informed of my progress, and tonight Class Struggle would be played for the first time at his home. The players were Sol, Adriane (his wife), Suzanna (their 10-year-old daughter), Paule, and I. Sol and Adriane were surprised that I had carried our old discussions to such "ridiculous extremes." But I had, and nothing remained now but to try it.

We threw dice to see who would play which class. Rather than allowing players to choose a class, I decided to leave this up to chance, since this is the way it happens in the real world, where one's class is largely determined by the family into which one is born. "But blacks and women have less chance to become capitalists. Is there some way to work this into the game?" Sol asked. Yes, the point could be made by having blacks and women throw the dice last when it comes to deciding who plays the Capitalists. "And if both are present?" Then let the players themselves decide which of these groups is less likely to spawn capitalists.

Sol became the Capitalists and Suzanna the Workers. Adriane, Paule, and I were left with the Farmers, Professionals and Small Businessmen. (I later added Students—who do not actually constitute a class—as a sixth class, another compromise with the requirements of gaming.) Through a series of adroit moves, Sol gathered most of the minor classes as allies, carefully avoided the nuclear-war square that would have blown us all to kingdom come, and stood poised on the edge of a smashing victory.

"We Farmers are paying too high a price for fertilizer," insisted Adriane as she pondered whether to switch alliances from the Workers to the Small Businessmen.

"Don't blame us," responded Paule, who was representing the Small Businessmen. "It's the Workers with their demands for higher wages who are at fault."

"What?" screamed Suzanna. "Unfair." She was even more incensed by the actions of the Capitalists. "Why didn't you put better safety equipment in the mines? And, Daddy, stop trying to smash my unions."

Sol tried to explain that he was very sad that workers died in mine accidents, but it was their responsibility to be more careful. He, too, was only doing his job. Given how our society works, this is what capitalists have to do in order to succeed. "Or else I'd lose all my money and be forced to become a Worker."

The amount of role-playing in the game exceeded anything I had expected. As I've since learned, neither Landlords (Monopoly) nor Wizards (Dungeons and Dragons) nor Heads of State (Diplomacy) provide such meaty parts for ham actors as do the Capitalists and the Workers in Class Struggle. The politics that evening at Sol's were light, funny, and apparently effective.

"The Workers want revenge," hollered Suzanna, bringing her little fist down on the Revolution square that had just been secured by the forces of Capitalist reaction.

"Yes, the struggle goes on," agreed Adriane, "but so does bedtime."

"Revolution now," insisted Suzanna, as her proud father and I exchanged subversive looks. What had I done?

"Good night, Suzanna. Power to the people," I called out.

"Night. Power to the children," came the reply. And had I really done it?

FOUR:
FROM CLASS STRUGGLE TO CLASS
STRUGGLE, INC.

If I had written another socialist book, I would have had no trouble getting it published. There are plenty of radical and even commercial publishers who seek out good socialist books. They sell. Most bookstores, as distinct from newsstands and supermarkets, carry at least some socialist works. But when was the last time you saw even a slightly controversial game in a department store? I was vaguely conscious of all this, but believed—no doubt with all other inventors—that if my creation was good enough, somebody would produce it. Class Struggle was unique. Its mere mention raised eyebrows, lowered jaws, and evoked the embarrassed awe that people show before a naughty trick. Informing the world that it existed would be enough to cause a run on the game. Or so went my thoughts at the time.

Didn't Art Rosenbloom's father own a toy company? I wondered if they would be interested. Art, who is an investment banker, was terribly amused, as he always is whenever I call him, which is about once every five years. His dad makes dolls and war toys, but no board games. But even if he did, Art assured me, he wouldn't touch a game called Class Struggle. It was from Art that I first heard of the mythical game-store owner in Iowa whose conservative tastes and prejudices set the standard for the whole industry. One complaint from his mostly middle-class customers is enough to set him reeling. He would be so angry at the company that produced my game that he would boycott their other products. The games industry, Art assured me, has little resemblance to publishing, where controversy is appreciated because it sells. It's more like TV, where everything is cut to fit the mind and tastes of the average 12-year-old. The accent is on fun, funny, and innocuous. The so-called adult games differ only in their greater complexity and, occasionally, smuttiness.

I don't think I expected to hear anything different from one of my more cynical friends, but the degree of certainty with which Art squelched my hopes forced me to reconsider. Had I been put-putting around the house these six or seven years only to end up with an anecdote that could not be told? A game that no one plays is like a voice that no one hears. Does it even exist? There were, of course, other companies to see, but now I was worried.

There are about 900 companies that make toys in the U.S., but four giants—Parker Brothers, Milton Bradley, Mattel, and Fisher-Price—account for over half of the $6 billion dollars' worth of sales in the industry. About 20 percent of this figure comes from board games. But only 60 firms produce the 2,500 to 3,000 board games that are on the market. "Marx Toys" sounded like it might be just right for Class Struggle, but Louis Marx, whose half-century in the business had earned him the title "King of Toys," was a close friend of Nixon's, and produced no board games. So, starting at the top, I wrote to both Parker Brothers and Milton Bradley, giving a brief description of Class Struggle and asking if they wished to see the game.

Art cautioned me to trademark and copyright my game before I showed it to anyone, "just in case." Several hundred new board games appear every year, but the number of new game ideas is very few. The fun industry is notorious for helping itself to other people's ideas. Here was one of the mysteries of capitalism I still could not fathom. Apparently, I had something that no one would buy but everyone might be tempted to steal.

Did I feel odd in taking out a copyright on the game? Many nonsocialists believe that socialists, who oppose the whole idea of private property, shouldn't own any. Something, I suspect, about consistency and hairshirts. But operating in a capitalist society, socialists have to play by the same rules as everyone else, even as we go about trying to convince people that these rules should be changed. Of course, I would prefer a system where new discoveries and inventions belong to everyone, but setting a good example is not a strategy that works. Two thousand years of Christianity should have taught us that. Taking out a trademark on Class Struggle, on the other hand, almost blew a fuse in my socialist head. Some things just don't mix very well, and here I was merrily mixing away. Now I was about to corner the market on a phrase that had become almost synonymous with Marxism.

The next move was up to Mssrs Parker and Bradley. What would I do if *both* wanted the game? I foresaw a bidding war ... the bids go higher and higher ... Parker offers me shares in the company ... Bradley promises to produce a whole line of socialist games ... Parker says if I sign with them, they'll stop selling games to South Africa ...! POP! Who was I kidding? I recognized Art was probably right. Maybe a small struggling company would take it ... Maybe I'd have to produce it myself. This last thought came slowly, painfully to the surface: Business. The idea wasn't completely new, but I had never looked it, really looked it, in the eye.

Whatever route I took, I now needed a full-scale mockup of the game. When I mentioned this to my friends Michael and Marie Brown, they said in one voice that their karate teacher could do the job. "Your what?" I must have said, though living so long in Greenwich Village, I was used to people combining a weird assortment of talents. As it turned out, Linda Lutes, their karate teacher, is also a professional designer of dresses, ads, and signs. While visiting her in her Soho loft, I also learned that she does a nightclub act for which she lies on a bed of nails while her equally talented husband chops wood (blindfolded) on her stomach! Her design work made it clear that she could do the game, but we agreed that Marie Brown, who is an imaginative painter, would do the drawings for the player pieces, the money, and a half-dozen key squares on the board.

It was a good decision. Marie's visual for the Revolution, which appears on the final square of the board, was particularly inspired: a closed fist pointing toward a rising sun. The problem here was as much political as aesthetic. Most Americans think of revolution as a necessarily violent uprising with a lot of killing and destruction. But, as the etymology of the term suggests, a "revolution" is a full turn of the wheel, or—in politics—the replacement of one social order by another. This transformation can be accomplished in various ways, including—where it is available—through the democratic process. The form of any American revolution will depend less on the workers and their allies than on the means the capitalists use to defend their privileges at that moment when the long-suffering majority have decided they have had enough. On the other side of the struggle is a new, more egalitarian society. Marie's drawing captures equally well the flexibility of means and optimism of ends that characterize any true understanding of socialist revolution.

Far more than books, games often succeed or fail as a result of their packaging; especially important is the image on the cover. It is what sticks in people's minds. For most, how they react to it carries over to how they think about the game. From the first, I thought that Marx arm-wrestling with Nelson Rockefeller offered the perfect image of what Class Struggle is all about. When real enemies are presented playing, is it play or is it for real? Like calling class struggle a game, it explodes existing distinctions, scattering shock, outrage, laughter, and puzzlement in all directions. Thrown off-balance, people have difficulty responding in standard ways.

I spent months scanning magazines for photos of Rocky, and even made a pilgrimage to the state GOP headquarters, where my enthusiasm for "our governor" added a poster to my collection. I finally settled on a well-known heroic pose for Marx and a nicely ambiguous one for Rocky, where it isn't clear if he is smiling or cringing in pain. Each viewer's unconscious is left to fill in the rest.

Next, I had to find the right bodies to go along with these heads. I thought it too immodest to play Marx, but I couldn't resist the temptation to play Rocky. The chunkiness, at least, was right. When the day for taking the photo arrived, I slipped into my good suit, pinned a couple of $20 bills so that they seemed to be popping out of my vest pocket, and put on three watches and all the fake rings Raoul had saved over the years, no doubt for just such an occasion. My friend Ira Shor, whose taut muscles suggested unyielding strength, was drafted to complete the picture. Ira, who has written the classic work on socialist pedagogy, has since acquired a kinky notoriety in New York radical circles as the trusty left arm of Karl Marx.

Once I started working on a mockup of the game, I knew that somehow or other Class Struggle would get produced. If "somehow" did not come through, then "other" would, had to. The Milton Bradley Company finally responded to my letter, saying that they did not even look at games coming from independent inventors. I soon received similar replies from Parker Brothers, Ideal Toys, and two other game companies I approached. It seemed that the big companies employed their own inventors and didn't consider it prudent to examine all the bad games that people wanted to send them. Not knowing other game inventors, I was shocked to learn that thousands of games were invented every year and that the major companies had been forced to protect themselves against being inundated with our shoddy products. Refusing to look at any game submitted by an outsider saved them both valuable time and possible involvement in a lawsuit later on. In an industry noted for theft, every potential thief has to be concerned about his reputation.

With the game-company route blocked off, at least temporarily, I swallowed hard and began the search for investors in all seriousness. If there is a business bug, I never caught it. If there is a business suit and face, I never wore them. If there is a typical businessman—and there are a lot—I never liked him. Now it was my turn. Annoyed and a touch disgusted at the thought of starting a business, I was also convinced there was no alternative. It helped me to recall that Engels, too, was a businessman. The $10,000 to $15,000 that would be necessary to produce and market the game, I felt, would be easy to find. I didn't know at this time about the innumerable game inventors who have taken this route and gone bust. But I had read about the extraordinary success of Anti-Monopoly, of how Ralph Anspach had turned a $5,000 initial investment into sales of $250,000 games in less than three years. (This was before Parker Brothers sued him for infringing on their Monopoly trademark, and sent him into near-bankruptcy.) Could a game called Class Struggle do any worse?

My previous contact with the world of business had been

limited and rather bleak. As a kid, I shined shoes in bars and dispensed lemonade on street corners; in high school, I worked in a shoe store, and graduated while in college to selling encyclopedias, lemon juice, and typewriters (all to unwilling buyers). Dollar for hour, I probably did best shining shoes, where a drunk customer once told me, "Kid, you've got a great future as a salesman." Now I would find out whether he knew what he was talking about.

When Faust made his pact with Mephistopheles, he was sure he would find some way to get out of performing his part of the bargain. I was no less sanguine in accepting to become a capitalist to further my socialist goals. There was no chance that I would really lose myself in my new capitalist role, for, as a Marxist, I knew all about the effect of function on character. No, I might have to go along with what the part required, but I could extract myself from it at any moment. Knowledge would protect me. My pact with the devil was made with my fingers crossed behind my back. The advantage was to be all one-sided—or so I thought.

Years earlier, I had raised the possibility of investing in the game with a few friends who had some spare dollars: "a way to raise consciousness and make money, or at least not lose any—a have-your-cake-and-eat-it-too proposition if ever there was one." I wasn't asking for a political donation, nor was I selling silver futures. Most of those I talked to were interested but noncommittal. Howard Polsky, a former All-City basketball center for North Division High School in Milwaukee and currently a professor at Columbia University's School of Social Work, was immediately taken by the idea, by both halves of it. Watching Howard's huge frame take to the boards, spin, and pump in two was one of the treats of my early adolescence. More recently, he had accumulated a modest savings by consulting with various corporations on how to keep their managers' emotional problems from interfering with their search for profits. As a former student radical, Howard felt the need to do something more for our society than apply balm to disturbed managerial souls. So if the game could really raise consciousness *and* sell, then why not?

But first he wanted to see the finished game.

When I completed the game, Howard was one of the first to see it. He loved it, and agreed to invest a few thousand dollars if I chose to produce it myself and if I could get the rest from other people. After the disappointing reception from the game companies, I called up Howard and told him we were in business. Working from what we knew of book publishing, we settled on 5,000 games as the figure to aim at. It seemed that to produce, market, and publicize this many games would require an investment of $15,000 to $20,000. From there, we would see.

Howard began to take a closer interest in the final form of the game and arranged a testing session with a half-dozen social workers whom he had trained. Fresh from paying rents for welfare mothers and buying shoes for their kids, they used Class Struggle to vent a lot of their hostility to the capitalist system. The game, they said, was too true not to be painful as well as fun. "But do you guys really expect stores to sell it?"

The mockup of the game was finally ready, at a cost of about $500, roughly double what I had anticipated. It was a bad omen for my new career as a businessman, but I was too excited by the material result to take much notice. My dream had become a colorful, tangible, playable reality. I couldn't resist taking it to my office at NYU, and—with all the casualness I could muster— showing it to my fellow professors and other co-workers. My reputation as a socialist in a capitalist world had prepared them for occasional surprises, but a board game called Class Struggle? Marx wrestling with Rockefeller? The delight was general. "So this is what professors do after they get tenure?" "No, only Marxist professors," I remember responding. "The others invent games like Ratrace and Easy Money."

The time had come to call an investors' meeting to find out who, besides Howard, was willing to risk some money on the game. About a dozen people turned up at my apartment that Sunday morning. After a brunch of lox and bagels, we played the game and I answered questions on the rules. Then, rising to the occasion, I delivered a "White Paper" full of impressive estimates on costs, sales margins, and profits. The game would cost,

I said, about $3 to produce, $3 to market, and would earn us a profit of $3 if we sold each unit for $9. It all seemed so nicely balanced.

How little I knew at the time can be seen from the fact that stores in the toy trade receive a 50 percent discount, not 33 percent as I projected, and that I didn't even mention the expense of running an office, an expense that practically broke us later on. Of course, I expected most of our business to be mail order, where the profit margin is much higher, but here, too, I guessed wrong. Nor did I know then how our finances would be affected by the lengthy time lag between selling goods and getting paid for them. Were we more naïve than other small businesspeople who are just starting out? I don't think so. Unfortunately, neither were we less naïve. Though the room was full of Ph.D.'s, knowledge of the game industry, as well as business acumen in general, was in woefully short supply. My talk was well received.

The meeting resulted in a few more people deciding to invest. Milton Polsky, Howard's kid brother, has been my playmate since we attended kindergarten together in Milwaukee. Unlike my parents, Milton's father was a small businessman, a jobber, and I recall how he used to force Milton to spend his evenings, and sometimes weekends, sorting belts and ties. Now a professor in the Theater Department at Hunter College, Milton has a keen interest in games and has even invented one to help teach creative drama to children. Overflowing as always with wisecracking good cheer and optimism, he agreed to invest $1,000. Ed Nell, a close comrade from my Oxford days, and now a professor of economics at the New School for Social Research, said he was in for $3,000. Ed laughs harder and thinks deeper than almost anyone else I know. There would be plenty of need for both qualities in the months to come. Several other people seemed to lean toward saying yes, but as it turned out, none did. A couple of weeks later, Jackie Simone, a sometimes professor of political science and writer on French affairs, added $2,000 more to our coffers. Howard and I had hoped that more people would invest, but the clock was running and Howard agreed to put up whatever more was needed to start us on our way.

Our form of organization was to be a corporation. The name? Class Struggle, Inc., of course. All of the above except Jackie, who preferred not to get involved, became members of the board of directors. We were joined by Paule, who was elected secretary-treasurer, and Isidore Silver, a longtime friend, lawyer, and professor of history at John Jay College, who became corporate counsel. It seems that Izzy, who secretly yearns to be a great comic writer like his friend Lenny Bruce, has been defending me against one kind of attack or another since our salad days as student radicals at the University of Wisconsin. In his new position, Izzy would get a lot more work than he bargained for.

The economics of our operation were simple: I received 51 percent of the corporation's shares for the work I had done in inventing the game and for what was going to be required of me to promote it. Izzy got one percent for his continuing legal work, and Milton, Jackie, Ed, and Howard got one percent, two percent, three percent and 15 percent respectively for the money they invested. Other shares would be sold as we needed money, with present investors getting a first crack at buying them—just in case the game took off. Everyone who invested agreed to give most of their profits above a certain amount to a Class Struggle Foundation that we would set up to channel money to worthy radical causes. And I began to daydream about all the good works one could do with a million socialist dollars.

Odysseus had just finished the Trojan War when his employers, the gods, sent him on a 20-year journey throughout the known world. Had he taken enough samples with him, his sales performance would have gone off the charts. As it is, he had to settle for doing market surveys and giving future salesmen a foretaste of what was in store for them.

Faust is for beginnings. He starts the motor running, but can't steer worth a damn. Odysseus had a lot of practice steering. The world of business is full of Lotus Eaters, Cyclopes, Sirens, and enchantresses with binding spells and poor credit ratings. Progress in this world is a matter of not losing one's way or courage, risking neither too much nor too late, and tempting and tricking all who bar the way. Odysseus had spunk, chutzpah,

ODYSSEUS

luck, friends in high places, and a good product line. He knew when to help his business associates and when to ditch them. Tossed hither and thither by the market into one scrape after another, he got out with his skin and made it home in the end. A model successful businessman.

Are these the footsteps of the nobleman from Ithaca? The world of business with all its monsters and siren songs held no dangers for the intrepid Odysseus, only adventures. So it would be for me. The stakes were high, but the economic winds were gentle, and a reading of the entrails propitious.

"To the boats," I yelled. "To the boats!"

FIVE:
INTO THE ENTRAILS OF THE TOY BUILDING, OR HOW DOES ONE PRODUCE A GAME?

At six feet six inches, Howard was the tallest person there. And with mustache and beard, I guess I was the hairiest. Our wrinkled grays and browns were also out of place among the checkered polyester pants and buff briefcases that surrounded us on all sides. This was the Toy Building, a 15-story Mego-block structure on Twenty-fourth Street and Fifth Avenue in the heart of Manhattan, where America's fun moguls decide what will be put under next year's Christmas trees. "How's business?" The president and chief financial backer of Class Struggle, Inc., had come to pay their respects ... and to find out how to produce our game.

We wandered through the halls looking at display rooms filled with stuffed pandas, electric yo-yos, lead soldiers, rubber badges, magic wood/glue/gum/guk, and the occasional game: Beat/Attack/Destroy ... The proportion of plain tacky to expensive trivia was about two to one. It was a supermarket full of striped dreams and polka-dot promises. Something for every taste and tastelessness. "How's business?" No toy was less exciting than "dazzling" or less wonderful than "super." As a kid, I would have liked nothing better than to be let loose in such a playhouse. As an adult, I couldn't help noticing the big price tags and bored expressions on everyone who worked here. My colleagues all! I am now a part of the industry, I thought, feeling strangely excited and wanting to greet "Harold" and "Jake" (names I overheard on the elevator) with a hearty "hello" and a slap on the back. "So, how is business?"

With Class Struggle, Inc., all but launched, I found myself getting an indecent amount of pleasure from "fulfilling my socialist duty." No denying it. Starting a small business is setting out on an adventure. There are exotic places to visit and important decisions to make. I could understand why many people whose whole lives consist of being told what to do are so attracted by a chance to become their own boss. Maybe becoming a businessperson is not like taking castor oil, after all. Or maybe I was just pleased to be doing something at long last of which my parents approved: "Nowadays," they told me, "everybody needs a second job."

"Can I help you gentlemen?" asked a practiced voice.

"No, we're just looking."

"Sorry. We're not open to the general public. Just to store buyers."

"Well, we're not quite general public either," I replied, a little uncertain of my footing. "You see, we have a game and we're looking for someone to manufacture it. Do you happen to know of a company that makes board games?"

He did. But they didn't. They, however, knew of Juvenile Packaging, a company in Brooklyn that does make board games. Howard and I also visited several game stores, seeking advice form their owners. Games Gallery on Fifty-Seventh Street and Eighth Avenue is New York's premier game store, with wall-to-wall, floor-to-ceiling games, just games, every possible variety of games. Its whiz-kid owner, John Stevenson, made us our first offer to produce Class Struggle. Not himself, of course—he sold finished games. But he knew the industry and had connections. The idea of a game called Class Struggle struck him as more ridiculous than funny, and not the least threatening if it helped him turn a buck.

"Look, this is like a vanity press," Stevenson said. "You want your creation produced, you pay the man and take your chances." The comparison with a vanity press, where people pay to publish their books just to see their names in print, didn't help our confidence any. Financially, it's a nonstarter.

"But do you think a game called Class Struggle will sell?" Howard couldn't help asking. "Stranger things have happened," was the honest reply. For a 10 percent commission off the top, which sounded quite reasonable, and one third of all profits (just in case it took off), which sounded unreasonable, Stevenson said he would take the whole thing off our hands, and sell the game in his store.

Leads also turned up in back issues of industry magazines. We called them, and they in turn gave us the names of several companies that we called or visited. I even phoned Ralph Anspach, whose success with Anti-Monopoly had so impressed me. Ralph told me that Anti-Monopoly was produced by a small firm in Minneapolis. No, the owner was politically very conservative and would not be interested in any game called Class Struggle. Ralph asked me if I knew how many new board games fail every year. I didn't, but said yes, believing that my game was so different that such statistics would not be relevant—why get frightened for no reason? If I knew all that and still wanted to go ahead, Ralph said, well, then, good luck. (I have since learned that at least 95 percent—some estimate 98 percent—of the 300 to 400 new board games produced each year fail.)

Within a couple of weeks, we came up with five full bids, three from companies that manufacture games and two from middlemen, like Stevenson, who would "prepare a package" and take their cut. What greatly amused us was that everyone warned us to be careful in dealing with others in the industry: "People steal, don't pay, break promises, etc." The implication always was, "I am a person you can trust." The bids ranged from $2.49 to $4.50 per unit for the production of 5,000 games.

In choosing a producer, we tried to be guided by three criteria: quality, price, and a union shop. None of the companies that bid on the game had a union shop, and they all assured us we wouldn't find one that could do the job. Quality was something everybody promised, but until we saw the finished product, there was no way of knowing. That left price, and with bids varying as much as they did, price became the decisive factor.

The lowest bid came from Sam Gouldner of Juvenile Packaging. He would do all the components of the game except the dice and rule booklets for $1.95. *The Guardian* newspaper, which is unionized, agreed to print the two rule booklets for 23 cents and Athol Industries, like Juvenile Packaging not unionized, would make the dice for 30 cents—for a total cost of $2.48 per game.

There were also some major one-time expenses. The mechanicals, negatives, printing plates, setups, and cutting dies—I didn't know what they meant either—would cost about $3,500. This in hand, we could make as many games as we wanted. An injection mold to make plastic markers for the different classes turned out to cost $10,000, so we decided to go with pieces of colored cardboard attached to little wooden blocks. "We'll get a mold when we do an edition of 100,000," I jested.

Gouldner smiled. He had a full, welcoming smile, just like that of Arthur Godfrey, whom he strikingly resembled. Dressed in a spiffy light gray suit, gold tie clip and brilliantine-shined shoes, Gouldner ruled over what looked like a functioning junk pile in the middle of the grimiest industrial section of Brooklyn. Juvenile Packaging produced several toy items, boxes for clocks, and now ideological weapons for the revolution.

Gouldner had been a member of the Young People's Socialist League in his youth. After becoming a businessman, his politics drifted rightward. "It's something that happens to the best of us," he said in a baritone voice so low that it seemed to require instrumental accompaniment.

"We don't expect to stay in business that long," I protested. "In for a quick million, and out before the virus takes hold."

"It doesn't take that long," and this time he laughed. As a former socialist, Gouldner readily admitted the social inequalities described in the game. His sense of fun was also tickled by the humor. But as a businessman ... well, it was our money. No, he wasn't interested in buying shares in our corporation. "You fellows are going to have quite a job getting stores to carry a game called Class Struggle. They also don't like to buy games from a one-game company."

"We professors have a secret plan," I assured him.

"It's called 'faith,'" Howard added, grimacing in pain at his own insight.

We liked Gouldner, and trusted him. I admit to feeling a little uncomfortable when he wouldn't sign the contract that Izzy drew up, which simply stated the terms we had already agreed upon. "What if a key machine breaks down? I'll do my best to get the work done in two months as I promised. You'll just have to trust me." We paid Gouldner half of the money in advance, with the other half due when he showed us the finished prints—that is, just before the games were due to run off the assembly line.

How did I feel doing business with a non-union shop? Not that good, but not that bad either, since I didn't think we had much choice. Less than 20 percent of the workers in America are unionized (down from a high in the 1960s of about 36 percent). In Class Struggle, the role of unions in securing Workers' interests is clear and urgent, but Class Struggle, Inc., the business, had to operate in the world as it is. Wishful thinking is bad business and worse politics. Beyond that, we never sought to be a model Marxist business, whatever that is. Our aim was not to teach by example, but to convey a socialist understanding of capitalism to many people who had never heard one, to convey it to them in a game that they bought in stores. This meant starting a business and acting like businessmen. To us, lower costs did not mean higher profits, but lower prices and more sales, more people being introduced to Class Struggle (and class struggle).

During this period, meetings of the board of directors of Class Struggle, Inc., were held every Sunday evening in my Greenwich Village apartment. Following our family's French traditions, we all gathered around a table replete with Camembert, Roquefort, Boursin, and Jarlsberg. Good cheese quickly became a Class struggle tradition. Howard, who has a passion for cheese, ate enormous portions of the stuff whenever things got rough, but in these early meetings he was content to share his favorite cheeses with the rest of us.

After settling on Gouldner as producer, our attention shifted to problems of distribution and publicity. For a fee, Juvenile Packaging had agreed to mail the games out from their plant—the details were still to be worked out—but who would take the orders, answer mail, place ads, and the like? All members of the board agreed to help with selling and publicity, so it didn't seem as if there would be much to do. Someone working 20 hours a week, we thought, could do it all.

Little Shawn Thomas's parents, Jo Ann and Paul Gullen, had

just finished with one traumatic birth experience and seemed ready, if not very eager, for another. Paul, my friend for over a decade, is a published poet, who speaks in cadences and dreams about having enough free time to write a novel. The market for poetry and first novels being what it is, he worked at the time in a bookstore. Jo Ann had already run an office for an architect. Together, they said, they could handle one part-time job, and even agreed to work out of their apartment. It would be easier for Jo Ann, who had the baby to care for, and of course cheaper for Class Struggle, Inc.

"But what credentials do they have in business?" Howard asked.

"They once owned a bookstore," I replied.

"How'd they do?" he persisted.

"They went bankrupt."

"Terrific." After meeting the Gullens, Howard was quickly reconciled. Jo Ann had kept books before. She was quick, bright, well organized, and answered the phone with the authority of a radio preacher.

As friends we related as equals. Paul and Jo Ann were now my employees. It was for me to decide how much money they made and how they were to spend the time I paid for. He owed me something and there could be no messing up. Could I forget this when we talked as friends? Could he? At the time, I consoled myself with the fact that this was only a part-time job, that it was still the bookstore where he worked that put most of the bread on his table. Paul was a friend first and an employee second, and I was determined to keep the priorities straight.

One of the earliest problems the board, which now included Paul and Jo Ann, had to resolve was whether to take on Nelson Rockefeller. Izzy informed us that by putting the face of a living person on the cover of the game, we were infringing on his privacy and breaking the law. He could sue us. Everyone agreed that one of the most attractive features of the game is the photo of Marx arm-wrestling with Rocky. Particularly in New York, where Rockefeller's face is well known, this picture guaranteed us instant notoriety.

There were really three questions here. Would Rocky sue? If he did, would he win? And if he won, what would he get? Izzy recalled that the Rockefellers forced some fast-food chain to change a radio jingle that used the family name.

"A David versus Goliath suit would only result in a lot of publicity for Class Struggle," Jo Ann observed.

"And for the class struggle, not Rockefeller's favorite cause," Ed added.

"Maybe he has a sense of humor," Paul suggested. As a poet, nothing seemed too farfetched.

"Settled," and I brought my coffee cup down with a bang. "He won't sue ... but if he does?"

"Then," Izzy replied, "we claim the game is really a kind of book, something educational. It's legal to use the face of a living person in 'educational material.'" "You mean we might even win such a suit?" Howard asked.

"I wouldn't bet on it. Better if he doesn't sue," said Izzy. His legal training had made him more cautious than the rest of us.

"It depends what he wins if he wins," Ed countered. "Doesn't he have to show that our action caused him financial loss to collect damages?"

"Right," Izzy admitted. "If he won, probably all that would happen is that the judge would make us take his face off the cover of the game."

"Then on with the suit," Milton exclaimed, giving voice to our common sentiment. "It's a small price to pay for a chance to wrestle with Rockefeller. Why should Marx have all the fun?"

From that moment on, the fear that Rockefeller might sue us was replaced by an even stronger fear that he might not. Until Rockefeller's abrupt demise a year later, David never gave up waiting and hoping for Goliath to make his move. Alas, to no avail.

Setting a price for the game was also a matter of long, involved discussions. In the toy industry, the standard practice is to charge a retail price that is four to five times what it costs to produce any item. When we first heard of it, this struck us as an outrageous rip-off. We would be satisfied with much less profit, so we could charge less for our game. That most of this difference went to pay storeowners, sales representatives, jobbers, shippers, warehousemen, advertisers, accountants, bankers, and landlords (we could never afford insurance) is something we didn't fully grasp at the time. I think it is hard for anyone who hasn't actually been in business to realize how much of what comes in has to be paid out to other businessmen. A planned society would greatly reduce these expenses, helping small businesspeople and consumers alike—but that is another story.

Our chief concern at this moment was to get Class Struggle into as many hands as possible, so we approached the problem from the other end. What would people, particularly workers and students, be willing to pay for a board game? No one in our group had bought a board game in years, and $10 struck us as a kind of psychological barrier, an outer limit of acceptability that we should honor at all costs. Looking back on these discussions two price hikes later, I'm struck by how little attention we paid to determining our exact costs and how much time went to unraveling the ideological and psychological ramifications of a $10 price. Amateur night in the boardroom!

Our ideas about distributing the game ranged from business to politics. No one knows how many Americans consider themselves socialists of one sort or another. Estimates range from a few hundred thousand to a couple million. This is "the Movement." Neither an opposition party nor a counterculture, it has aspects of both. Wherever they are and whatever their number, we felt certain that people in the Movement would all want to get a copy of the first Marxist board game, particularly as Class Struggle avoided sectarian answers and stressed themes different socialist tendencies have in common. After all, what simpler, less threatening, and more amusing way to introduce children, friends, and relatives to radical ideas? The problem was how to contact all these unseen comrades. We decided to place mail-order ads in a dozen Left publications and to try to sell the game directly in the couple of hundred radical bookstores now spread throughout the country.

To sell Class Struggle beyond the Movement, to workers, students, and others, meant getting the game into toy and department stores. Between the producer and the stores lay the distributor, salesmen who sell the product to stores for a commission. Parker Brothers and a few other major toy companies do their own distributing, but everyone else uses professional distributors, most of whom have their offices in the Toy Building. Stevenson, Gouldner, Anspach, and others to whom we talked all said that our success would depend to a large extent on our distributors, on how large and well connected they were, and on how much they pushed the game.

I recall Stevenson explaining, "A sales rep may work for five to 10 companies. Each one has a dozen or more items, that's 100 toys and games. In the 15 or even 30 minutes that he's talking to the buyer, how much time do you think he is going to devote to your game?" Howard had just said that it would take a little time to point out to a store buyer how Class Struggle is different, how funny it is, and why it will sell. "No," Stevenson went on, "you guys are going to have quite a job getting salesmen to give you that kind of time, assuming you find someone who's willing to take on such a controversial game in the first place."

"And if there are a lot of favorable press stories?" Howard asked.

"Well, with good publicity," Stevenson admitted, "anything is possible."

From this and similar discussions, we concluded that this was not the time to get a good distributor. Once Class Struggle had burst upon the public and picked up a couple of good newspaper stories, then, we figured, we could get the distributor we wanted and maybe a deal that was something less than blackmail. That put a lot of pressure on us to begin life with a Big Bang.

A press conference, we decided, was the perfect occasion to carry the message of Class Struggle's availability to all America.

"But will the press come?" Jo Ann asked.

"Did TV cover the Kennedy assassination, the Normandy landing, the trip to the moon?" was Milton's quick response.

"Yes," Jo Ann came back, "but did they cover Heinz's

announcement of a new, improved chicken-noodle soup?"

"Hopefully, we fall somewhere in between," I broke in. "It will depend a lot on how it's handled. We have to do a professional job. Who has ever run a press conference? Antiwar demonstrations don't count."

Izzy said his friend Irwin was a PR specialist who would be glad to advise us. We began to list what we needed to know. Whom do we invite? Where do we hold it? What day and time of day is best? What do we do besides display the game? What do we dine and wine them with? Newspapermen, all seemed to agree, were heavy drinkers.

"I know just what to feed them," Milton said. "Class Strudel."

We all groaned, but Milton went on, "And we'll serve drinks in glass muggles."

"This has to be fairly serious." Paul's aesthetic sense had been ruffled.

"Why?" Milton asked. "We have to show that we can laugh at ourselves, too."

"Funny and corny are not the same thing," Paul insisted. Puns, slogans, and publicity gimmicks tumbled out of Milton's mouth without letup and, like a spring rain, were wet, soggy, and refreshing in turn. I liked a lot of Milt's suggestions and tried to look at each one on its own merits. I think Milton would have made Class Struggle a household word in no time—if we'd only had a couple of million dollars to spend on advertising. "And who is going to record the event?" Milt wanted to know. The wife of one of his friends had dreams of becoming a professional photographer. She would do it. "Cheap?" "Free," he answered us. "Maybe a couple bucks."

We also decided that we needed a slogan, something that said it all quickly and attached itself to the memory like glue. After an evening of weighing the relative merits of "Highest Marx?" and "Recommended by the Bored of Education," we finally settled on "Class Struggle Is the Name of the Game." Almost immediately, we placed teaser ads in *The Village Voice* and in microscopic print at the bottom of the front page of *The*

New York Times which simply read, "Class Struggle Is the Name of the Game." We ran six of these in the hope of setting the whole town abuzz with a question to which the game's appearance would be the welcome answer.

In these final weeks before the press conference, I remember feeling a little uneasy about my new role and its responsibilities. The joy and excitement I felt as expectant father about to witness the birth of a long-awaited baby couldn't obliterate the pulsating doubts I had buried under the practical tasks of each succeeding moment. On the contrary, the imminence of what had been so long promised brought these worries to the surface. Class Struggle had already begun to take up much more of my time than I had expected. As thankful, too, as I was for Howard's largesse, I was not at all comfortable with so much of my friend's money riding on my creation. We had to succeed.

There was also the question of how my new game and business would affect my reputation at NYU and in the academic community at large. In the university, reputation is legal tender; it equates with money, security, and influence. Only scholarly achievements contribute to it. Works that a lot of people read, that are understood too easily or enjoyed too much, works that make money, cannot be "serious." They are not respectable. Professors who do such work are taking a walk at the edge of the abyss. In a hokum world, credibility is an increasingly fragile asset.

A talk I had with my friend Ray Rakow around this time contributed to my growing malaise. Ray is a former psychoanalyst who recognized that the socially induced maladies that crossed his couch require a social cure and exchanged his personalized craft for political activism. When I told Ray I had gone into business selling revolution in toy stores, he looked sadly disappointed. Ray was invited to the open house for potential investors a couple of months earlier, but had not come. "Business is unhealthy for children and other living things," he advised. "You're not going to come out of this unscarred. Besides, class struggle is too serious a subject to play games with."

I was taken aback by the cold water that Ray threw on both the game and my idea of going into business. It may have been the first really negative reaction I got from someone whose opinions I respected. I wanted to hear more of Ray's doubts and to explain more fully my own position, but I had an appointment with Gouldner to discuss production delays and couldn't stay. We agreed to meet again soon. Ray was not lacking a sense of humor or political sense. I couldn't figure out what was bugging him. Why couldn't he understand? His words nagged at me and fed my own uneasiness at becoming a businessman. It was almost two years before Ray and I met to finish our discussion.

On my way to Gouldner's, I couldn't help but reflect on the sad fate of another academic turned businessman, Bob Bonic. Bob, who had grown up with me in Milwaukee, reached his 40th year a respected professor of mathematics, but he, too, had another passion. In his case, it was darts. Feigning more nonchalance than even he could have felt, he walked away from a tenured position and with his life savings opened up a bar for dart players in an untraveled corner of Soho, Manhattan. Bob's second wife, Jill, an aspiring actress who enjoyed being married to a college professor, had little interest in darts and less in helping build and run a bar, an activity that began to take up all of Bob's time. Dart players, as it turned out, don't drink very much. Business never took off, but Jill did. After a couple more years of dashed hopes and unrelenting penny-pinching agony—almost as painful for Bob's friends to watch as for him to go through—Bob lost the bar and went bankrupt. There are a half-dozen morals one can draw from this story, but the one that stuck in my craw concerned the damage that business misery can inflict on family life. Unlike Jill, Paule understood why her husband had gone into business—that would help. But I was determined to keep Paule and Raoul as far away from Class Struggle, Inc., as geography and cohabitation allowed.

When I arrived at my appointment with Gouldner, he informed me in a perfectly matter-of-fact tone that a rise in the price of paper made it necessary for him to raise the price he had quoted us to produce his part of the game.

"By how much?"

"To $2.75," Gouldner said, avoiding my eyes.

"From $1.95?" My voice dropped to the floor, where my heart had preceded it. "That's about one third more."

"Sorry, Bertell, but I really have no choice. Should we go ahead?"

With no contract in writing, it was I who had no choice, and Gouldner knew it. So much for going with the lowest bid! Our band of super educated professors had been given a first, painful lesson in the ways of business.

SIX:
LITMUS TEST IN MARYLAND:
ACADEMIC FREEDOM IS ALSO CLASS
STRUGGLE

On April 18, 1978, just two weeks before our Class Struggle press conference, the *Washington Star* newspaper announced, "The University of Maryland is expected to appoint perhaps the first Marxist to head a U.S. college political science department." Three days later, on April 21, *The Washington Post* reported, "The nomination of a Marxist political scientist to head a University of Maryland department has provoked a growing campus controversy that yesterday spilled over into the arena of state politics as Acting Governor Blair Lee III questioned the wisdom of the appointment ... Lee warned that the appointment 'could kick up quite a backlash.'" Lee also said that the state legislature might react to the appointment by trying to cut the university's budget. A loud echo came from State Senator Roy Straten, chairman of the Appropriation Committee of the Maryland Senate, who said the university "may have gone too far this time."

About five weeks before, on March 15, I had been offered the position of chairman of the University of Maryland Department of Government and Politics, "subject to the approval of the president," by Provost Murray Polokoff. A search committee that included 10 professors from the Department of Government and Politics had chosen me out of approximately 100 candidates for the job, and Chancellor Robert Gluckstern, the top administrator on the University of Maryland College Park campus, had ratified their choice. All that remained was the approval of President Wilson Elkins, and Polokoff and others assured me that this was a mere formality, since Elkins had never disapproved of any chairman appointment.

What is especially remarkable here is that none of the people who had anything to do with my nomination, not the search committee, not the provost or the chancellor, indeed none of the 41 professors in the Department of Government and Politics,

46

were Marxists. They were professors and administrators who honestly believed that a person should be judged on the basis of his scholarship and character and not his ideology, and were ready to act on this belief—to the point of recommending a Marxist colleague for a position of academic leadership. American universities, I proudly reflected, had come a long way since the intolerant days of Joe McCarthy.

Given the chance to expand this new tolerance even further and to advance ever so slightly the cause of critical thinking in the Academy, could I turn it down? Class Struggle, Inc., I was certain, would be able to operate quite well without me by the end of the summer. After a couple of intense family councils and a visit to Washington (College Park is a suburb of the nation's capital) to look into schools and housing, I called Provost Polokoff and accepted his offer.

In early April, a half-dozen of the older, academically less productive and politically more conservative members of the Department of Government and Politics wrote to President Elkins about the calamity that was about to befall the University of Maryland, to wit, the hiring of a Marxist chairman. They also alerted the student press, and on April 18, the University of Maryland *Diamondback* ran the banner headline, "Marxist Eyed for Top Post." The story was picked up immediately by the Washington, Baltimore, and—with the help of Governor Lee—New York papers. I couldn't help but recall my imbroglio at the University of the West Indies, but I quickly dismissed it. This time the outcome would be different.

Putting polemic aside, the question was a simple one of freedom to teach and research as one wishes, and to rise in the Academy to the level justified by one's abilities. It was a question not only of my own academic freedom but also that of the scholars and administrators who chose me and of the students whom I would eventually teach. A leading American political scientist, Michael Parenti, has said, "We should want the same good things for Americans (students included) that we so passionately desire for the Russians and Chinese, namely that they have the opportunity to hear, express, and advocate iconoclastic, anti-establishment views in their media and educational institutions without fear or reprisal." Otherwise, how do we differ from THEM?

The people who recommended me for the job obviously agreed with this sentiment, as did a large portion of the press that commented on this subject. In an editorial entitled "Litmus Test at College Park," the *Baltimore Sun* said, "We can never tell if the avowed American respect for academic freedom has reasserted itself until a toleration test arises." This, the *Sun* claimed, was such a test.

Opposition to my appointment was also spreading. Its more vocal spokesmen included leading state politicians, several members of the University Board of Regents, and a broad phalanx of conservative newspaper columnists, including Kilpatrick, Buchanan, Drumond, and Evans and Novak. It became clear that a lot of people favor academic freedom in principle on the condition that no one use it in practice, at least no one they seriously disagree with, and especially not Marxists. What Marxists do or say that is so terrible was generally left very vague in the attacks on me, but by calling myself a Marxist I had clearly put myself beyond the pale.

A member of the University Board of Regents, Samuel Hoover, J. Edgar's younger brother, said, "I just don't think a Marxist should be a state institution in a position of that caliber. He'll never get on there." But when asked by a reporter what he understood by "Marxism," he replied, "I really don't know what it is. I'll be honest with you."

Others who thought they knew what Marxism is attacked me for not being "objective" (as if other professors don't also have a point of view), or for being intolerant in the classroom (against all the evidence gathered from my decade of teaching at NYU), or as an enemy of democracy (when I have defined "socialism" again and again as the extension of democracy into all walks of life). No one accused me of being a pawn of the Soviet Union, but a document that was sent to President Elkins by the U.S. Labor Party, a small, right-wing sect, suggested that I might be part of a British conspiracy to overthrow the American government. My repeated assurances that I would run a pluralist department and not do anything that other chairmen don't already do did not satisfy my critics.

What they were really objecting to, of course, was the content of my Marxist views and to the fact that if I became chairman these views would get a wider hearing. My opponents could not say this in so many words, because this would clearly identify them as enemies of academic freedom and of free speech generally, principles that are still so popular in America that few dare attack them openly.

Michael Olesker, a columnist for the *Baltimore News-American*, saw clearly through all the disguises: "Ollman's made it clear," he said. "If he's appointed, he will teach socialist ideas in the classrooms. So that's why all those True Believers are upset. It doesn't matter that virtually all other courses are taught by non-Marxists. What matters is all these college kids who might become tainted. They might find something in this one course, and this one man, that is far more appealing than anything else they've gotten in years of academic and political indoctrination. And that's the final absurdity of what the Ollman detractors are saying: There's something so juicy here, so enticing in this Marxist business, that we're absolutely terrified of letting anybody hear it." Better to present me to the public as a fox who had been hired to guard the chickens (the headline over a page of hostile letters on my case in the *Washington Star*) than to have them mistake me for the little boy in the story of the emperor's new clothes. But if they think that one or even a few Marxists could wreak such havoc on the minds of the young, what are they saying about the truth and power of their own ideas?

There is a danger in stopping here, and viewing the opposition to my appointment as just another expression of political reaction. The *Baltimore Sun* may have been right in editorializing that "in Mencken's old precincts ... the Boobus Americanus" was waging one of its perennial wars to preserve "the blue crap harvest," but there is a deeper meaning that needs to be uncovered. For the struggle over my appointment reflected not only differences in people's acceptance of academic freedom, but also several conflicting tendencies, or contradictions, within the university itself.

On the one hand, universities function to transfer knowledge from one generation to the next, to teach critical thinking and to allow scholars to study and discuss the most important questions of the day. Readers will recognize this as the stuff of every Commencement Day speech. In order to perform these functions well, universities require some Marxists as well as supporters of other critical perspectives, and an atmosphere in which people feel free to follow their interests and insights wherever they may lead. If professors and students know that some ideas are barred from the university, they naturally become skeptical about what *is* taught.

What is generally left unsaid in Commencement Day speeches is that our universities also function to produce learned rationalizations for the status quo, to do the basic research required by both industry and government (especially in the area of defense [sic]), to provide custodial care for young, unemployed workers (to serve as what Ira Shor has called a "collegiate warehouse for unneeded labor"), and to teach students the skills and attitudes that will make them effective, model workers for their future capitalist employers. Scholars, who try to relate these functions to the workings of our social-economic system, to understand what groups benefit most and what groups least, and to explore alternatives, may actually undermine the effectiveness with which these less recognized functions are being carried out. From the point of view of the people for whom this is the decisive work of the university (chiefly members of university boards of trustees, businessmen, politicians, and conservative ideologues), the presence of any Marxists constitutes a dangerous threat.

Fortunately, many of these same "academic statesmen" also understand that the activities they consider primary require for their own effective implementation the pursuit of a program in which knowledge gets transferred, critical thinking is taught, and basic questions are discussed. Otherwise, we don't have a university but a technical school, and a bad one at that. Students need to believe, in other words, that they are getting a *real* education—one where different opinions can be heard—if they are to submit willingly to the ideological indoctrination and job training that constitutes the standard fare of their college years. Likewise, professors must believe they are more than trainers, ideologues, and warehouse attendants if they are to do these jobs well. And the general public has to believe that the ideas that filter down from universities have won out in fair and open combat with other ideas if these notions are to receive the credence that their sponsors require. In sum, the opponents of Marxism are limited in what they can do against Marxists by what they want and need to do for themselves.

Conservatives, then, need academic freedom—albeit for their own peculiar ends—as much as radicals. Similar ideological work is done by the notion of "consumer sovereignty," which helps mask and render acceptable an economy dominated by large corporations, and by the idea of "democracy," which helps legitimate a government dominated by Big Money. In America, where everything is bigger, we have fig leaves that hide mountains. Hence the paradox that those who consistently oppose real democracy, genuine consumer sovereignty, and thorough-going academic freedom are often found among their most vociferous defenders.

American universities, then, need some Marxists. The key question is, when and at what level of authority do some become too many? From the start, the real controversy over my appointment has been over where to draw the line and, to a lesser extent, over who should do it. To be sure, the two sides in this battle also disagree over what are the most important functions of a university and the kind of society worth preserving or building. For the most part, it is the liberals who once again are trying to preserve what is best in American traditions (aided by radicals who hope to build upon them), while so-called "conservatives" do their best to destroy these traditions in the name of preserving them. While the labels are confusing, the conflict is all too familiar. My battle for academic freedom at the University of Maryland turns out to be part of the broader class struggle.

In the spring of 1978, the class struggle had progressed far enough for a Marxist to be nominated for the post of chairman in a political science department at a major university. This was a greater surprise than the subsequent attacks on my appointment. The widespread support I enjoyed among University of Maryland students and faculty also convinced me this battle could be won. How would President Elkins react to the enormous political pressures that were being brought to bear on him? For the moment, events were out of my hands—and luckily so, for these hands were becoming increasingly occupied with the work of Class Struggle, Inc.

SEVEN:
MAYDAY 1978, 4:30 PM:
"YOU ARE INVITED TO A PRESS CONFERENCE ..."

"Did we buy enough class strudel?" No one winced anymore at the pun. Milton had convinced us that punning was one of our strongest suits and that we shouldn't be afraid to play it. The world's press was coming, or as many of them as could fit into Ed's Soho loft, and we were anxious to put our best foot forward—the one with the red, white, and blue slipper. The first hundred games of Class Struggle had arrived from Juvenile Packaging just yesterday, still warm from the shrink wrapping and as bold and brassy as the hopes that had nurtured them into life. They were arranged on a long table that also sported two large wicker baskets of red and black "Class Struggle Is the Name of the Game" buttons. Delays in production and all the extra dollars Gouldner plucked from us were immediately forgotten in the warm glow I felt in holding the newborn on my knees. "Look, Paule, it already talks."

"What does it say?"

" 'Feed me' ... no, it's 'Read me, you who would be free.'" We laughed and hugged each other. It was the laugh of people who had come to the end of a long and tiring journey. Because all of our efforts had been aimed at producing and unveiling the game, Paule felt that our experience with Class Struggle was coming to an end. Never as interested in games as I was, and even more hostile to everything connected to business, she had looked forward to this moment in ways she would only now admit.

Not everything was ready. It was 10 minutes after 4 P.M. and the beer, wine, soda, nuts, crackers, and strudel were still fighting with each other for space on the overcrowded bar. Milton was squeezing the last pun into the punch as Ed brought out more ice and cups. Jo Ann was directing traffic. "The bar can't come out that far. It doesn't leave enough room for the TV cameras." More chairs were displaced and the bar pushed farther into a corner, leaving a 15' x 15' space in front of the huge blow-up of the Class Struggle board that would serve as the backdrop for my remarks to the press. Milt's friend the photographer arrived and immediately started taking pictures.

Ed's loft had once been the headquarters of the American Silk Exchange, which accounted for the mahogany floors and the pieces of marble jutting out of the walls. Ten floors below in the same building, our friend Bob Bonic had tempted fate with his darts bar. It was a coincidence we preferred on this occasion to forget. From the huge egg-shaped picture window in Ed's front room one looked over the checkered roofs of the Lower East Side, the site of some of New York's most intense class struggles.

"Throw the Genetic Die to see who plays what class."

"Maybe we should wait until some press people arrive."

I had just entered one of the bedrooms where a game of Class Struggle was about to get under way with Raoul, by now a sassy adolescent, John Birnbaum, Ellen Chase, friends from the NYU Center for Marxist Studies, and a few of my students who had volunteered for the occasion. "No, I think it's better if you begin now," I said. "This way you'll be in the heat of battle when the press comes along. And don't forget to enjoy yourselves madly."

"Dad," Raoul asked, "do I have to laugh even when I don't find it funny?"

"You have to laugh the loudest." Turning to John, I instructed, "Report to me if Raoul doesn't laugh loud enough."

Margaret, Ed's wife, poked her head in the door and announced that the band had arrived. And in walked Perry, Les, and two friends they had invited to play along with them. Perry is an accomplished jazz clarinetist with a couple of esoteric records under his belt, while Les plays guitar and sings, most recently dressed as a chicken, on the Greenwich Village street corner circuit.

"Greetings, minstrels. There are no press here yet. Margaret, could you take them to the other bedroom? The Class Struggle T-shirts are there."

For some reason, which I don't now understand, we thought Class Struggle needed a theme song, and that the press conference was the perfect place to introduce it. With a dozen last-minute details contesting for my time, I had spent the previous evening with Les distilling the essence of Class Struggle into song while Perry improvised a jazz accompaniment.

"Gouldner's here." A cry rang out from the front hall. And a moment later, in walked our beaming producer, sporting a powder-blue suit, orange tie, and what seemed like spats. Deeply tanned from "a couple of days out on the boat," he looked every studied inch like the Hollywood mogul. No one would guess from his appearance or from the Mercedes Benz he arrived in ("It saves me a fortune in upkeep") that he was turning out subversive games. Gouldner had come to our opening to see how many rabbits a socialist professor could pull out of a hat. We had assured him that the press could not fail to see the novelty of our venture and would turn out in droves for the press conference, but he remained politely skeptical.

"Good luck, Bertell. Nice crowd," he greeted me warmly, gesturing to all the friends, relatives, and students who were milling about. "Who's here from the press?"

Before I could find my voice for an answer, Paul rushed in with his news: "There's a guy here who says he's from *Toy Magazine*." I exchanged knowing winks with Gouldner, and urged him to help himself to a drink in the next room. I would speak to him later. Then, to Paul: "Send him in here. No, let me go out to greet him."

"Too pushy," Ed stopped me. "Play it cool, like it's the biggest story of the decade. Someone go tell the guy that Professor Ollman is in here."

"Yeah," Howard agreed. "This way we hit him right away with the image of people enjoying the game. I'll go get him."

A few moments later, a thirtyish, baby-faced man about five feet high entered the room, followed by Howard, who supplied the introductions while looking down on the top of his short-cropped, well-scrubbed head. "Bertell, this is Davis Winfell of *Toy Magazine*. Mr. Winfell, this is Bertell Ollman, the creator of Class Struggle."

Warmly shaking hands with our slightly overwhelmed guest,

I continued, "And this is Ed Nell, who is also on the board of directors of Class Struggle, Inc., the producers of the game, and Jo Ann Gullen, our general manager. That's John, Ellen, Bill, Raoul—my son—Irma, and Philip playing the game. This is ..."

Raoul let out a wild youp, followed by three quick guffaws, which I was able to stop only by giving him the dirtiest of looks.

"As you probably know," Winfell began, "*Toy Magazine* is the largest publication in the industry. It has 100,000 readers including most of the people who buy games for stores."

"Sounds like the ideal place for a good story on Class Struggle." Milt smiled, only to receive a kick from Howard, whose lips I could see mouthing the words, "Too pushy."

Hoping to recover from Milton's *faux pas*, Jo Ann broke in, "The press conference should start in about 20 minutes, but if you have any questions to ask Professor Ollman now, I'm sure he'd be pleased to answer."

I nodded assent. We were about to hear the first question asked by the press about Class Struggle. It was a historic moment. Milt called over our court photographer to make sure it wasn't lost to posterity. She snapped two, three, four photos.

After a slight hesitation, Winfell began, "Have you gentlemen considered the importance of advertising in selling your product?"

Howard, Milton, Ed, Jo Ann, and I looked at each other, puzzled, and then back at Winfell. "Sure," I answered, really unsure of what I was hearing. "Do you want to know how Class Struggle works?" Howard asked. "Or why Professor Ollman invented it?"

Not to be sidetracked, Winfell pushed on: "A study of the companies that have advertised in *Toy Magazine* shows an increase ..."

Ed interrupted, "Aren't you a reporter for *Toy Magazine*?"

"No," Winfell replied, looking very sheepish all of a sudden. "I'm with their advertising department."

Not sure that he heard him correctly, Ed persisted, "You don't write?"

"I write ads, well, really sales agreements for ads," Winfell corrected himself. "Someone else writes the ad copy." The noise from our deflating balloon might have frightened him off his feet if the band hadn't begun playing at that moment in the other room. The cool jazz made the party atmosphere complete. I apologized to Winfell and said that I had to greet our other guests, promising to discuss advertising with him later on.

Jo Ann, who joined me, swore once again that all the invitations had been sent out 10 days ago, over 100 of them. "I followed up," she went on, "with phone calls yesterday to ABC, NBC, and CBS news staffs, and to the dozen New York papers, TV and radio stations we singled out."

"Then I don't understand it," I said. "Could Irwin have been so right about 4:30 P.M. being a bad time for a press conference?" (Our other "experts" had disagreed).

A noisy crowd of people had just gotten off the elevator outside the front door. It sounded like a welcome burst of rain in the middle of a long drought. Whoever they were, they really enjoyed being here, judging from their rapid-fire talk and frequent bursts of laughter. The door opened and in came a smiling Milton, waving his hand behind him as he announced to us, "Board members of Class Struggle, Inc., meet the ladies and gentlemen of the press." And in walked two, five, 10, 14 in all, black and Puerto Rican teenagers 14 to 16-years-old, each holding a notebook and pencil, and all looking dead serious, the fun having stopped at the door. Following the troop in was Milt's friend Joe Leonard.

I think it was Ed who recovered first. "Who are these kids?"

"They are students at the New York High School of Printing," Milt replied. "Joe teaches a class in reporting there. This is their first press conference. I thought it would be a good idea if they came. It kinda gives us the crowd effect." Then, addressing the ladies and gentlemen of the press, he added, "Go into the back room, kids. The press conference will begin in about 10 minutes."

"Milt, aren't you supposed to check out your good ideas with us?" Jo Ann was brimming with annoyance.

"It makes no difference, Jo Ann," I said. "We have lots of

room. I wish we didn't, but we do."

"And lots of class strudel." Milt smiled weakly.

Paul rushed up. "It's 4:35 P.M. Are there any press here yet?"

As I slowly shook my head, I began to feel what seemed like strong hunger pains in my stomach, though I knew I had just eaten. It was no time to show anxiety. A general has to swallow his panic. My troops were watching, ready to take their cue from how I reacted. For someone who had always made a fetish of letting it all hang out, setting an example of calm in the midst of a growing storm is a grueling experience. Easy, I thought, it's still early. The loft may have been hard to find. A lot of press will come late. *The Guardian* and *Seven Days* surely will come late. Radicals are never on time to meetings. My native optimism began to reassert itself.

"There is a guy in the bedroom watching the Class Struggle game whom nobody seems to know." Paule, who had just emerged from the room, added, "I saw him ask Perry and Les some questions earlier."

We went back into the bedroom, and sure enough, there was a solidly built man with straight black hair and a navy-blue double-breasted suit peering intently over Raoul's shoulder watching the game. I don't know how I could have missed him, but I did, and so, apparently, did Howard, Ed, Izzy, Milton, Jo Ann, and Paul.

"Are you enjoying the game?" I asked.

"Very much. A game called Class Struggle, very interesting idea." Not wanting to miss any of the action on the board, he hardly glanced in our direction. The accent with which he spoke was slight, but noticeable.

"Where are you from?" I went on. "Are you a reporter?"

"Yes, I am a reporter." Every head in the room was now turned in his direction waiting for his next words. "I represent TASS, the Soviet press agency."

An unexpected pleasure, I assured him. Along with the other major foreign press agencies, TASS received an invitation to the conference, but we'd had little hope they would attend. An article in *Pravda* wouldn't sell many games in New York City, but the idea of it boosted our flagging morale just the same.

With the introductions out of the way, Mr. Borosov asked me, "Why did you make a game of class struggle?"

"To help teach people about the real class struggle in America," I answered. "Don't you think it's needed?"

"But tell me truthfully, Professor," his tone had become very skeptical, "do you really believe the capitalists will allow such a game to be sold?"

"Yes, they'll let it be sold, but whether they'll *help* us sell it is the big question. And only time will tell." My answer brought a doubting smile to his lips.

"It's a quarter to five," Margaret said, joining us. "Perry and Les want to know if you're ready for the Class Struggle song."

"Yes, I think we'd better begin. Will everyone please come into the living room?" Turning to the man from TASS, I added, "We can continue to talk during the question and answer period of the press conference."

•••

In the front room, Milton, our emcee for the occasion, was conducting the Class Struggle raffle—first prize, an all-new Class Struggle T-shirt. To his embarrassment, his own 9-year-old son, Jonah, emerged the winner. Having weathered the audience's cries of "cheat," "fix," "fake," Milt began to introduce the members of what he had baptized "The Class Strugglers," Perry, Les … They looked resplendent in their red T-shirts with black "Class Struggle" lettering across the front. After a brief instrumental intro, Les started to sing.

"Move over Monopoly, you capitalist game.
We've had enough of your greed, it's time for a change.
CLASS STRUGGLE, THAT'S THE NAME OF THE GAME
…"

Well, at least the music was good, and Les has a pleasant baritone voice. The audience responded warmly to the song. It was now 5 o'clock, or about a half-hour after the press conference was scheduled to begin. We could not delay things any longer. I nodded my assent. Milt welcomed the ladies and gentlemen of the press and assembled friends. Then he introduced me, handing me the wooden pointer that he had insisted was a necessary implement in every successful press conference. I began by asking each member of the Class struggle team to stand and take a bow. Howard took advantage of his moment to say how proud he was to be a part of this "unique undertaking." I'm sure he chose the word "undertaking" as a happy compromise for "business" and "politics," but in the circumstances I could only hear "undertaker." Under the professorial calm, my stomach was hurting so much that I had to loosen my belt.

I took only four or five minutes to explain why I had invented Class Struggle and to outline the mechanisms of the game. The large empty space we had put aside for TV cameras became more and more oppressive as I spoke. "Fun, funny, politically relevant"—I strove mightily, but my heart wasn't in it. "Are there any questions?"

After a decidedly unpregnant silence, one of the reporters from the New York High School for Printing raised his hand: "How does one invent a game?" he asked. "What are you going to do with all the profit you make?" Rex Wiener, an ex-Yippy friend of mine who was writing a book on the counterculture, wanted to know. I thought it odd that Rex or anyone else should be interested in our profits when we hadn't yet sold a game.

Two questions, one from Milton on problems connected with playing the game, followed, and then nothing. I looked hard for the man from TASS, but he seemed to have left. Ordinarily, the sea of young black faces down front would have inspired me to heights of socialist oratory, but not now. When our court photographer signaled she had finished her last roll of film, I opted for a swift ending (in keeping with the rest of the occasion, only a couple of the photos came out, but the bill was a royal $500!).

The band resumed playing. "No, Les, I don't think it's a good idea to sing the Class Struggle song again." I wanted nothing so much as to leave, to go home and sleep. My whole body felt heavy, weighted down with bags of sand. But most of our guests felt obliged to say good-bye and wish me good luck, often adding something about "the terrific party." Some more sensitive souls, like Ira, wordlessly patted me on the back, or simply waved from the door.

Howard approached. His long face never looked longer. "Where were *The Guardian* and *Seven Days?*" he asked plaintively. "Even the radical press let us down."

Later that evening, Paule, the Gullens, Izzy, Milt, and I retired to drown our sorrows in Chinese tea at the Hong Fat Restaurant down the block from Ed's loft. "Well, let's hear it. What next?" I asked.

"I got it," Milton erupted with what seemed like genuine excitement. "How about issuing a news release saying that press from around the world, ranging from the New York High School for Printing to TASS, turned up today to greet the birth of the world's first Marxist board game?"

EIGHT:
ROCKY GRAPPLES WITH MARXIST:
THE MEDIA DISCOVER CLASS STRUGGLE

"Have you seen today's *New York Post*?" Jo Ann asked excitedly.

"Were they at yesterday's press conference?" Her call caught me in the middle of a meeting with a student.

"No, but I talked briefly to a woman there on the phone a couple of days ago, and I sent her a copy of the game. Listen to this—it's under the heading, 'Rocky Grapples with Marxist.' 'Nelson Rockefeller locked in an arm-wrestle with Karl Marx? Well, that's the delectable combination gracing the cover of a clever new board game called Class Struggle, which proves (if nothing else) that even Marxists have a sense of humor. Even a Marxist socialist like NYU professor Bertell Ollman, author of such sober works as *Alienation: Marx's Conception of Man in Capitalist Society*, and the fellow whose appointment to head the University of Maryland government department has that state's governor hopping mad. Ollman, it turns out, is the theorist behind Class Struggle, wherein you must cooperate with other classes to win—but if a Capitalist lands on a square called "Nuclear War," the game is over. And, of course, you can't pick which of the game's six classes you'll be: That's handled by a toss of the "Genetic Die." This nifty game will go on sale at a capitalist's dream price of $9.95.'"

"Hey, that's really good," I responded, still a little dazed and depressed from yesterday's press conference.

"Good? It's terrific," Jo Ann shot back. "It's on page six, the gossip page. Everyone reads it."

That afternoon, I received my first call from a radio station, WNEW in New York. Would I be willing to talk to them for a few minutes about my new game? Roger Simon, who writes a syndicated column for the *Chicago Sun-Times*, called the next day. Under the headline, "A Real Class Game If You Dig Struggle," he summarized the game and quoted extensively from the Chance Cards. His main message was—socialist yes, but above

62

all very funny.

Other calls from papers and radio stations followed, one or two a day at first. Richard Weiss called from the St. Louis *Post-Dispatch*. In a long piece on games, he spoke of me as someone who ignored all the rules on how to produce a successful game, and stressed that Class Struggle was unique in its rejection of the core capitalist values of greed and competition. In New York, *The Village Voice* and *The Villager* both ran favorable articles on the game that first week. Alex Cockburn of the *Voice* found the game "good sport" and "very instructional," if also a "shade prim" for calling alcohol and marijuana opium's of the people.

Meanwhile, Jo Ann and I were kept very busy sending out more press releases to media around the country. No, we didn't announce that our press conference had been attended by the world's press ranging from the New York High School for Printing to TASS, but we did try to include blurbs on the game from stories as they appeared.

How would the media relate Class Struggle to the events still building in Maryland? The danger was that my academic-freedom struggle might make the game appear too political, too dangerous; while the game, if treated too lightly, might make me appear frivolous and undermine my reputation as a serious scholar. The first reaction of the Washington and Baltimore press registered surprise and genuine amusement that someone who was being depicted by his enemies as a sinister influence on the young could have a sense of humor. *The Washington Post* called Class Struggle "Marxism for fun and profit," and said "all the proletariat may soon be playing it." The *Baltimore Sun* said it had both good news and bad news for those worried about the appointment of a Marxist to a chairmanship at Maryland. The "good news is that Ollman is a capitalist. The bad news is that what he is selling is a game called Class Struggle."

The New York Times chose this moment to write a welcome editorial supporting my cause at Maryland. Entitled "The Marketing of a Marxist," it skillfully interwove the two themes that were coming to dominate my existence. Perhaps Ollman's opponents, the *Times* said, "will be less fearful once they play his new board game, Class Struggle ... He expects to do well with it—a clear sign that he is, for practical purposes, safely devoted to the system that Mr. Hoover, Governor Lee, and the vigilantes in the legislature are so anxious to protect." Some socialist friends considered the editorial an underhanded attack on my politics. They had missed the point. At that moment, it was not my socialist credentials that needed the *Good Housekeeping* Seal of Approval as much as my candidacy at Maryland and my Marxist board game.

Then, on May 17, *The New York Times* ran a half-page article with a big picture of me and the game board on the front page of its Metropolitan Section under the heading, "NYU Professor, Marxist Game Inventor, Finds Art Imitates Life." (To provide, I suppose, political balance, the other half of the page was given over to the mass murderer Son of Sam.) And with this, the dam broke. After noting the resemblance between the game and events in Maryland, the *Times* reporter quoted a few Chance Cards and concluded that "good humor keeps the game from turning into pure propaganda."

After this article, which was reprinted in over a dozen major papers around the country, I was inundated with calls and visits by media from around the world. My home phone began ringing at 8 A.M., and calls would come in as late as midnight. One Australian and three Canadian radio stations called in that first week. At my NYU office, I would be on the phone with two, three, and even four reporters at the same time. People who passed by my office saw a juggler at work.

I was invited on the *Today* show, where Tom Brokaw mixed funny questions about Maryland with serious ones on Class Struggle. The *Tomorrow* show, with Tom Snyder, where I shared the stage with Ralph Anspach and a lady who makes chocolate Monopoly sets for $600, followed a month later. No, I didn't think a chocolate Class Struggle set would make Marxism sweeter to the American palate.

Some interviews broke out of the traditional format. On WBAI, New York's progressive radio station, six people played Class Struggle for two hours while a reporter talked to me about the game and related issues. It was the first time, I was told, that a board game was ever played on the radio.

Wires occasionally got crossed: "Is that 'Marks' with a 'k'? And you say you're the president of what Marxist country?" asked an assistant producer (!) of a radio talk show in Los Angeles. A lady vice-president at the Finance Corporation of America called to say that *Business Week*, which had just published a piece on the game, gave me as the source for another story they did on the imminent bankruptcy of several major companies. The financial community, she said, was very worried by the story, and wanted to know how I had come by my information. When I denied knowing anything about it, she became very persistent, promised to protect my sources, even appealed to my patriotism. I have the feeling that, if I had played my cards right, I could have brought the whole of Wall Street crashing down that same afternoon.

Not everyone liked what I said during interviews about the game. The host of a Denver radio talk show got very upset by my comment that capitalism is undemocratic because a small group of bosses make all important economic decisions. "Where in the world is it better?" he wanted to know.

"James Thurber tells a story," I said, "about a friend who asked him, 'How is your wife?' Thurber replied, 'Compared to what?'" When the man from Denver started to laugh, I added, "Yet many people make just this mistake when reacting to criticisms of American capitalism ... The history and conditions in each country are different. Instead of asking 'Where in the world is it better?' and setting up irrelevant comparisons, we should be asking 'Can we make things better here in America, on the basis of advantages that we alone have got?'"

"I've had enough of this," my interviewer shot back, and hung up. Just like that. In the middle of a live broadcast.

There were also slips between the cup and the lip. *Fortune* magazine sent over for a copy of the game, saying that their editors wanted to play it. Their photographer spent an hour taking pictures in my office, but the article on Class Struggle never appeared. (Did the editors learn something on playing the game?) Neither did the promised article in *Newsweek*, nor, a little later—and most vexing—the article in *Time*. Here, the piece was not only written but in print when Pope Paul VI died and the whole issue was redone, leaving out such inessentials as Class Struggle to make more room for His Holiness, who had succeeded in carrying his struggle against Marxism into the hereafter.

Still, with few exceptions, the overwhelming response of the media was, "Here is an amusing game about, of all things, class struggle." Or, alternatively, "Here is a Marxist who is funny." What a surprise! Not that anyone missed the serious political message in the game—how could they? Socialist tracts were nothing new; a socialist tract in the form of a game was. And just because it was amusing, the socialist arguments were somehow less threatening, perhaps even less objectionable. In light of this, the square on the Class Struggle board that speaks of the capitalists' control of the media and its use to present the capitalist point of view requires at least this small qualification.

The almost total absence of political criticism took me by surprise. I had hoped for a positive response, and feared teeth-gnashing hostility. The degree of acceptance, indeed, of enthusiastic support, threw me slightly off-balance. What was at work here? Why were the capitalist media so enthusiastic about my anticapitalist game? Why are people pleased to learn that socialists (or capitalists) have a sense of humor? Why don't people want others with whom they disagree to take themselves too seriously? Is having a sense of humor incompatible with taking oneself seriously? These questions started me thinking about the role of humor in politics, and particularly about the function of radical political humor. I seemed to have accomplished something good, possibly important, that I didn't completely understand.

The literature on humor gives three main reasons for why people laugh: because they feel superior, as a relief from tension or an indirect expression of forbidden urges, and as a results of the juxtaposition of two incongruous ideas. Class Struggle is constructed out of incongruities, juxtaposing as it does Marx and Rockefeller, struggle and play, politics and games, growth in trade unions and losing a turn at the dice. The amusement most people get out of playing and sometimes just on hearing about Class Struggle comes mainly from experiencing these incongruities.

Everyone likes to laugh, and we all appreciate and generally like the people who make us laugh. Liking them, we tend to react more favorably to whatever is identified with them—a country, a race, an ideology—or at least to be less hostile. With Class Struggle, I began to benefit, only half-knowingly at first, from this psychological predisposition. It is not easy for socialists to be funny. We are known to the general public as dour, often angry, superserious people—and with good reason. Life isn't funny. It is hard to be light-hearted in a world full of human tragedies, especially if one believes that most of them are the result of faulty social organization. Weighted down by this knowledge and its accompanying responsibility, most socialist humor takes the form of bitter irony, whether directed against capitalists or against oneself for being so ineffective. In either case, the potential inherent in a humor that nonsocialists can laugh at for "winning friends and influencing people" is lost.

Another lesson I gleaned from Class Struggle's ready acceptance by the media is that people are more ready to listen to "disagreeable" ideas if they are presented in a humorous manner: "Smile when you say that." It removes some of the discomfort and anxiety associated with dissonance of all sorts. People construct ideological, emotional, and even physical defenses to protect themselves against such discomfort, but these same defenses also make it difficult to understand and sometimes even to hear contrary opinions. Humor gets people to lower their defenses not only because laughing is a relaxing activity, but also because humor is associated in our minds with what is nonserious and nonthreatening. In this way, a little space is opened up for genuine communication.

Then—and this is something I still don't understand well— leaving aside outright nonsense, people are more likely to believe the truth of whatever makes them laugh. For example, if you tell people that statistics distort reality, you'll get qualified agreement at best. But if you substitute, "When your head is in the freezer and your feet are on the stove, statistics is what tells you that the temperature in your stomach is just right," agreement is likely to be general. (Remember this joke the next time an economist says something about the average income.) Political speakers of all persuasions have made use of this bias in favor of the humorous version, but to my knowledge no one has adequately explained it. Is it too much to hope that Class Struggle, not despite but because of its clowning, actually taught some members of the Fourth Estate a thing or two about the class struggle?

We soon learned that getting publicity in the press and selling the game were two different things. To be sure, the one prompted the other, but there was no simple cause and effect relationship. If the games were not available in local stores, interest could not translate easily into sales. Some stores contacted us for orders as soon as the avalanche of stories hit. They were getting many requests for the game. They didn't care what it was about, whether it was good or bad—customers were asking for it. Nothing else counted. About a hundred of the requests received by Bloomingdale's, Macy's and F.A.O. Schwarz, those from the most disappointed customers, came from members of the board of Class Struggle, Inc. Sometimes public opinion needs a little goosing.

Many individuals also called us up asking for games. The day after the story in *The Washington Post*, we got a call from Sargent Shriver's office ordering seven gift copies that Shriver wanted to take with him on a trip to Moscow. Did Brezhnev get one? Did he learn something? I hoped so.

Board meetings during this period were celebrations of our successes. I would begin each meeting by passing around the latest stories from the press. *Business Week*, *Money*, and *The London Financial Times* had just done favorable stories. *Fortune*, *Playboy*, and *Gallery* had just interviewed me. The business and skin magazines made an unbeatable combination, American to the core. It seemed now we couldn't miss.

Howard would shake his head disbelievingly. "Look at this. How did we do it?" Iz announced that his friend Irwin, from whom we had sought some PR advice, was dumbfounded by our achievement.

Then Jo Ann would announce what stores had ordered games that week, and whom we had appointments to talk to the following week. Brentano's chain of book and game stores, Bloomingdale's, which had the *chutzpah* to ask for an "exclusive," and the Eighth Street Bookstore in Greenwich Village were among our first and best customers. All the members of the board took part in the selling.

Right from the start, we accumulated as many bookstore customers as game and department stores. Most of these bookstores sold no other games. It just became clear to their owners, as it had to us, that Class Struggle was the kind of game that had a special appeal to book buyers. In contacts with bookstore people, we stressed that Class Struggle is really "a book in a box, a humorous book about capitalism that one reads by picking up Chance Cards rather than turning pages."

A special problem arose over what sales terms to use in the book trade. Bookstores follow a policy of returning books that don't sell to their publishers, whereas game and department stores pay for all the games ordered, whether they sell or not. We opted for a compromise: first orders were returnable; subsequent orders were not. This satisfied the bookstores, and gave added appeal to our product in game and department stores.

The American Booksellers Association's annual fair was held in Atlanta in late May. Howard went and set up a display of Class Struggle. We had no idea what to expect. Judging from the press explosion and our quick successes in New York, we thought Howard might sell thousands of games. In fact, he sold only a couple hundred, but he reported that a lot of bookstore owners showed a keen interest. They preferred to watch and wait for a while to see how well Class Struggle sold in the stores. Their caution should have made us more cautious, but things were going too well in New York and in the media. Howard's most exciting news was that he had been approached by a representative of Mondadori, Italy's largest publisher, about an Italian edition. They promised to contact us shortly.

Just back from a combination lecture tour and Class Struggle promotion trip to California, the first week of June found me in Washington, D.C., selling games and trying to learn what was happening at Maryland (the decision, I was told, would be coming any day now, since President Elkins was scheduled to retire at the end of June). It was there that I met Rodney Sokol. When he is not being a gentlemanly painter, Rodney is a top-flight literary agent whose stable of clients includes Erich Fromm, Gar Alperowitz, and several other important radical and liberal thinkers. The world of business is full of people who talk as if they know it all. They've seen it, lived it all before, many times. They know all the angles, have all the connections. They say it in words, in their tone of voice, in how they smile and lay their hands on you. Sokol—thirtyish, pudgy and baby-faced—was a master at this game.

Rodney was immensely impressed by the media attention given to Class Struggle. And when I told him that Mondadori had expressed interest in doing an Italian edition, he said that what we needed was an experienced agent to negotiate the best possible deal with Mondadori and then to duplicate this deal in other countries. Though he had never handled a game before, Rodney said he would make an exception for Class Struggle.

That very Sunday, Rodney came to a meeting of our board of directors. The talk was all about the million games we could sell if we did it right, thought big, and went with the pros, like him. He went over his track record, his special relationship with Dick Snyder, president of Simon and Schuster—there was the possibility of a co-production deal here—and again, the numbers game. "Hundreds of thousands," "millions." Of course, the picture of Marx and Rocky on the cover would have to go. We could do much better, he said, with cartoon figures.

Only Jo Ann and Paul refused to be impressed. They didn't like Rodney's style and they didn't appreciate the condescension he showed toward us "boychicks," us "poor amateurs." Still, we made Rodney our agent, giving him 10 percent off the top of any foreign licensing deal he would arrange. Rodney wanted to buy into the business itself in order to have a major voice in our future development and also to make what he considered a sure financial killing. On this, we stalled. Yes, we needed money to finance another, bigger edition of games, but we had to give existing investors a first crack at buying more shares. Howard, in particular, insisted that having invested so much money in Class Struggle when it was an extremely risky venture, he should have the option to buy as many shares as he wanted now that we had a "sure thing" going.

How much more money was needed would depend on how many more games we decided to produce. In May alone, we had sold over 3,000 games, and all indications were that this was just the beginning. We needed at least 10,000 more games, but decided 25,000 was even better, if we could afford it. Whether we could would depend, in large part, on how much we had to pay for each game and on the terms of payment. Very little money had come in, and we were beginning to understand that there was a big difference between selling games and getting paid for them, though how great this difference was we had still to learn.

This left the question of who would produce the next edition. We felt no commitment to continue with Juvenile Packaging. Hadn't Gouldner raised the price on us in the middle of the run? We all felt badly burned by this incident. If we got a better offer from another manufacturer, then, as businessmen, we would have to take it.

Through a friend in publishing, Izzy heard of the Finn Company of Hoboken, New Jersey, which publishes mainly religious books and tracts, but also produces a number of games, Scrabble among them. Howard and I visited Bill Finn, the small, elf-like, sexagenarian owner of the company. There was a marked contrast between the respectful reception he gave us and the odd looks with which toy-industry people had greeted us a few months before. We were told that no game in the history of the industry—and that includes Monopoly—had ever received the kind of press coverage we were getting. Finn offered to produce 25,000 Class Struggles at $3.09 a game. Covered in this price were a number of improvements, the most important of which was a cardboard tray to hold the money and the player pieces. All this, including the price, would be stated in writing. He also promised us that if business continued to improve and we wanted an additional 25,000, they would cost us only $3 a game (this was not in writing).

Finn said he could not store and ship the finished games for more than two months. Going with Finn, then, meant assuming the responsibility for storage, shipping, and billing, which Juvenile Packaging had been doing for us for an additional fee. Because of the numerous delays and foul-ups we were experiencing, this was something we were about to do in any case.

I told Gouldner that we were taking a bid from another company to produce an additional 25,000 games. From the way he reacted, it was clear that he thought this was simply a ploy to get him to lower his price. He had taken the measure of these socialist professors; he knew what we could and couldn't do. Besides, he had taught us most of what we knew about the games industry, and had become our friend. In all this, Gouldner was not far off the mark. All my business relations with board members, employees, and even buyers were still primarily personal relations. I responded to them in ways that they evoked from me as people, being who they were, with all their individual foibles and needs. Warming to his pleasant personality, I had begun to treat Gouldner as a good friend. What could possibly change this?

A week later, Gouldner came to my NYU office to deliver his "lowest possible" bid and to take away—he was certain—an order for 25,000 more games. His bid was $3.07 per unit on the identical game he had produced before (no improvements). Everything would be in writing this time (what happened to the machines that might break down?), but there was no assurance on the price of the next order. This last, in particular, weighed heavily on my mind.

"Well, Sam," I told him, "if that's the best you can do, I'm afraid we'll have to accept the offer of the Finn Company." My heart was pounding fast as I strained for calm.

"What?" His usually jovial expression froze on a note of genuine shock. "Don't you owe it to me? After all I did ..."

"Sam, they've made us the better offer. What else is there to say?"

Collecting himself, he looked at me with as much sadness as controlled anger. "Bertell," he almost whispered, "you've really become a businessman." I accompanied him to the elevator. We didn't exchange another word. He got on the elevator, looked at me, and slowly shook his head.

The accusation in his words did not bother me, but the compliment did.

NINE:
STRIKE AT BRENTANO'S BOOKSTORE

The order for 25,000 more games made it necessary for us to come up with $78,000. Most of the stores that had bought games from the first edition had still to pay us. Sensing a runaway success, Howard and other members of the board bought another 110 shares in the company at $300 a share (the price had tripled since our first offering), which brought in $33,000, or slightly less than half of what we needed. There was no telling when the money from Mondadori would become available, or from Sokol, if we chose to sell him shares. Before Finn handed over the finished games, he would have to be paid the full amount. Would the banks lend us money to produce (promote) Class Struggle (class struggle)? It was an intriguing thought. I began to investigate whether it was also a real possibility.

In early July, Macy's and Gimbels department stores decided ' that Class Struggle was respectable enough for their customers, and Brentano's, which had already sold several hundred games, began ordering for their 25 stores throughout the country. Then—out of the blue—a call from the working class.

"Is this Bertell Ollman?" my caller asked.

"Yes."

"Do you support striking workers?" he went on.

"Yes." The question was puzzling, but easy to answer.

"Do you know there's a strike at the Brentano store in Manhasset, Long Island?"

"No, I didn't," I said.

"The strike is for recognition of the union, and it's been going on for over eight months." The voice on the phone hardened.

"That is a long time." I remembered the escalating anger my father felt during a long summer strike when I was still a kid. "The Brentano stores in New York City are unionized," I said, "and I assumed the others were as well."

"No, some of their stores are unionized, but some are not.

The difference to Brentano's is over a dollar an hour in wages, so they have put up a stiff resistance on the strike. I am one of the strikers. My name is Jim Evans." In Class Struggle, the Workers receive three assets for going on strike. It's their best weapon. I was really pleased, even a little excited, to receive Jim's call.

"Well, what can I do for you?" I asked.

"The Manhasset store," Jim said, "has sold a lot of your game, Class Struggle. They've even put it in the window. Imagine how we strikers feel marching in front of the store with picket signs having to look at Class Struggle in the window. Yesterday a woman apologized for crossing our picket line, saying she just had to buy a copy of Class Struggle. That was too much. So we are asking you, as a socialist who supports the workers, to stop selling games to Brentano's until they settle the strike."

Somewhat taken aback, I managed to reply that this was a big order, since Brentano's was our largest customer, and, in any case, this was a matter for the board of Class Struggle, Inc., to decide. I invited Jim and whomever he'd like to bring to come to the next meeting of our board to make his request in person.

That Sunday evening, I told the board members who was coming and what they wanted. Something wasn't going according to plan. A fly, quite a large one, had fallen into the ointment. Howard, in particular, seemed very uncomfortable. Before long, Jim turned up with three of his fellow strikers, all tall, long-haired men in their twenties.

After the introductions, Jim began by telling the history of the strike. Overwork, rotten pay, no security. It didn't take long for everyone in the room to be convinced that the strike was right and necessary.

Bob, another of the workers, interrupted to say that no one seemed to know anything about their strike. "A small strike—there are 11 of us—in an out-of-the-way corner of Long Island gets no attention from the press. If something about the strike got into the papers, it might help us."

Then came the request: "You guys say you're socialists and that you support the workers. Well, we need your support where it counts. Call a press conference and announce that you're boycotting Brentano's for the duration of the strike."

After some moments of silent reflection, Ed, our resident realist, asked, "What is your union doing to help?"

"We belong to the Teamsters and they give us some strike benefits and help print leaflets, that sort of thing."

"Most truckers belong to the Teamsters. They have the muscle to stop all deliveries to the store. Why aren't they doing more?" Ed wanted to know.

A couple of the strikers threw up their hands as if to say, "That's a good question. I wish we had the answer."

Izzy interrupted to ask, "Who else are you asking to boycott Brentano's? I'm sure they buy books from a number of progressive publishers, like Monthly Review Press and International Publishers."

"Class Struggle is in the window. It's Class Struggle that's in the public eye right now. If you boycott Brentano's, the press will take notice," Bob said.

"What effect do you think our boycott would have on Brentano's?" I asked.

"Probably none," was the honest response, "but they can't be completely indifferent to bad publicity."

"Let me get something clear," Howard said. "You guys are asking that we boycott the whole chain, not just one store, right?"

Jo Ann, who had the best grasp of the mechanics of distribution, replied for them: "We don't sell to individual stores. We ship the games to a central location and they decide where to send them. Brentano's wouldn't accept a demand that they withdraw the game from a particular store."

Jim cleared up any doubt there might have been on this score: "It is necessary to boycott the whole chain to have maximum impact."

"So," Howard continued, "we're talking about cutting off about 15 percent of our market."

"Probably more than that," Jo Ann said, "when you consider the other store owners who will be frightened off by a boycott of Brentano's. Remember, many of our customers think they're selling an ordinary game and not the revolution."

"Look," Bob said, "the matter is really very simple. You guys talk a lot about workers and class struggle. Here's your chance to combine theory with practice, to do something you say you believe in."

"We're already doing something we believe in by selling the game," I said. "You fellows have seen the game, have read what's inside, I take it."

Our guests looked at one another and then at us, each in turn shaking his head. "No," Jim said, a little embarrassed, "but we sort of know what it's about."

"What it's about," I continued, surprised that they had not even looked into what they were so willing to sacrifice, "is how capitalism works for the few and what can be done to change this."

Sensing that I was about to deliver a favorite lecture, Ed broke in. "What you fellows have to understand is that we went into business because of our politics. Business is just a means to our end, but it's a means that sets limits to what we can and cannot do. We can't, for example, do anything that would make us go broke."

"It's a strange means for socialists to be using," Jim replied, with a touch of contempt in his voice.

"Well, it's a means that hasn't been tried before," Ed came back. "So far, for us, it seems to be working."

Somewhat annoyed at the turn in our discussion, Bob broke in to say, "That's all well and good, but the question remains— are you going to give us the support we're asking for?"

Paule, who had been quiet until now, was the first to respond: "The day after we announce our boycott to the press could be our last day in business. Do you fellows understand that?"

"Yes, we do," Jim answered, "but what a way to go!"

We all laughed, but at this point it was clear to everyone that our differences could not be reconciled. We went on to explain the financial investment that had already gone into the game and that we were in the midst of producing 25,000 more. If our business went under, all this money would be lost. They argued, once again, that we should live up to our ideals, and offered to help us promote the game if we agreed to boycott Brentano's, though how they could help us was unclear. We parted amicably enough, and I promised to call Jim the next day with our decision.

As our meeting with the strikers neared its close, I began to experience a tearing of my seamless conscience. Finding myself, if only momentarily, in opposition to strikers left me feeling exposed to a class guilt that was altogether new. At the same time, I felt deeply indignant about their apparent indifference to our project. My career as a Marxist businessman was beginning to pull me in two directions. Would it end up splitting me in half?

The consensus on the board was that boycotting Brentano's at this moment would sink us. Committing suicide, we decided, is bad business and even worse politics. Our answer had to be "no." The attraction we all felt to be in solidarity with the strikers, no matter what, had to be resisted. Nothing, not even supporting a group of workers, is unambiguously radical. It all depends on context, outcomes, alternatives. In this case, our larger, longer-term goals had to be given priority.

The next day, I called Jim with our decision, explaining that it was our view that a boycott would probably mean the end of Class struggle, Inc. Later, when we were less dependent on Brentano's, or if the strikers organized a larger, more inclusive boycott, we would reconsider our position. For now, I said, because we considered the strike a good one, we would like to contribute a couple hundred dollars to the strike fund and a few of us would like to join the workers for a day on the picket line.

Jim was very disappointed but said he would get back to me about our counteroffer. A week passed without hearing from him, when I got a call from Barbara Ehrenreich of *Seven Days*, who wanted to know, "Is it true that Class struggle has refused to support the Brentano strikers?" I explained what had happened and why we had decided against a boycott. The next day, Alex Cockburn, who had already written on Class Struggle in his *Village Voice* column, called with the same question. It seemed as if our friends at Brentano's had decided to use Class Struggle as a springboard into the media, if not one way, then another.

Barbara Ehrenreich's article came out in the August issue of *Seven Days*, which at the time was second only to *Mother Jones* in its Left readership. It was entitled, "Class Struggle: Only a Game? Marxist Professor's Game Collides with Real Class Struggle." After a humorous summary of the game, she related the story of the Brentano strike, concluding with their request to us that we boycott the chain: "Chance for Class Alliance between Professionals and Workers," she comments. But we only offered them money and help on the picket line, the article went on, which one striker was said to have found "disillusioning, to say the least." Then, I was quoted as saying that pulling the game from Brentano's "might get us a few plaudits, but it would ruin the business." Ehrenreich concluded by asking, "Did the players take the game too seriously? Or not seriously enough?" The story itself was accompanied by a large picture of a striking worker pointing out a copy of Class Struggle in the window of the Brentano Manhasset store, with the caption, "Caught in the act: Class Struggle crosses the picket line in Long Island."

The *Village Voice* article on Class Struggle and the Brentano strike appeared the same week. Cockburn's account, however, simply presented the facts, without the snide putdown that characterized the *Seven Days* piece. The attention in the press that had carried us so far was about to boomerang. The effect of these two stories was immediate. First, three Left bookstores canceled orders for the game, because "Ollman crossed the picket line in the Brentano strike." *Seven Days* had ordered 500 games to use in a subscription drive. After the Ehrenreich article, their interest in the game flagged, and a few months later they canceled their order. And the majority of the reporters who interviewed me over the next six months wanted to know, "Why did you let the workers down?"

Several friends also called or wrote me to express their dismay. I was especially pained by the letter I received from Victor Wallis, who was then chairman of the Caucus for a New Political

Science, the Left alternative in the American Political Science Association. Victor and I had struggled together in a variety of causes for over a decade, and I much respected his commitment and political judgment. Victor wrote, "I think the key issue is that of the actual consciousness of the strikers and the question of how it can be raised beyond the level of their immediate interests. In one sense, their decision to ask for a significant gesture on your part (i.e., temporarily withdrawing the game) does the game an honor by suggesting that they do see its subject matter as being related to what they are doing."

The Brentano strike even invaded my place of work. Someone posted the Ehrenreich article on the elevator I take up to my office at NYU. Each day I would remove it, and the next morning it would be back. Like my seething anger, the article just wouldn't go away. "Unfair," I wanted to scream.

Instead, I wrote to *Seven Days*, emphasizing that Class Struggle, Inc., did not cross the picket line, an extremely damaging charge in Left circles, but that we refused to engage in a one-company boycott, and not, as the article suggested, because it would cost some money, but because it would probably mean the end of both our business and our political project. No progressive group, be it a union or anything else, has the right to ask another progressive group to commit *hari kiri* on its behalf. The editors and publishers of *Monthly Review Press*, America's largest socialist publisher, also wrote *Seven Days* to protest the article as a "smear," adding that they considered the strikers' request both "frivolous" and a "publicity gag." If the strikers were serious, the Monthly Review letter said, they would have tried to organize all radical suppliers, and this they never did. "Brentano's will operate with or without Class Struggle, but they could not operate without books."

But the damage was already done. Other papers both in the U.S. and abroad picked up the story without the qualifications and corrections carried in subsequent correspondence. Aside from the distortions of fact spread by these stories, I was also very disturbed that so many socialist publications waited to comment on Class Struggle until our success could be presented

in the form of a scandal. Whatever one might think of its contents, Class Struggle was a unique socialist cultural event, and
we had counted on the interest and support of the socialist press.
Instead, *Mother Jones*, the most widely read socialist magazine,
never reviewed the game. Neither did *The Guardian*, nor the
Progressive, nor the *Militant*, though *The Guardian* marketplace
section sold close to a thousands copies of Class Struggle over
two Christmas seasons. *The Daily World*, the newspaper of the
Communist party, did publish a review, but it began by asking,
"What can you expect from a country that has toilet seats in 70
different colors?" Then, after quoting at length from the game,
the review concluded by pointing to my major political error,
which was not to give the Soviet Union any credit for the
progress of the class struggle in the United States.

Other than a favorable article in *The Nation*, whose main
focus was on events at the University of Maryland, the one serious, positive piece on Class Struggle in the socialist press
appeared in *In These Times*, where the game was said to be an
"ironic form of Marxist education" that was "ingenious, original, and entertaining." Beautiful! Except the review happens to
have been written by my close friend Ira Shor. Given the widespread and generally enthusiastic reception Class Struggle
received in the capitalist media, the indifference and even hostility with which it was greeted by many radicals was as puzzling as it was painful. The reaction to our refusal to boycott
Brentano's offered some clues to what was going on.

Presenting class struggle in the form of a game was seen by
some on the Left as a trivialization of the real thing. For these
critics, the bourgeois media's enthusiasm for the game only confirmed their interpretation. I recalled how surprised I had been
a few months before, when Ray Rakow first argued this point.
But class struggle is not the kind of thing that can be trivialized.
It happens, is real; it's how our society works, though most workers don't know it. Enhancing people's understanding of this
struggle, through whatever means are available, is what most
socialist politics is all about. The accusation that my game triv-
ializes the class struggle bespeaks a kind of sacred attitude

toward the concepts of Marxism that belongs in church, not in the socialist movement.

One could argue, of course, that our inability to satisfy the demands of the Brentano strikers shows that socialists have no business going into business. And I will admit that this thought passed through my mind, but I quickly rejected it. The rapid spread of the game through the marketplace gave evidence that our strategy could work. We would push on.

In mid-June, Mondadori made us a concrete offer to do an Italian edition of the game. Large picture stories on Class Struggle had just appeared in three Italian magazines, led by *Epoca*, their version of *Life*. When Ricardi, another large Italian company, expressed an interest in the game, Sokol got Mondadori and Ricardi to bid against each other. Mondadori won out with an offer that included an advance on royalties of $35,000. We were elated, thinking this was but the first of many such contracts from overseas. Already, publishers and game companies from eight different countries had written asking about foreign rights to the game.

In the midst of our controversy with the Brentano workers, and just as negotiations with Mondadori were coming to a head, the bubble at the University of Maryland burst. President Elkins retired from office on June 30 without taking any action, but on July 20, his successor, Dr. John Toll (a physicist), rejected my appointment, stating that I did not come up to his high standards for the job. He refused to specify in what ways I fell short, but assured everyone that political considerations had nothing to do with it. Wrapping himself in the mantle of academic freedom, Toll proudly took credit for resisting all the pressures that had been exerted on him to confirm the appointment, and conveniently neglected to mention the far more powerful political and business figures who had urged my rejection.

I told the press that anyone who doubted the political motivation behind Toll's decision must also believe in Santa Claus, and immediately filed suit against the University for violating my First Amendment rights. Did Toll want to reject me?

Probably not. He buckled under to business necessity, his business being the university, and the necessity having to do with getting enough money from a conservative state legislature to pay for all its programs. Fortunately, it is unconstitutional for a public university to deny someone a job because of his political views. Maryland's infraction of the law was sufficiently serious (and obvious) that the prestigious Washington law firm of Arnold and Porter offered to take the case on a *pro bono* basis, asking me to pay only what they called "incidental expenses."

In an editorial, *The New York Times* expressed the view of many, even in the liberal establishment: "For now, Professor Ollman has lost a job and must seek justice in the courts. The members of the university community have lost the right to choose their peers and have been put on notice that deviation is dangerous. And the rest of us have been challenged in our faith that the spread of divergent ideas can never hurt as much as their suppression."

At the same time, I started a $5 million libel suit against the conservative syndicated columnists Rowland Evans and Robert Novak, who had strung together a necklace of falsehoods about me in a column they wrote about Maryland. *Time* magazine had just branded this duo the least respected members of the Washington press corps (in the eyes of their peers), and related how their column had been dropped by *The Los Angeles Times* because the editor could not trust the authenticity of what they reported. To help Evans and Novak understand Marxism better for the next time they wrote on this subject, I also sent them a copy of Class Struggle.

From the very start, the board recognized that distribution beyond the radical market would be our greatest hurdle. How would we get Class struggle past the political prejudices of store owners and the outraged cries of conservative customers into the store window? Gouldner, Stevenson, and others to whom we had spoken about producing our game explained that all but the biggest toy companies use professional distributors, who take anything from 7 percent to 15 percent for their trouble. What you're buying is their connections, which in the case of a good distributor, Gouldner said, "are worth their weight in gold." The reigning motto in business seems to be: Anything that sells is good; any way that sells it is better; and he who sells a lot of them is best of all.

Once the game came out and immediately after the first favorable stories in the press (we now had a "hot" item), Howard and I visited several distributors. The first of these was Holiday Distributors. Ronnie, middle-aged and stout, and Herb, 10 years older and very slim, greeted us in what must have been the smallest office in the entire Toy Building. It was tucked away in the back corner, next to the freight elevator and just behind the men's room, on the tenth floor. The two small desks hugged each other for dear life in the center of the room, leaving just enough space for their occupants to squeeze around behind them and take seats facing the two folding chairs that leaned up against the front door. The walls were lined with display cases showing stuffed giraffes, metal building sets, and such world-famous board games as Buffo and String Them Up. To compensate for their unimpressive surroundings, Ronnie wore the brightest green blazer and the shiniest red trousers in the industry, and Herb, who dressed more modestly, sported a waxed RAF mustache, which came out an inch on either side of his face.

"Sit down. Make yourselves at home. No, there. Just call me Herb."

"I'm Ronnie. No misters here. Yeah. Sit down there. Gimme your coat. Herb, take their coats."

"Two professors, huh?" Herb continued. "Do they look like professors to you, Ronnie?"

TEN
SELLING REVOLUTION OVER THE COUNTER

"Who knows what professors look like nowadays? Well, look at this." Ronnie began turning Class Struggle over in his hands. "Does this look like a game to you, Herb?"

"I can't think or do business on an empty stomach," Herb replied.

"That's not all he can't do on a empty stomach," Ronnie smiled and winked at us.

"Once I eat, I can do anything, and I do it all better than this *momser* here," Herb said, showing mock anger and giving Ronnie a gentle elbow in the ribs. "We'll send down for sandwiches. Four corned beef, okay?"

Howard and I were interested in learning what they had done, how well they had done it, and what kind of connections they had with the main department-store buyers.

"Trudy told me just the other day ..." Herb began.

"That's Trudy Max, the buyer for Gimbels," Ronnie interrupted. "We sold her 50 gross of PooPoo last year."

"Trudy said, 'Herbie,'" Herbie went on, "if all the reps knew their line of goods as well as you do, I could save 10 hours a week."

"We've been dealing with Trudy for six years. She trusts our judgment," Ronnie added, pumping his chin up and down for emphasis.

"How many years have we been selling to Harry, eight or nine?" Herb asked his partner.

"Ten. That's Harry Salzman of Korvettes," Ronnie informed us. "Herb, did you go to his boy's bar mitzvah? Two bands. What a shindig that was."

"No, that was Solly Weiss's boy's bar mitzvah." Then, to us, Herb added, "He used to be the buyer at Klein's, God rest his soul. Run over chased by a mugger, just outside of Klein's on Fourteenth Street."

"Nobody's safe. So stay home and play more games," Ronnie concluded. "That should be your slogan, Mr. Professor Bertell. Where did you say you came from?"

When we finally got around to business, Herb spoke for Holiday Distributors: "Sell? We sell to everybody, from Boston to Washington. And we got top connections in other parts of the country. The way it works is like this. You give us 15 percent, and we set up sales people all over the country for you. All the big store buyers will see your game. Why did you have to call it Class Struggle, by the way?"

By the time the corned beef arrived, Howard and I had come to the conclusion that Holiday was not for us. I then made the mistake—before finishing my sandwich—of saying that naturally we wanted to check out a couple other distributors before deciding whom to go with.

"What's there to check out?" Ronnie shot back in some annoyance. "You want we should help you or not?"

"Ronnie, these professors are not serious," Herb said, standing up. "Look, Professor Bertell, and you, too, Mister, go eat your sandwich someplace else. Who needs the headache?"

Ignoring us and pointing an angry finger at his partner, Ronnie almost shouted, "You made this appointment, Herb. Next time you'll know better. Headaches."

I apologized, mumbling something about not thinking I had said anything wrong, but, as the argument over who was guilty of inviting us heated up, we eased our way out, and finished our sandwiches in the hall.

Harvey Wolkowitz was a distributor friend of Sam Gouldner's. We met him, too, in the Toy Building, in a big and plush office, which, as we soon discovered, was not his. Wolkowitz had been ill and out of work for some time. He shook our hands with some difficulty; his leg was in a cast. In his day, he had been a "titan," Gouldner told us, but that was the day before yesterday. "Who do you think made the hoola hoop a household woid?" He was tight with Ed Greenberg in Cincinnati, and even worked with his father, "Old Ed." When no sign of recognition crossed our faces, Wolkowitz told us that Eddy controlled Ohio's top department stores, "like in a vise." Wolkowitz was putting together a unique package of new toys and games, and from what he'd seen in the press—several stories had now appeared—Class struggle might just fit. No, he didn't visit bookstores or, which surprised us, stationary stores. "That's another rep."

In discussions with stationery and book reps, we discovered that the 120,000 outlets that make up the game market are divided into three parts: 1) toy stores, supermarkets and drugstores, 2) stationery stores, and 3) bookstores—and each is visited by different representatives, who also visit the corresponding sections of department stores. As a rule, toy stores, toy departments, supermarkets, and drug stores carry children's games; stationery stores and departments carry adult games; and bookstores, well, they usually don't carry any games at all. Right from the start, however, Class Struggle's biggest customers were bookstores. Also, as a game that could really be played by "kids from eight to 80," Class Struggle was being ordered by both toy and stationery stores. In Bloomingdale's, one of our first department-store customers, Class Struggle was sold in both the toy and stationery departments, the only game to be so honored. All the reps we talked to would only venture into their special areas. At the same time, each wanted a geographical exclusive, which meant they would get a commission from any sale in their territory no matter what kind of store sold it.

It seemed that no one was ready to sell the game to all the stores that were already buying it except ourselves, and we were nobody, or a half-dozen nobodies, who were already taxing ourselves to the limit. Could we organize the distribution of Class Struggle ourselves? In this way, we wouldn't have to hand over the commissions for stores, including some of the major ones, which had already become our customers. If we could only find the right person to put it all together. Paul Gullen, who was fed up with his job in the bookstore and already helping Jo Ann as our part-time manager, presented himself as that person. It seemed like a perfect, if probably temporary, solution to our problems.

We agreed to pay Paul $15,000, guaranteeing the job for one year. We also gave him 10 shares of Class Struggle stock, then worth $3,000, to make him that much more than a simple employee. Howard in particular, was very pleased with this arrangement. As we shook hands on the matter, I couldn't help but reflect—with some trepidation—that I was now responsible for putting all of the bread on Paul's table. (That's the boss thinking. As a Marxist, I know, of course, that it's the other way around.)

Hiring Paul as manager coincided with Class Struggle, Inc.'s move into its first real office. Actually, we only moved from Paul and Jo Ann's Class Struggle-cluttered bedroom to one of Ed's, but since Ed's was larger and no one was using it regularly, it seemed as if we now had a real office. Of course, Ed's two little girls were constantly running in and out, but that only added to the spice of a working day (again, that's management's view). Our new office could also hold several hundred games. Another 1,000, for which we needed to find a place, were crammed into my living room. "It's just for a couple of months," I promised Paule.

Every industry has annual shows where it displays its latest wares. It was at the American Booksellers Association Fair in late May, as we saw, that Howard made contact with Mondadori. In June, New York's Coliseum housed the Stationery Show; September saw the National Mail Order Show; October, the College Bookstore Show, and in February there was the big Toy Fair. We attended all of them in both our first and second year.

These shows are "for the trade." The general public is not welcome. There is nothing to buy, nothing to take away. Storeowners come to look at what the producers' imagination and resources have concocted for the American public. Owners of the littlest stores and buyers for the chains and department stores come. So does the trade press. The foreign competition comes to see what they can steal (and what was stolen from them). They all come to look, to compare gimmicks, prices, advertising campaigns, and, occasionally, quality. They come to think it over, sometimes to order, though the usual practice is to order later from the manufacturer's representative, who visits them in their stores.

A "booth" at one of these shows, that is a 10'x10' space fronting on one of 50 or more block-long aisles, costs anywhere from $500 to $1,000. In most instances, we couldn't afford to get a booth for ourselves. Also, applying late, which translates as less than a year before the show, means getting a booth in an out-of-the-way corner. At the National College Store Show, where we rented a whole booth, we were put on another floor along with other latecomers, with the result that almost no one saw the game. In selling, position is next to godliness.

The Coliseum is a large factory like space on Fifty-ninth Street and Seventh Avenue just across from Central Park. Its huge marquee is always announcing one world fair or another. In front, a long line of taxis never stops disgorging and swallowing up the nattily attired commercial gladiators whose battleground this is. I had never been to the Coliseum before the Stationery Show. To get in, I had to line up with other "out-of-towners" and show my Class Struggle, Inc., business card, which we had printed up for just such occasions.

Once inside the main exhibit hall, I searched through the numbered aisles—so this is what they sell in stationery stores?—for Harold Rossman, a friend of Gouldner's, who said he might rent us a corner of his booth. "No space," but Rossman suggested that other booths might be less congested. The Coliseum management explicitly forbids such transactions, but "What they don't know ..."

A center aisle on the second floor had exhibits on three games, including a huge three-booth extravaganza on Mastermind. If only we could get a place on that aisle. After three or four refusals, I approached Matt Halveh, whose booth featured expensive leather chess and backgammon sets. Whether he was really sad about our plight, or so amused by our game, or just wanted company, I don't know. It certainly wasn't the money, because he asked for only $200 for three days, which is less than we ever paid for "piggybacking" on someone else's booth in one of these shows.

There was room in the booth for only one Class Struggle worker at a time. I took the first stint. Who were these people walking by? Cincinnati, Miami, Hoboken—I could only make out the cities on their name tags. The Class Struggle game lay open on a small table in front of me, and the cover of the game box hung from the side of the booth announcing to passersby who we were. What was I expecting? Why was I so excited? Did I really think that once these store owners saw what we had, they would stand in line to give me orders? Most of the people walking through the aisle didn't seem to see me. They were looking for ashtrays or doilies or fountain pens, and a booth exhibiting games did not interest them. Even Class Struggle? Some buyers looking for ashtrays did notice Class Struggle. If that happened once, it usually happened twice. Heads snapped back. Some who walked by would stop and come back to look, often from a safe distance, to see if our game box really said what they thought it said. Sometimes they would smile, a little embarrassed to be caught showing an interest in something so risqué

"Hi, can I interest you in Class Struggle?" No, too political. "Did you see this article on our game in *The New York Times*?" worked better. Or, "Hottest selling game in Greenwhich Village." Paul, when he came on duty, preferred, "Psst, buddy. Do you want to buy a hot game?" The trick was to turn their momentary shock or amusement into a dialogue, and from that into a sale.

Their first question was almost always some variation on, "Are you serious?" If this was followed by another smile, a sale frequently resulted. Unless it was the type of buyer who smiles coming in, smiles during the whole sales rap, and goes away still smiling. Some people, of course, are completely lost at fairs. Their loneliness often translates as aloofness and even hostility, because they don't want to be the first ones to be rejected. A sharp smile to the chin will often daze them sufficiently so that they stop and listen to what you have to say. Then, so thankful for the human contact, even in the inhuman form of a sales pitch, they take a dozen.

By the second day, we had made friends with people in all

the booths around us, though the heavyset man who sold Mastermind continued to eye us suspiciously for the entire show. The talk was all about "good deals" and "specials" and "Christmas seasons that were better [or worse] than others." Matt, who had kindly taken us into his booth, fancied himself a "Willy Rogers," and used every break in the flow of customers to lecture "the professors" on everything from a more soothing name for our game to the sex habits of Russian Communists. He was getting back at all the teachers who had ever bored him to tears and never let him leave his seat until the bell rang for the end of class. "See, you don't have to have a fancy education, right?"

"Sort of right, Matt ... and sort of wrong." I couldn't afford to get into an argument and get thrown out of the booth. This was business. I had to be realistic. Smile. Be nice, be nice. I needed him. It was a humiliating introduction to the world of the salesman.

"Really," Matt insisted, "why don't you give your game a good American name, like Class Change?"

"That's an interesting idea," I said. "Let me think about it."

Our efforts at display reached their Madison Avenue heights in the National Mail Order Show in September. We rented a whole booth and put a 6'x 6' photo of Marx as high on the back wall as we could reach. People were struck by it immediately on entering the hall. Just four weeks before, the picture had hung on the wall behind Tom Brokaw when he interviewed me on Maryland and Class Struggle on TV's *Today* show. Afterward, the producer explained it would probably be some years before they had another Marxist on the program, so if I wanted the picture ... I did, and the Mail Order Show was the first chance we had to use it. Marx's austere visage certainly made our booth stand out from the picture-frame, wax candle, and toiletry exhibits in our area. And I'm sure Marx enjoyed looking down at the hustle and bustle of the capitalist exchange that went on below.

"Who's that?"

"Karl Marx."

"What's he doing here?"

"He's coming later to autograph his game, Class Struggle."

In the first and even second trade show I attended, I felt exhilarated. I knew I didn't fit and would never fit, but these people were going to help us bring Class Struggle to the American public. That was what counted. My tie disguise didn't seem to fool anyone. My suit was too wrinkled, my beard unkempt. I stood out to them, but not as much as they stood out to me. These were not the crowds I was used to seeing at academic and radical meetings. The clothes were newer, with a lot more color, their checkered patterns often causing me to blink. Pants were pressed highwaters. Shoes were always shined. Only a few senior citizens wore glasses. Their hair was short and combed into submission. Overironed, overwashed—I thought only choir children were so clean—everything was in place. Nothing was left to chance or fantasy. In an academic or political meeting, I am generally aware of the faces with their nuanced, pensive expressions, and can never remember what people were wearing. At the trade shows we attended, all I can recall is what people wore.

Still, I could not help but feel a little uncomfortable being so much an outsider. I felt much worse, though, a year later, when we returned to the same aisle in the Stationery Show and were greeted as old friends by the other exhibitors. For them, the "odd-balls" had survived a year in business and must be doing something right, must be "real businessmen." Had we really become a part of all this? Was I now a businessman?

Was it worth it going to all these shows? The question was debated at length at board meetings, but we could never say no to a chance to open up a new market. The fact is that the number of games sold at a show never paid for what the show cost us. Publicizing the game, of course, always helps, and we did make a number of contacts, some of which—as in the case of Mondadori—paid off. There were many other calls on our limited funds. We bought ads in *The New York Times* and in 10 Left and counterculture publications for a total of about $4,000.

Instead of a flood of orders, we got a dribble. The media stories on the game were doing a much better job of acquainting people with Class Struggle than the ads, which we soon stopped, except for Christmas.

We also sent out several large mailings to book and game stores: "Has Monopoly Met Its Match?" Included were blurbs from a dozen publications to show how universally we were loved ... or, at least, accepted. Letters also went off to trade-union officials and social-science teachers and professors, offering them the wholesale price on bulk orders. Again, the several dozen people who responded to our offer did not make up for the cost of the mailing.

Radical publications were approached to run per-inquiry ads—they print the ad free and we split with them the money that comes in. A few, including *The Nation*, agreed, but the results were disappointing. We wrote to the book clubs: "Are you ready to offer your members something completely different?" They weren't. Taken together, all our promotion efforts, the shows, the ads, mailings, etc., cost us over $15,000 in the first year. Some of the evidence was slow coming in, but it all pointed in one direction. The best way to sell games is to visit buyers in the stores.

From the start, we had also taken this route, but, having rejected professional distributors, for the reasons I gave earlier, our options were limited. Our first idea was to develop a network of radical salespeople in all the big cities and important university towns across the country, people for whom Class Struggle was a way to do politics as well as a means to earn money. Given the extra time it took to explain the game to potential customers (and to display the growing pile of clippings), some degree of commitment to our cause, we believed, was essential. Paul would visit most of the stores in New York and I undertook to visit major stores in the cities where I gave lectures, usually about once a month.

Brentano's and Bloomingdale's are the pacesetters for games in New York City. The fact that Class Struggle was in these stores and selling extremely well—the manager of the Brentano store in Greenwich Village said it was his fastest-selling game—gave us a wedge for opening up other accounts. Orders were often cautious at the start, but going into that Christmas season a couple hundred New York stores were willing to sell the game.

Outside New York, the situation was very different, except in radical bookstores, where owners had already heard of the game. Most of these owners had also heard of the incident with the Brentano strikers. After I gave my side of the story, they generally ordered a dozen games. The buyer in Hirsch's Department Store in St. Louis, however, looked at me as if I were a madman. None of my funny lines worked. He seemed relieved when I left without assaulting him.

Kramer's, Washington's largest bookstore, set up a big window display on Class Struggle, and sold over 50 in a week. But Woody's and Hecht's, the two largest department store chains in the Washington area, insisted that the game had not proven itself. What did they want—blood? Their proximity to the University of Maryland suggested as much.

It's dangerous to make appointments at a distance. Paul set up an appointment for me in Los Angeles with Shaffer's Department Store. After a 20-minute ride into the heart of Los Angeles's black ghetto, I arrived at a small Chinese general store, which, for some ancient historical reason, is called Shaffer's Department Store. Amazed that I should come all that way to see him, Simon Yuan, the owner, ordered a dozen games.

My friend Bob Bonic's niece is married to the son of a grand muck-a-muck in the Toys-R-Us organization, who got me an introduction to the buyer, Hy Steinway. Until then, he had refused to see us. At last, a connection. I decided to handle this one myself. Later, while waiting in Steinway's outer office, I overheard two salesmen talking: "Gotta bump 'em up to a car load ... pass along allowances ... if they feature it, that's so much P.M. money ... the competition is testing their product in high markets ... dealer's choice ... kick back on some of the A.I. but never on the M.I. ... only a big ad program will firm it up" (from my notebook). I was reminded of a nonsense lecture that I sometimes give to students in "Introduction to Political Theory" just to see if they're critical enough to recognize nonsense when they hear it. I had always liked Hemingway's definition of "education" as a "crap detector." My natural bent is critical, but I suspected this wasn't nonsense, just a new language I had yet to learn.

"Hello, I'm Professor Bertell Ollman, president of Class Struggle, Inc. I'm sure you've already heard of our game, Class Struggle."

"Oh, yeah. I saw something about it in the *Post*," Steinway replied. He was 40 going on 20, with a huge hippy neckpiece hanging from a red-freckled, well-manicured head. "You're a friend of Cy's?"

"Well, actually, I'm a good friend of Harold, his son. Wonderful kid, Harold." I swung easily into what I thought was expected.

Opening up my packet of newspaper clippings, I moved quickly to the business at hand. "*The New York Times* and over 50 other publications have had stories on Class struggle, practically all of them are favorable." I held my breath for a second, hoping Steinway hadn't seen the article that had just appeared in '*The National Star* under the heading, "Marxist Professor Out to Get Our Kids." I went on. "Right now, it is the fastest selling game in Brentano's in New York. Bloomingdale's ..."

"Where are you a professor?" Steinway broke in.

"NYU," I answered, trying not to miss a beat in my salesman's patter. "Let me show you how Class Struggle works. The game revolves around a contest between ..."

"I don't like the box," Steinway interrupted, holding the game up in front of him.

"What?" I felt my jaw drop.

"Black. It's a bad color for games. Games are yellow, red, bright colors. They stand out in the stores. Steinway was giving me a lesson in basics.

"But with all the other games in bright colors, a black game will stand out. No?" My composure had returned, and I wasn't about to cede the point.

"And why do you have the word 'EDUCATION' in such big letters?" Then, reading from the box, " 'AN EDUCATIONAL GAME FOR KIDS FROM 8 TO 80'?"

"Because it is," I said.

"'Education' doesn't sell the game," Steinway intoned with authority. "It puts people off. 'Fun,' 'exciting,' 'super,' sells games. People have enough education in school. They don't want to take it home with them."

"The word is used ironically," I explained. "Most people can see that. It's part of the humor in the game."

"I don't see anything funny about education." And with this, Steinway took out a tape and started measuring the box. "Yeah, I guess it would fit," he finally said.

"What?" I wasn't sure I had heard him right.

"On our shelves. Space is at a premium on our shelves," Steinway repeated. Then, lifting and shaking the game, he added, "Nice weight. Games have to weigh something, need to feel right in the box. People buy what feels right."

"Is there anything else you want to know about the game?" I inquired. My enthusiasm was rapidly waning.

"Do you plan any TV advertising?" Steinway asked.

"I appeared last month with the game on the *Today* show, and am scheduled to be interviewed on Tom Snyder's *Tomorrow* show. There has been a lot of local TV stuff, news programs and a few talk-show appearances. But advertising on TV is beyond our budget." Reeling off more of our media successes helped perk me up.

Steinway was unimpressed. "Advertising on TV is what sells games. People need to be told to go out and get it."

"But our game is already selling very well," I assured him.

"That's New York." Steinway was beginning to show annoyance. "We're talking about 30 stores spread around the country."

I persisted. "Class Struggle is a terrifically exciting and funny game. People all over will ..."

"Look, Professor," Steinway interrupted, "save that kind of talk for the cover of your game. It's for customers over the counter. Me, I'm interested in color, weight, and above all advertising budgets. Between you and me, I couldn't care less how the game is played, whether it's fun or not. Who knows why people have fun? It could be shit. A lot of times, it is shit. I just want to sell it, and I know what sells games."

I obviously had a lot to learn about games, and fun, and selling. This was not the crackerjack salesman that the drunk oracle, whose shoes I'd shined so many years back, had predicted. Still, Steinway closed our meeting by saying he'd take a couple of dozen for stores near New York and try them out. We should call him next month to get the order. After the dent Steinway made in my self-confidence, I considered myself lucky to have gotten any order at all. At least we had opened an account with the chain. The game would prove itself in the "trenches," Paul's favorite name for the stores.

When we called the next month, Steinway's line was busy. It was busy for a week, two weeks, four weeks. We left messages, but he never returned our calls. Nor did he respond to our letters. Three months later, after I hollered at his secretary that he had chosen a stupid and impolite way of saying no, Steinway took the phone and said no politely—"Maybe next year."

As I traveled through the hinterlands, I found that buyers were much more willing to state their political objections to the game. The buyer at Scott's Department Store in Chicago found Class Struggle very amusing. Then, pen in hand about to write up an order, she looked at me quizzically and said, "I just hope that no one learns anything from the game." Do I reassure her? A businessman would, if that's what she wants to hear, if that will clinch the sale. I hesitated—the words wouldn't come. She put the pen down. "Call back in a couple of weeks for an order." Another empty promise.

At Swallen's discount chain in Cincinnati, the buyer was impressed enough to order four dozen, but before I left, he decided to check with the manager who, after a hurried conference, vetoed the deal. "Mr. Swallen is a very religious man," the buyer explained in some embarrassment, "and he wouldn't like us to sell a socialist game." "But Jesus was a socialist," I protested. "Not Mr. Swallen's Jesus," came the reply.

As a rule, the higher one ascends in the hierarchy of business, the friendlier, more relaxed, and confident the person. Owners and managers of bigger companies were often interested in me as a professor. I heard a lot about kids in college, and occasionally words were exchanged on the state of the nation. If we talked about capitalism and socialism, they generally took pains to let me know how hard they worked, how they took all the risks and had all the ideas and worries and, therefore, why they deserve everything they've got.

I never doubted what they told me, or wondered how these experiences gave rise to such views. Unfortunately, life has little to do with "deserving." Otherwise, other small businesspeople who worked equally hard would not have lost everything (and they are the majority); and most big businesspeople, who never worked at all and who inherited the sizeable wealth with which they began, would not be where they are; and workers, who have worked long and faithfully for their employers, would not now be losing their jobs and incomes. But I was here to sell games, so I acted suitably impressed and either said nothing or mumbled something about "agreeing to disagree."

Visits with buyers and assistant managers were usually briefer, more to the point. Less secure in their jobs, they have all sorts of status signals to live (and suffer) by. They are uncomfortable meeting a salesman-professor; "Just what kind of hybrid monster is this?" Low on self-confidence, many cannot afford a sense of humor. They may laugh at the wrong time or too much, so they don't laugh at all. Newer buyers often want big discounts on shipping and advertising to show their bosses they are doing well. Everyone's concern is with the bottom line.

One evening while I was on the road, I tried to reread *Death of a Salesman*, but it was too painful. I had to put it aside. The indifference, the return calls and promise of orders that never come, the abrupt refusals, the recorded voices stalling—"Call after the show; before the show; later in the fall." No funds, no place, no call for it. And always the subtle signs of who has power over whom—too polite, too haughty, too suave, no time, another appointment, someone waiting downstairs, an impor-

tant call, "Excuse me, please." The adventure of starting a business had been replaced by the weary and worry ridden routine of
running one. It was also very tiring playing the merry Marxist—
"Who, me, dangerous?"

The long, slow walk back to my car. Sitting there, trying hard
to keep the overall picture in mind. Seeking comfort in clichés—
"One battle does not a war make." The efforts of the noble
Odysseus also came to mind more than once. Business had not
become any less hazardous in the intervening centuries. I had a
need to fix my attention on something warm and natural, like
that rabbit running by the edge of the wood ... or, better still,
like the big sale Paul made last week to Gimbels.

But I have been moving ahead of my story. In late summer of
1978, selling Class Struggle in New York was like pulling ripe
apples off a tree, and a few stores in Washington and Boston
were selling games as fast as they came in. Sales in July and
August (traditionally a slow period) had moved up to 2,000 a
week and were increasing. Susan Kronick, the buyer at
Bloomingdale's, said that it looked as if Class Struggle was
becoming the game of the year. If the interest continued, she was
thinking about featuring it for Christmas, which meant an additional order of 10,000. At this pace, our second edition of 25,000,
which we had just received, would soon be sold out.

At a Sunday meeting of the board in early September, we
discussed the need for more games. Paul told us he had just got
a call from a buyer in Holland who wanted 5,000 games, though
the details of the deal still had to be worked out. It would be
politically irresponsible, we agreed, to be caught without games
just before Christmas, but we were practically broke. Very little
money had actually been received for the games we sold. How
could we pay for new games? Thirty-five thousand dollars was
due soon from Mondadori, stores owed us almost double that
amount, we could sell more shares in Class Struggle, Inc. (Sokol
still wanted to buy into the business), Simon and Schuster might
advance us something as part of a distribution deal then pending—(more on this later), and with our track record there should

be no problem borrowing—if we still needed it — $25,000 to $50,000 from the bank. In the euphoria of the moment, there was no doubt about the issue. We would order 25,000 more games from Finn.

I saw Finn a few days later and told him we wanted another 25,000 games at the $3 per game figure he quoted me when we made our first agreement. Not so fast! Or so easy! He apologized profusely but said that the price of paper had risen so much in the last month that the best he could offer me now was $3.37 per game, or about $8,000 more than we expected to pay. I was dumbfounded. Another squeeze play. Gouldner was wrong—I still wasn't a businessman. "However, if you want 50,000," Finn added, "I can let you have them for as little as $3.20 per game." After a hurried conference with the board, we decided, with only Jo Ann dissenting, that the best thing to do was to swallow our resentment and order the larger number. "Look," I recall saying, "the way the game is selling, the worst thing that can happen is that we'll have a few left over after Christmas!"

The public's reaction to Class Struggle, as expressed in hundreds of letters, was more varied and interesting than the almost unanimous praise the game received in the press. On the whole, it was also better written. One student wrote me, "I bought the game for a friend who is a strong believer in the capitalist system, and he loved it at first sight because he thought it would be a joke. After playing the part of the Workers, he admitted the game was anything but a joke, and for the first time was able to see there could be life after capitalism." Another satisfied customer wrote, "Playing Class Struggle was the most fun I have had in my entire learning experience."

Not everyone shared this judgment: "Class Struggle is the most boring game I have ever played ... Your socialist conscience should be bothered by your rip-off price ... Bertell, how can you sleep?" A professor at the Harvard School of Business declaimed, "Accountants of the world unite. You have nothing to lose but your net balance," and delivered a technical lecture on the meaning of "assets" and "debits." Some found fault with the underlying social analysis: "Giving the workers a 50 percent chance to win doesn't, unfortunately, represent the real historical situation in the U.S."

Most of the critical letters, however, were addressed more to my Marxist views than to the game itself: "After reading over the instructions which accompany your game, Class Struggle, I had visions of school-age children marching through Wall Street singing songs about 'barbaric parasites' and carrying banners with your face and long pledges dedicating themselves to be firm believers in Ollmanism ... No, Mr. Ollman, I won't buy your game, and if I ever see it again, I'll probably burn it." Equally perceptive was the letter that began, "I am on disability, which means I get a little over $300 per month. I do not feel alienated. Since you are a Marxist, are you going to shoot me for saying that?" I couldn't help but reflect on how well the capitalist media and educational system have done their job, when even such a wretched soul perceives me as the enemy.

One correspondent claimed to know the source of the game's humor: "How can anyone be surprised to find that a Marxist can

ELEVEN:
VOX POPULI

be funny? It is to laugh. Why else would the capitalists pay your salary at NYU?" Another came right to the point: "Asshole." That was it, except for a signature and return address. This was the only really hostile letter for which the writer took full responsibility. Was he hoping to begin a serious exchange of ideas? For a few who couldn't bother to write down their abuse, there was always the telephone. Obscene calls started coming in, sometimes as many as three or four a day.

Typical of the many religious letters I received is this one: "Please, my friend, humble yourself and come to Jesus before it is too late. Time is fast running out. Check out what you have placed your faith in. Marxism will pass away, but the Lord is forever. Marx never healed anyone, raised anyone from the dead, or raised himself from the dead—Jesus did ... Jesus is the day of salvation—not Marxism." Such letters often contained helpful religious tracts, and in one case a comic book on hell for nonbelievers.

Criticisms from the Left were not lacking. Objecting to the Chance Card, "Stealing is no answer to poverty," an anarchist writer argued, "Better to steal than to make no response at all to oppression and exploitation. I steal whenever I can."

Especially gratifying were the reactions of teachers who had used the game in their high school and college classes, in subjects ranging from politics to nursing: "With some other teachers at Glasgow University, we have had a tournament of Class Struggle with our students ... I was very impressed with the game as a way of getting across new ideas." A high school teacher from Boston wrote, "We played Class Struggle in class today. There was much excitement. Once the students got the hang of alliances, they took off with it ... I had a number of students rooting for the Workers all the way, and they felt let down when they had to ally with the Capitalists." An Australian high school teacher even gave an exam on the explanations found in the game, and sent me his students' papers to correct.

The large majority of the letters I have received on Class Struggle have been friendly and positive; while just the opposite is true of the letters that poured in during the same period in response to my academic freedom controversy with the University of Maryland. Criticisms tended to be angrier, often with a bite that was meant to draw blood. One correspondent wrote, "I'm terribly sorry to hear that Dr. Toll of the University of Maryland rejected you for the chair. I really wish that there were some way we could give you the chair, but you know the death penalty has been eliminated by the rest of the Marxist scum in this country even though most commie *cun*tries still keep it, since they know how to deal with their traitorous slime. It shows how far the U.S. has degenerated when they even consider a miserable sonofabitch like you for a university job of any kind. Happy coronary infarction and drop dead." Someone with a more poetical turn of mind asked, "Who wants to go to bed with a prickly porcupine? Even on a cold night, he makes a dubious bedmate."

Another, for whom socialism and Russian Communism were synonymous, wanted to know, "Do you think you would be hired as head of the Department of Political Philosophy at the University of Moscow if you were an avowed espouser of the capitalist philosophy?" It's odd how often people who oppose the Soviet Union fall into using what they do there (or are perceived as doing) as a model for what we should do here in the U.S. I was also reminded of a recent experience on the Larry King radio talk show, where a good three quarters of the people who called in asked hostile questions about Russia. Here I was talking about the need to give people more power over the decisions which affect their daily lives, here in America, and the next caller would spew hate at me and rant once again about Russia. As far as America's rulers are concerned, if Russia didn't exist, it would have to be invented. Maybe it was.

The one letter that went to my heart more than any other read, "Hey, Berty. Love your game. Just stole it from a friend's pad. Good luck. Professors that invent games are the greatest teachers in the playground of America. Your student—Abbie Hoffman." I had met Abbie briefly about 10 years ago, but so had a million other people. We don't really know each other, but yet on the deepest human level I feel I know him very well. As someone who has given new life to the tired anarchist notion of propaganda by the deed, and has uncovered new ways of using the system against the system, Abbie may just be the most creative socialist teacher of us all. He is our own Evel Knievel, the shadow who walks out in front of us to test the dangerous waters, a whole army including a drum and bugle corps, and an intelligence service, all by himself. Abbie's role in inspiring the creation of Class Struggle and our media strategy was considerable. To receive word from the Underground that he knew and understood was one of the high points of my Class Struggle career.

A couple of months later, Abbie sent me outlines of two games he was working on, inspired—it seems—by my example. One was called the Down Game, which he described as "A game of chance—Loser takes all—The bottom of the bummers—Death wins (for all ages: 65-75)." Players start out with a house, a job, good health, a family, etc., and move around the board losing them one after another. The first player who arrives at the last square, which is called "Death," having lost all that makes life worth living, wins. That is a downer. Always the visionary, Abbie had produced the first primer on Reaganomics.

The other game was called Fugitive. It was meant to show all the problems Abbie had in being a fugitive and the ways he overcame them. Since, at that time, he was still overcoming them, there were tricks that could not be revealed. So the game was full of gaps. Now that Abbie has surfaced, maybe he can finish this game. With more chances to develop strategies, I think it has a lot more promise than the Down Game.

Abbie was not alone in sending me ideas for games. The word had gotten out that Class Struggle had made it, and with it, our company. I must have received close to 50 letters and calls from game inventors asking me to produce their game or for advice on how to get it produced. Some inventors had been inspired by Class Struggle, but others had been working on their games for some time. Because of the character of Class Struggle, many of the inquiries were about progressive games. One professor offered us a game called Utopia, in which players learn about the advantages of life in a society without private property. Another professor sent me rules for a card game on revolution that could be played with existing decks. We ourselves had given some thought to producing a card-game version of Class Struggle, so this idea triggered a lot of interest.

A reporter from a business magazine sent me two socialist games: Transition from Feudalism to Capitalism and Rent Strike. The first was an exercise in explaining "what," while the second offered lessons in "how to." He also had an interesting idea for a Bureaucracy Game, which needed no special equipment and allowed any number to play. "It's simple," he said. "The players sit facing one another, and the first one to move loses." A winner, but how do you package it? A game arrived called Unemployment—How to Survive It, which was full of practical solutions, but left out the most practical solution of all, which is to do away with the economic order that produces unemployment. It is the only solution, after all, that is guaranteed to work for everyone over the long term. This is, of course, what Class Struggle is all about.

One caller obviously got the wrong number. His game, "Public Assistance," was meant "to show how the poor were ripping off the system." "Public Assistance," he said, "was a natural to piggyback off the success of Class Struggle." Could it be that he didn't notice that my chief concern was with how the system was ripping off the poor? This game appeared on the market about a year later, and was pegged by some reporters as the conservative response to Class Struggle.

As interesting as some of these ideas were, we were in no position to produce another game. Not yet. Not until Class Struggle really took off and made some money. We were still pumping ever-greater sums into our own game. Those who asked for the names of companies that make dice or game boards got them. But our experience with Class Struggle, particularly as regards the media blitz, was so unusual that I didn't see much that others could learn from us. Without a lot of start-up money and connections with distributors, it is practically impossible for a small entrepreneur to succeed. Even with them, the odds are heavily against you. My advice? Go with the established game companies—if you can. If you can't, lock your game up in a drawer and throw away the key.

My newfound notoriety as inventor of a successful socialist game also brought me news of other games that share some of my values. I discovered two small family businesses, Animal Farm Games (P.O. Box 2002, Santa Barbara, CA 93102), and Family Pastime Games (R.R. 4, Perth, Ontario, Canada, K7H, 3C6), that produce a variety of children's games, like Save the Whale, which emphasize cooperation—everyone wins or loses together. The same principle guides the French Canadian game Co-op, which is sold by the Canadian Cooperative Movement as a means of teaching the principles of cooperative owning and living.

Games that promote group consciousness and urge struggle with other groups apparently have been on the market for some time. Starpower is one and Simsoc, which tries to simulate the origins of society, is another. I had not been aware, though, of any game that treats class as the most important of the groups to which we belong and the conflict between the working class and the capitalist class as the decisive social conflict in our society. Strike and Workers United, two games for young children invented by teachers at the Che Lumumba Grade School attached to the University of Massachusetts at Amherst, do just this. In Strike, players move through setting up picket lines, police repression, and strike breakers, to a conclusion that is labeled New Contract. Workers Unite offers a lesson on the great moments of workers' struggles—1848, 1917, and 1949, with imperialism and counterrevolution as occasions for retreat.

Puerto Rico has a game about life in a socialist society called Socio-Polio. Here, players compete to see who can serve the people best. The player who becomes a National Hero of Labor first wins. The takeover by workers of the Lip watch factory in France a few years ago gave rise to Chomageopoly, in which players repeat the steps by which workers occupied the plant and protected themselves from the police. And Germany has an anarchist game called Provopoli, which pits a red group using barricades and bombs against a blue group for control of a city. Though banned in some German states, it has become an under-the-counter best seller.

Most intriguing of all, I discovered an earlier American game that was called Class Struggle. It is listed in a pre-World War I catalogue of the Charles Kerr Publishing Company, then America's premier publisher of socialist books. There is no date on the form. At the bottom of a long list of books and pamphlets, we simply read, "Class Struggle game—25 cents." Obviously, prices have changed even more than the class struggle in the last 70 years. No one at the Kerr Company today knows anything about the game, and I have been unable to turn up any copies or anyone who has played it.

The idea that someone may have traveled on this path before me sends shivers of excitement up and down my socialist spine. I don't know which is greater, my curiosity about all that I don't know, or my sympathy for all that I can divine. To the reader who can enlighten me about this early 25 cent version of Class Struggle goes my warmest, comradely appreciation and thanks.

Why did Alice jump down the rabbit hole? Did she, too, mistake herself for Odysseus about to embark on a voyage around the known world? The reality she found was far less grandiose, upside-down, laced with a touch of the ridiculous. If I set out on my trek through the marketplace treading in the footsteps of the noble Odysseus, I gradually came to see that I was really a socialist Alice lost in a capitalist Wonderland, surrounded by March Hares and Mad Hatters shouting "Off with his game, off with his game." "Sentence first, verdict afterward" became my daily lot.

Why is the Cheshire Cat grinning so? Is he laughing with me or at me? I can no longer tell. It's all very confusing and upsetting. I had heard that the road to revolution is full of strange twists, but I didn't expect to find it looking like a pretzel.

Throwing a curve ball at capitalism (*Darleen Rubin* © 1983)

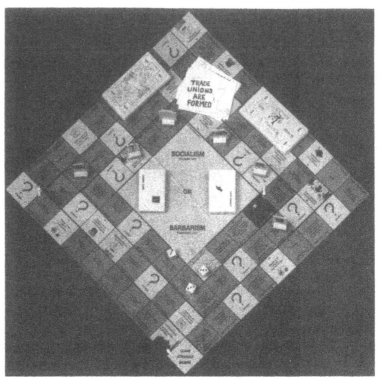

Board of Class Struggle Game (*Alan Orling*)

The original of the photo on the Class Struggle box, with Bertell
as Rockefeller and Ira Shor standing in for Marx (*Paule Ollman*)

The board of directors of Class Struggle, Inc.: (*left to right*) Isidore
Silver, Ed Nell, Howard Polsky, Paule Ollman, Milton Polsky, and
Bertell (*Alan Orling*)

Class Struggle tournament in Washington, D.C. University of
Maryland students express their views on an academic freedom
controversy raging at their university (*Mimi Levine*)

Family portrait: Bertell, Paule, Raoul, and Frisbee (*Mimi Levine*)

Are the banks ready to finance
the Class Struggle? (*Mimi Levine*)

Boxes of Class Struggle take
over Ollman's apartment
(*Alan Orling*)

Professor/businessman at work in NYU office (*Alan Orling*)

Debating Joe McCarthy's former sidekick, Roy Cohn, at the Yale Political Union (*Alan Orling*)

Santa Claus, in the person of Class Struggle board member Milton Polsky, wishing everyone a "Merry Marxmas"

Cartoon used to promote Class Struggle in ads and posters (*Frank Baginski*)

"Helmut Kohl [German Chancellor] Plays Class Struggle," or so the German press wrote when Kohl was caught in this position at the Frankfurt Book Fair. (*Werner Hewig*)

Ollman and U.S. Congress exchange greetings for the New Year
(*Mimi Levine*)

ALICE

This was the first time I had ever applied for a loan of any kind. Though I assured Howard, Ed, and the others that I could handle it, I had no clear sense of what that meant. Is there a special borrower's uniform that I should wear? Do I assure the bank that this is just a game, nothing serious, fellows, just a way to make a buck, you know how badly professors are paid? Or just give them the figures and say nothing? Do bankers have a sense of humor? Is that at all relevant to lending us money?

The elevator leading to Citibank's Small Business Loan Office on the fourth floor of their Twenty-eighth Street branch was so small that I felt they were trying to squeeze the interest out of me before I even got the loan. Or was this merely another symptom of my Marxo-neurotic reaction to banks, this super-shell game in which coins are moved around so fast that few can divine where they come from or where they go, this magic money tree that grows interest like other trees grow apples, this Mafia-run casino taking its percentage out of every bet? And always, everywhere, it is the most imposing house on the block, for those whose taste runs to blockhouses. While industrial capitalists use other people's labor to make money, banking capitalists use other people's money to make more money. Justice, on their lips, always means forgetting where their wealth originates. Are the banks ready to finance Class Struggle? Greed, we're counting on you!

Inside, Philip Miller, Jr., assistant vice-president of Citibank, greeted me and tried to put me at ease by taking note of my "interesting straw hat."

"Yes, the holes are for ventilation," I responded.

Miller, whose own conservative attire contrasted sharply with the kindly twinkle in his eye, led me to the leather-upholstered conference room, where we were joined by Thomas Thweet, his deadpan black assistant.

TWELVE:
ARE THE BANKS READY TO FINANCE THE
CLASS STRUGGLE?

"NYU. I've taken some courses there," Miller said.

"Did you?" Score two points for the old-boy network, I thought.

Then, following the rules of Class Struggle, the Capitalists threw the dice first: "Well, just what kind of a business do you have?" Miller asked.

I looked from Miller to Thweet and back, and as casually as I could, I took out a copy of the game and laid it before them. "It's a board game."

Just for a moment, Thweet lost his well-manicured composure, opening his eyes so wide that his eyebrows rose a full inch on his forehead. Miller glanced at the box and then back at me. His expression was completely noncommittal. Their silence seemed to call for more of something, but of what? I opened the box and took out the board.

"It's a kind of socialist Monopoly," I went on. "The players represent different classes, the main ones being Workers and ... Capitalists ... It's all very real to life ... and a lot of fun."

"General Strike." Thweet was reading out loud from the board.

"The first edition sold out in a month," I continued, wishing that Thweet had focused on something a little less explicit.

"Revolution." Thweet's voice had become barely audible.

"Here are a sampling of the over 50 stories that have been written on the game, almost all of them extremely favorable." And I spread newspaper clippings over the board to give Thweet and Miller something else to read.

Slowly, Miller broke into a broad smile. "Yes, I recall reading something about it. So you're the inventor. Well, well, well. How did you say the game is doing?"

"Great. So good that we have to produce more games fast. That is, of course, where you come in. How would Citibank like to help finance the class struggle?" No sooner had the words come out of my mouth than I regretted saying them. I had promised myself to be more serious, businesslike. Thweet was put off-balance and didn't know how to respond. He glanced over at Miller for his cue.

Miller hesitated, but just a moment. "If it's a solid business, why not? But that's what we'll have to find out first."

The next couple of weeks were spent drawing up a financial report of income, costs, receivables (money owed us by stores), and games on hand. Together with a Movement accountant friend, who organized numbers by night and workers by day, Jo Ann spent a couple of sleepless nights preparing neat rows of figures. However messy the facts, the figures had to be exact, and, above all, neat. Miller also asked that Howard, Izzy, Ed, and I, the four tenured professors on the board (two of whom own homes), co-sign the loan. In this way, in July, Class Struggle, Inc., obtained $30,000 at 14 percent interest to help pay for our second edition of 25,000 games. For a long time, Citibank had been making money out of supporting the capitalists in the class struggle, and now it had found a way to make money by supporting the workers' side as well.

But the decision in September to produce another 50,000 games, coming so soon after we had finished paying Finn for the 25,000, caught us fiscally unprepared. For the past month, we had been negotiating with Simon and Schuster, the giant publisher, for some kind of distribution arrangement in bookstores that we were hoping would include a hefty advance to help us produce more games. Using the bait of the Mondadori offer to do an Italian edition, Rodney Sokol had convinced S&S (the jargon of the trade came easy) that a lot of quick money could be made selling Class Struggle, especially overseas. Rodney had always made a lot of his personal connections, something we intended to discount as part of his selling style, until we saw a big picture of our agent hanging in isolated splendor on the wall of the office of Dan Green, a vice-president of S&S.

Friendship notwithstanding, the best S&S offered us was to take over the sale of foreign rights for a commission of 25 percent (Sokol's 10 percent would come on top of that), and to distribute the game in bookstores, also for 25 percent. Getting an offer of any kind was considered something of a coup. *Publishers Weekly* later spoke of it as a first for the publishing industry. It gave us considerable legitimacy and the widespread distribution network that we lacked. Promising that America's bookstores would soon be stocked to the ceiling with Class Struggle, Sokol urged us to accept the offer. Unfortunately, the numbers argued otherwise. The 25 percent that S&S wanted for their help in distribution was about twice what we were then paying, and did not leave us enough of a margin to continue running an office to sell the game in the areas they neglected. Publicity and promotional expenses were also to be our responsibility, and, most important, they refused to advance us the money or to guarantee the bank loan that we needed to produce more games.

Paul, Jo Ann, and the other people then working in our office were so incensed by the offer that they said they would resign immediately if we accepted it. After running through a half-dozen possible scenarios, the board agreed to make S&S our agent for the sale of foreign rights, starting with the Mondadori deal, which had just been concluded (a windfall for S&S)—Sokol had convinced us of their special clout overseas—but decided that we could do better on our own in the U.S. From that moment on, Sokol's interest in Class Struggle seriously waned. We were also right back at the beginning in our search for money to finance the next edition of the game.

The new contact with Finn called for paying $53,333 immediately in order to commence production, the same when he began to assemble the games approximately one month later, and the final third in 30-, 60-, 90-day installments after that. Our bank account at the time was $3,200. A little money could be raised by selling more shares. With sales still shooting upward, we raised the price of a share to $500 ($5,000 for a block of 10). In theory, investors had made a profit of 500 percent on the value of shares bought at $100 apiece in five short months—if they could find anyone to buy them. In practice, only Howard was willing to buy shares (20) at this new price. Even Sokol said no. Howard had never counted on digging quite this deep into his pockets to support Class Struggle, Inc. With this purchase of stock, he had come to the end of his middle-income savings account, to the keen discomfort of his wife, Zita, who had always harbored doubts about the game's ultimate success.

The sale of the Italian license for Class Struggle to Mondadori had just been consummated, and "the check was in the mail." Firms in Spain, France, Germany, Sweden, and Norway had expressed strong interest in doing foreign-language editions, and money from them could not be long in coming. Stores that owed us for games already bought would also start paying us at a faster clip. All this money was just out of reach. For the present, we had a serious "cash flow" problem, a lack of cash in hand to pay for the third edition of the game. However we cut it, in the short run we needed a loan of $75,000 to $100,000, depending on how quickly money from these other sources became available.

I had assured Finn when we signed the contract that there would be no problem in securing the needed financing from the bank. Hadn't they already shown their faith in our product to the tune of $30,000? And that was before Mondadori. In any case, we had investors who were prepared to raise their stakes. Look at these sales figures. Look at this week's press clippings. *L'Express*, France's equivalent of *Time Magazine*, had just written, "The star at this year's Frankfurt International Book Fair was not a book but a game, *Class Struggle*." Wasn't this evidence enough? Finn looked at me a little skeptically, but I managed to convince him that Class Struggle had indeed tapped the mother lode. In order to get production underway, I gave Finn a check for $10,000 (the money from Howard's latest purchase of shares), and promised to bring him the other $43,000 due as part of the first payment in a week.

And I really believed there would be no problem. I had already called my friend Phil, the banker, to tell him that things were going so well we needed money to produce another 50,000 games for Christmas. He seemed truly pleased at our success, but reminded me that $100,000 is a lot of money. There was something in his tone of voice that gave me a slight chill. Still, he expressed optimism that we could work something out, and invited me to the bank to lay out the figures.

Having been there several times, I felt quite at home in his office. This was my bank. Weren't these people here to lend a helping hand to small businessmen, even socialist businessmen, as long as Citibank got theirs? The contradictions of capitalism continued to work nicely in our favor. In the conference room, Miller began by informing me that the ground rules for loans of this size were different from the ones we had used before. A lot more information was required, including 12-month projections of income and expenses, and the final decision on whether to grant the loan would be made on a higher level. How the hell did we know how many games we would sell and how many foreign license agreements we would make in the next year? No matter— we had to guess, and guess accurately, numerically. Miller said his role was limited to helping me collect these materials and to making a recommendation.

There wasn't much time. The rest of the first payment was due in several days. If we didn't have it, production would be delayed, and there was a danger of not having games to meet the Christmas rush. Poor Jo Ann had to spend more nights with little or no sleep. It seemed as if our first accountant, whose authoritative style made up for his lack of formal training, had made a mess of our books. The amateurish, helter-skelter nature of our operation required a systematic overhaul now that we stood poised on the edge of the Big Time. Bob Ricca, a professional CPA, was called in to establish fiscal order at $50 an hour. By the time I delivered the materials to the bank, it had almost cost us the equivalent of a first interest payment on the loan.

I urged Miller to try to get us a quick answer, but he found that a description of our office and a copy of the contract with Simon and Schuster were still lacking. The next day, when I returned with this, he said we still needed the Social Security numbers of all the members of the board and their wives. "Couldn't I telephone that in later?" I asked. "No, it has to be written on these papers before the divisional manager will look at it." Miller was only doing his job, doing it well, so well that we would get our loan. I don't doubt that this was his intent.

When the week had passed, Finn threatened to discontinue production unless the rest of the first payment of $53,000 was made immediately. He needed it, he said, to buy the necessary materials. The following day, the Mondadori money finally arrived. With commissions our share had shrunk to $23,000—a substantial boon, but still not enough. Confident that a loan from Citibank would set us squarely on our feet, Howard took out an $18,000 mortgage on his home and Izzy scraped the bottom of his savings barrel for $3,500 to put us over the top. Finn got his first payment. Both Howard and Izzy were assured by the entire board that their loans would be repaid in a few weeks. What was the alternative? With this loan, Howard had now sunk close to $90,000 into Class Struggle. He stood there hovering over the roulette table like a seasoned gambler having bet everything on the red, watching the wheel turn, knowing that this time the ball had to land on his color. I was immensely thankful for his commitment; I greatly admired his courage, and tried hard not to think too much about what he must be feeling.

The days dragged by. I waited a week, and then called. The decision, I was told, would be made any day. Miller said he didn't expect any problems, but, of course, he couldn't be sure. As the tension built up, Paule noticed that I began grinding my teeth at night. To help me relax, she insisted on taking me swimming. Three days later, I called again. It was such a simple, obvious matter. The following day the decision was made—to deny us the loan! I was quite flabbergasted. "Why?"

"It seems as if the assets of the four co-signers don't justify a loan of this size," Miller explained, decidedly uncomfortable with his new role.

"I didn't understand. What about our booming business? What about all the money people owe us?" I asked plaintively.

"Too doubtful," Miller replied. "The bank doesn't like to take risks. Just the certainties are counted, like the assets of the co-signers, and for a $100,000 loan, they proved insufficient."

"Howard's house, Ed's loft, and Izzy's land in

Massachusetts," I persisted, "are worth well over $200,000."

"Yes, maybe," Miller went on, "but none of you have any stocks or cash to speak of, and the bank doesn't like to take real estate as collateral. It's a messy business taking a house away from someone. Besides, all this is already tied up as collateral for the $30,000 loan we made to you earlier."

"Yeah, yeah, sure." No speech, no joke, nothing more literate came to mind. My legs wobbled as I left the bank. Did the higher-ups decide against the loan for political reasons? Did they finally understand what Class struggle is all about? I'll never know.

•••

Production of the games was going according to schedule, which meant that in eight days we had to pay Finn the second $53,000. The machine had been set in motion, and my sleeve was caught in the conveyor belt. No time to panic. I called an emergency meeting of the board to discuss our situation. Howard was noticeably shaken by Citibank's refusal to lend us more money. Sales remained high. We wanted the new games as much as ever, but how to pay for them? Izzy had a friend who had borrowed $50,000 to start a record company from the Banco Popular: "No, he wasn't a Puerto Rican, and he had no assets to speak of." Apparently, there are banks that occasionally take a risk.

Ed wanted to know about going public with our stock. "Just what the New York Stock Exchange needs," Milton said. "Instead of buying kids a share of General Motors for their bar mitzvahs, their rich uncles will be able to buy them a share of Class Struggle, Inc."

Izzy remembered that there was an investment company called Carl Marks: "Maybe they'll handle it for us."

"Not likely," Ed responded. "It's a different Carl Marks. This one actually specializes in pre-World War I Czarist bonds."

Howard was too depressed to join in. Maybe I was, too. "Look," I finally said, "even if we could sell shares on the Exchange, it is not something we can do in a week or even a month. Ed, why don't you look into it as a middle-term possibility and also see how much it would cost us. Meanwhile, we still have to pay Fin $53,000 in a week or we don't get any games."

"And we lose the $53,000 we paid him last month," Howard added gravely. It was the first time anyone had mentioned the possibility of losing money.

"I'll go to the bank Izzy mentioned. There are also people who are looking for surefire investments, even if they are a bit kinky. I'll find them," I said in my most determined voice.

Why would another bank see things differently? Yet we had to try, and to try, we had to believe. The next day, I visited George Renert, who lends money to new record companies for the Banco Popular, which is located just off Rockefeller Center in central Manhattan. The bank's secretaries are Latins, but all the people with private offices seemed to be Anglos.

Renert showed genuine delight in meeting me. He had heard all about Class Struggle and thought it was a "gas." He went over the game in some detail, laughing in all the right places, and said he couldn't wait to play it with his boss. Yes, his boss, the director of the bank, would love it—"a real capitalist, but he has a great sense of humor."

In the world of "us" and "them," Renert put out all sorts of signals that he was part of "us." If he could take off this stuffy jacket and wear just a T-shirt, but ... Right off he wanted me to know that he understood, about everything. "We're in business to help small businesses, and to help Class Struggle would be a real pleasure." Meanwhile, he urged me to see the National Economic Development Administration (NEDA) to find out if we were eligible for a Small Business Administration guarantee on our loan. "That would make things easy," Renert said. "But even without it, I think your operation is sound enough for Banco Popular to give you the help you need. There are, of course, some materials you will have to bring me."

I went that same afternoon to the office of the NEDA and learned that an SBA guarantee—if we were lucky enough to get one—would take from six to 10 months to come through. But given the political tone of our game, the SBA guidelines made it very unlikely that they would help us even then. How could I have thought otherwise? Unfortunately, we only needed thousands and not hundreds of millions; and our name wasn't Lockheed or Chrysler. Yes, it would be lovely having the U.S. government helping to finance Class Struggle, but it was not to be.

I got to work immediately putting together the materials that Renert wanted, but other options had to be pursued at the same time. Michael Lehrman, who scouts professionally for venture capital (money in search of big risks and correspondingly big profits), offered to help for 5 percent off the top, but complained that his task would be easier if we wanted more money. Alan Petricoff, a Republican lawyer and venture capitalist, obtained a free game and a stimulating lecture on the need to hedge his bets against the possibility of a socialist victory in America, and said he would think it over. Everyone wanted numbers, lots of numbers, almost any numbers, but they had to "add up."

People I knew with money also received calls offering them a piece of our booming business. Kent Barber, a boyhood friend, had earned most of his small fortune as a psychiatrist treating welfare patients. His soul was badly in need of saving. By investing in Class Struggle, he could save his soul and make money at the same time. How could he resist? Barry Schwartz, an anarchist friend from Milwaukee, who spends his days as a stockholder playing hide-and-seek with the market, offered to help. "If it makes money," he assured me, "my Jewish clients will invest in guns for the PLO." "Forget the guns," I told him. "The big money this year is in Class Struggle. But you've got to act fast."

I also called up people I know who edit radical publications or run progressive institutes: "Who has helped you out in a pinch? Where are the radical rich? Do you know anyone who might be interested in buying into Class Struggle, Inc., or lending us $100,000?" The names most frequently mentioned in answer to my questions were Samuel Rubin and Stewart Mott. Rubin was terminally ill at the time, and Mott, whose money came from a General Motors legacy, filters all requests for help through his assistant, Daphne Stewart. I made an appointment to see Daphne the next day.

I suppose I should have felt among comrades, but I didn't. Class Struggle was a stiffer political drink than any I knew Mott to have tasted. Daphne was an intense, attractive woman, who had the self-assurance that comes from knowing who had come to ask for money and who had it to give. Her young assistant, Carol, who was present at the meeting, was very enthusiastic about the whole project: "What a good idea to make a game about class struggle." Daphne stuck to questions about the business, saying finally, "Well, it's quite different than anything Stewart has done before, but maybe ... The main problem, as I see it is—is it an investment, or a political donation?"

"It's an investment. A good one, a safe one," I responded, "but one with a political thrust."

Daphne went on: "Stewart invests to make money and gives money to promote good causes he believes in. This seems to fall between two stools."

"No," I insisted. "This is a way of sitting on both stools at the same time. A super trick, you must admit, if it can be done, and it can be done. All it takes is the kind of flair for which Stewart is famous." (Ouch. There I go sounding like a salesman again. Now I'm selling Stewart Mott to his own assistant.)

"Well, bring me a copy of your financial report," she listed several other documents, "and we'll get back to you as soon as we can."

"We need a positive answer by Thursday," I responded, and my throat tightened as I realized how little time we had left.

Thursday came, and Friday. No decision yet from Banco Popular or from Mott or from the friends and businessmen who had promised to think about investing in Class Struggle. On Monday, I went to see Finn to explain the delay, sounding as optimistic a note as I could. Finn was very grim. There was no folksy exchange of news about our families, no anecdotes about the religious books he was publishing. "Look, I put a lot of my own money into this. The games are ready to be assembled as I promised. We're on time. You said you would have the money by now." His eyes would have scorched my face if I had let them.

"Bill, it's not time to worry, really worry." I punctuated each phrase with deep, labored breaths. "We had an unexpected problem with Citibank, so we lost some time. There is no question but that we'll come up with the money. It just might take another week ... or so." My words bounced back at me from the walls. I had experienced this echo effect before, whenever I gave a particularly bad lecture, whenever my words and feelings seemed to lack synchronization. Yet I had no doubt that the money would turn up somehow. Business was going gangbusters. How could Renert, or Mott, or someone else, fail to see that? But I was beginning to have doubts about how soon that would be. Christmas was slowly sneaking up on us. It was essential that Finn not halt production, that he go ahead. My hope was that he was already too committed to pull back. Finn's breathing was fast and shallow. "Get me that money in a week, one way or another."

That evening, after giving my graduate class on "Marxism," I attended a fundraising party in a posh Park Avenue apartment for Tom Harkin, the liberal congressman from Iowa. With the frequent changes of role, the multiple demands on my time and emotions, my energy level was dangerously low, but just thinking of business was generally enough to recharge my batteries. Susan Weyerhauser, a former student at NYU, was one of the hosts. Susan knew of my business needs and encouraged me to come: "A lot of moneyed liberals will be there, including Stewart Mott, and well, who knows?"

The abrupt transition from explaining the theory of exploitation to being surrounded by some of its more striking effects left me momentarily numb. It was my visits to Citibank that first suggested the analogy with Alice in Wonderland, but it was only now, watching the Lobster Quadrille, that I realized how far I had wandered down the rabbit hole. Calm, mustn't run. Even Alice, I tried to reassure myself, eventually emerged from her weird adventure. But she had been asleep, while I was—and here I pinched myself to make sure—quite awake. (I don't know if it was the pinch, or the recurring image of Finn, or the lemonade brought to me by a uniformed maid, but I snapped out of my reverie and began to mingle.)

The 100-plus "beautiful people" in the crowd seemed so confident of their own importance that no one took much notice of Robert Redford, who sat in a far corner munching on hors d'oeuvre. Susan was pleased to see me and introduced me to a group as "the professor from Class Struggle." I winced, but who could say that she was wrong? The moment had come for the congressman to deliver his typically inspiring liberal talk: The country is going to hell in a roller coaster, the conservatives having greased the track, and only liberals know how to apply the brake. Worsening poverty, unemployment, inflation, war, were all blamed on bad people when not viewed as unavoidable facts of nature. Solutions lay in electing better people. Of course, to grasp—even as Ma Bell has—that "the system is the solution," Congressman Harkin would have had to recognize the way in which he and his audience were also part of the problem. How I wished they had given me 15 minutes to respond. But, at the time, ideology seemed less important than finding cash.

"Bertell, this is Stewart Mott." Standing in front of me was a tall, rugged-looking man who could have been a professional football player only recently put out to pasture. "Stewart has a great interest in alienation." Then, turning to Stewart, Susan went on, "Bertell has written the definitive work on alienation, but of course you must know it." Stewart shook his head, with more than a touch of embarrassment. Not a good beginning.

Susan left us to find our own way out of the void. "What a coincidence seeing you here tonight. I met with your assistant, Daphne, just the other day, to talk about a project that I hoped would be of interest to you. It's about Class Struggle, the game. Did Daphne ...?"

"Oh, yes. Daphne spoke to me about it." The casual encounter had turned into a business meeting, and Mott immediately became very defensive. "There's been no time to look into it."

"Have you seen the game?" I asked.

"Yes ... well, no. I've heard about it."

Damn. I should have stayed with alienation. My remarks had categorized me as just another indigent in need of money. Mott's whole adult life has been spent dodging people who want something from him. It's the price he pays for occasionally saying yes. He had become very cool and correct. I looked in vain for a sign of interest, a smile. Making polite noises about how good it was to meet me, he promised to look into my proposal very soon, and moved on. Like Casey at bat, I had struck out with the bases loaded. I felt silly, small, foolish. Then angry at myself. What should I have said?

Mott and I collided like two icebergs in the Bering Sea. I didn't want to talk to him about games or money. What I really wanted to ask was—how does it feel playing God? Happy? Lonely? Frightening? Funny? Judging from his works, Mott is a better god than most, but what interests me is how he feels in the role, something Moses, too, neglected to ask of Jehovah. Instead, I stood in line with my cup like the others, a *schnorer* for Class Struggle, for those who had their hopes and marbles in it, and for the political pay-off it promised. It's bad enough having to ask, but worse having to ask the wrong question, and worse still getting put off, having your pressing needs ignored. I felt humiliated, and resented Mott for the power of his indifference.

After the party, about 25 of the biggest tippers and I were invited by Susan to join Congressman Harkin for a late supper at Pierre's Restaurant. My dinner partner was Jerry Wexler, president of Warner Records. His old mother, he told me, was once a Communist, but he is content to make records and money.

"It's not too late to make the old lady proud of you," I consoled him. "Don't let her die thinking of you as a failure. Invest in Class Struggle." Wexler got a good listener for his old yarns over supper. I got nothing.

As we were leaving the restaurant, another guest pulled me aside to boast, confidentially of course, that his son had been a member of SDS. "Buy the kid some shares in Class Struggle. Show him his dad isn't as reactionary as he thinks," I suggested, trying my best to bring the generations together.

"What an interesting idea," he smiled.

After 10 days of "tomorrow for sure," "probably okay," "just one more figure,"—the telephone wire between us was being burned to a frazzle by my anxiety—the Banco Popular decided to invest its funds in more traditional enterprises. Records, *sí!* Games, *no!*

"Don't take it personally," Renert advised.

Rejections were still too new to me not to hurt, not to take personally. I tried to step back and see the bigger picture: Socially, a small business was getting screwed by the banks; politically, the capitalist class had struck another blow against the forces of socialism. The relief was only temporary. Where to go now? Whom to see? Later, later. I'll call Howard and Paul tomorrow. Don't want to talk now. Don't want them to see me so low, so worn, so short on hope. I felt an overwhelming sense of exhaustion that comes when you discover you've been walking a whole day, a whole week, in the wrong direction. So much energy, so much time—and in this case so much wasted civility. Too frequent sales raps had burned the initials "C.S." in my throat. I needed a drink of cool water, a change of air, of people, of ideas—fast.

Some days before, a friend had invited me to attend a talk by Manuel Azcarate, a leading member of Spain's Communist party, who was visiting New York. I was much too busy to attend, but I noted the address. Now it seemed like a window opening onto the world beyond my petty business concerns. I needed to stretch, and forget.

The first half-dozen people I met at the meeting all asked me about Class Struggle. "We're doing fine. Of course, we could use $100,000." "Ha, ha, ha. Ollman sure has a sense of humor," went the refrain.

The talk offered some relief. Azcarate didn't mention Class Struggle once. Afterward, while I was drowning my sorrow in a second cup of tea, an elderly Communist union organizer turned Jewish businessman came up and introduced himself: "Nat Levine. I've been in the toy business many years, so I know what you're going through." There was something in Nat's look that suggested he might be right.

"I'm sure you know what it's like to sell games," I responded, "but how about needing $100,000 in a week, or else?"

Nat nodded. "Most small businessmen know that. If you were to make a doll of a small businessman, he would have his hand out like this." And he opened his palm.

"That leaves out the stomach pains," I said.

"No," he replied, "we show that with a facial expression— like this." And he pointed first to his face, and then—with emphasis—to mine.

I had done enough selling that day to appreciate a chance to unburden myself to an understanding comrade. Then in the middle of my sorry tale, Nat interrupted—"I'll help you." I must have looked at him with such disbelief that he said again, "I'll help you. How much do you need?"

"One hundred thousand dollars," I answered, still unsure of what I had heard.

"Well, probably not that much, but I think I can get you out of the hole you're in. Come to see me tomorrow morning."

"Why?" I asked. In the emotional din set off by Nat's remarks, it was my curiosity that dominated.

Nat laughed. "Well, if I told you it sounded like a good business proposition, I'd be lying. No, I like what you're trying to do with the game. All my life, I've been a fighter in the class struggle, though I haven't had a chance to do much lately." Then, becoming very animated, he added, "If I can give capitalism just one more good *stauch* before I die ..."

The very next night, Nat came to my house to meet the Class Struggle board. How much he would help us was still unclear. That morning, Ed and I had gone with him to see his banker in Brooklyn. The banker said he would only make us a loan if Nat co-signed the note. On the drive back, Nat said he himself would lend us $15,000. Only, we mustn't tell his wife. "And then," he said, "and then we'll see."

Our meeting uncorked all the laughter and good cheer that had been bottled up in the last month of worries. Nat, who loved telling anecdotes about his life as a Marxist businessman, never had a more appreciative audience. Then, with the coffee poured and cheese spread, Nat began to grill us on the business side of our business. "How many orders did you have when you put in the request for another 50,000 games?"

I looked at Paul, who looked back at me, and we both looked at Howard. Howard began, "The games we had were selling very fast."

"And the buyer at Bloomingdale's told us she was thinking of taking 10,000 sets for Christmas," I added.

Paul chimed in: "We also got a call from Holland asking for 5,000 ... Of course, it hasn't been confirmed yet."

"The Bloomingdale order hasn't come in yet either," I said, beginning to feel uncomfortable.

Nat's jovial manner turned icy cold. And he repeated his question: "How many definite orders did you have when you asked Finn for another 50,000 games?"

"If you mean firm orders," I said, "I guess the answer is none."

Nat shook his head in disbelief. "You bought 50,000 games at a cost of $160,000 that you didn't have on the basis of no orders?" With these words, something snapped. I heard it. We all heard it. Howard has confessed that for him this was the most frightening moment of our entire venture.

"And if the expected orders don't come through?" Nat asked, after a long moment of silence.

"Then, we're in bad shape," I responded. "Though even then ..." And I repeated, but with waning assurance, the long litany of our successes and possibilities.

In America, the centerpiece of the month-long Christmas pageant is the "gift." Sold in a thousand shapes and textures, possessing a hundred different hues and prices, it can be eaten, worn, or played with. It breaks and tears easily, and is generally put away and forgotten once the "thank yous" are over. For the recipient, the symbol of these glory days is the tie that is never worn and the game whose rules are too complicated for anyone to figure out. Yet, without the Christmas present, many American businesses would simply roll over and die. According to fun-industry sources, over 60 percent of all games are sold in the month between Thanksgiving and Christmas.

At Class Struggle, Inc., we had been dreaming of a red Christmas from the start. What could we do to help America's shoppers see that Class Struggle is the perfect Christmas gift? A catchy phrase, a slogan that would drive our message and product into every brain, is the way the market works.

Capitalism has long filched people's idealism and even socialist sentiments to sell its products: Ma Bell's "The system is the solution"; Buick's "Dedicated to the free spirit in just about everyone"; and General Electric's "Progress for the people." It was only fitting that we should return the favor and use the market to sell socialist ideas. Right now, for it to work, we needed a slogan that would put Class Struggle under every Christmas tree in the land.

"Merry Marxmas," Milt burst out. "Class Struggle wishes all America a Merry Marxmas."

"Great," Ed said, "but how do we get Santa Claus to bellow it out on TV?"

"No, too light," Howard shook his head. "We need something more in keeping with the seriousness of the occasion."

"Yeah," Izzy smiled, taking Howard at his word, "like—Put Marx Back Into Christmas." Conversation, all movement stopped. I fixed my most appreciative stare at Izzy, and nodded my head. He couldn't believe we were taking his suggestion seriously. "Yeah," he went on, "and we'll get Jerry Falwell to bellow it out on TV." But it was too late: "Merry Marxmas" and "Put Marx Back Into Christmas' had just been baptized our season's greetings.

The New York Times balked at printing a "Merry Marxmas" ad for fear of "offending Christians," though they didn't seem to mind capitalism's repeated efforts to package Jesus as Santa Claus. Even without their help, we managed to spread our slogans to store windows and car bumpers throughout the country.

Though we needed more money immediately to survive, we needed expanded sales to justify anyone lending us more money. Neither effort could be neglected. I would just have to talk and eat faster, and sleep less. Some time had to be put aside, too, for

THIRTEEN:
PUTTING MARX BACK INTO CHRISTMAS

the antidraft movement, which was then getting started, the Center for Marxist Studies at NYU, my "Visits with Marxist Thinkers" monthly radio talk show, out of town lectures—including a Yale Political Union debate with McCarthy sidekick, Roy Cohn, on the red menace in our schools—and conferences with lawyers in preparation for my upcoming trial in Maryland. Through all this, I continued to meet my classes and keep my office hours, but students found that I had become very stingy with time, "very businesslike," as one student put it.

After teaching, my main commitment was to promoting Class Struggle. But after inventing slogans, placing ads, visiting shows and buyers, and giving innumerable interviews to the press, what else can one do to sell games? Hard sell, soft sell, funny sell. We tried them all. Attracting customers in whatever way you can, making the sale—that's what business means. Of the businessman of his day, Marx remarked, "No eunuch flatters his despot more basely or uses more despicable means to stimulate his dulled capacity for pleasure in order to sneak a favor for himself than does the industrial eunuch—the producer—in order to sneak for himself a few pennies, in order to charm the golden bird out of the pockets of his Christianity-beloved neighbors. He puts himself at the service of the other's most depraved fancies, plays the pimp between him and his need, excites in him morbid appetites, lies in wait for each of his weaknesses—all so that he can then demand the cash for his services of love." Who, me? Surely—I gulped when I reread this quote—our operation was different.

When consumer advocate Bess Meyerson, for example, starts peddling blurbs to all and sundry, she appears to be simply cashing in on her reputation. The product seems to be irrelevant. Likewise, capitalists are only interested in making a profit, not a product, or rather in making any product that will make a profit. Hence, we should not be surprised when the Pillsbury Company buys Weight Watchers, or General Mills (originally a flour company) buys Parker Brothers (a game company), or when the oil companies buy everything in sight. For us, on the other hand, the product and its message was everything. But to sell Class Struggle, if we wished to maximize our sales, we had to adopt the same mechanisms and manners of the system we were criticizing.

Hoping to counteract the anonymity of the market, many buyers of books, paintings, and pottery like to get their purchase autographed by the creator. I guess it makes them feel important, as though they count for something more than the money they have just shelled out for the product. Along with computer dating and fan clubs, it is capitalism's way of breaching the gaps between the lonely souls who inhabit our competitive society. So, putting our critique of alienation off to one side, we set up a series of game-signing ceremonies. The first one was held at Abraham and Strauss Department Store, which caters to a black middle-class trade in the heart of Brooklyn. The signs posted on the outside doors read, "Dr. Bertell Ollman, inventor of the world-famous game Class Struggle, will be autographing his game in ..." When I got to the game department, the crowds had not yet arrived, nor had they come yet four hours later when I decided to leave. In between, a half-dozen people came and bought games, though hundreds more peered at me rather suspiciously out of the corners of their eyes as they hurried down the corridor where I was stationed.

"Why did you put your face on the cover of the game?" one teenaged girl wanted to know, mistaking Marx's bearded countenance for my own. "Don't bother the man with foolish questions, girl," interrupted her mother, yanking her away. "The man has a right to advertise his game the way he likes."

At a Macy's store in Brooklyn, the manager set up a small table just in front of the escalator and asked me to play Class Struggle with the assistant manager. After a half-hour, the assistant manager was replaced by one of the salespersons, and she by another salesperson a half-hour later, and so on until 6 P.M.

Nothing kills like repetition. My arms got sore from throwing the dice, my back from bending over to move the markers, and my brain became numb from explaining the rules again and again. What probably saved my sanity was questioning the workers about conditions in the store and asking them if they saw any connections between what was going on on the board and their lives. Once I realized that Macy's had invited me into the store to help unionize their workers, I felt considerably cheered. Just another way of wishing everybody a Merry Marxmas.

My busiest autograph-signing session took place in Macy's flagship store at Herald Square in Manhattan just two weeks before Christmas. For this occasion only, we gave away "Class Struggle Is the Name of the Game" T-shirts. The day began on a note of struggle. A conservatively dressed, middle-class woman listened to my rap, while, off to the side, her 10-year-old daughter was reading some Chance Cards. When she noticed what her daughter was doing, Mom got semihysterical: "Stop! Don't read that," she screamed.

Just then, another woman came up and announced proudly that her young son knew all about politics. "He knows the names of all our senators and representatives."

"But does he know," I asked, "whom they *really* represent?" Smiling uncomfortably, she backed off.

Arthur Ashe's lovely young wife wanted to know what the game is about. When I told her, she shook her head and confessed that she is a capitalist, because she, too, wants to make money.

"But everyone wants to make money," I replied. "In our society, we need it to live. Do you own factories or stores or big tracts of farmland? No? Well, then you're not a capitalist."

A young man who had been watching from a distance approached hesitantly. "A game called Class Struggle. Are you a socialist?" The voice was slow and heavily accented.

"Sure," I said. "Where are you from?"

"Russia. I immigrate two years ago from Russia."

Afraid to scare the fellow away, I quickly pointed out, "The socialism I favor is an extension of democracy into all walks of life. It has little to do with what's called 'socialism' in Russia."

"And what's wrong with socialism in Russia?" he shot back. "Is much better than this rat race." And he stalked off in anger.

Two South Africans bought games, which they said they would have to smuggle back into their country. A woman trade unionist bought two for friends who were union officials. "They need a little of this to top up their courage."

"It will also help clear up their acne," I added. All in all, I sold close to 30 games in three hours. But this time, I also had a lot of fun. The mood was jovial and accepting, almost like Christmas.

Seeking to solidify our identity in people's minds as a "real game," we also held a series of Class struggle tournaments—similar to those Parker Brothers holds for Monopoly—in Washington, New Haven, and Ann Arbor. The first and largest of these took place in Kramer's Bookstore in Washington in October 1978. About 50 people turned up including a sprinkling of Washington's progressive intelligentsia and several University of Maryland students wearing "HIRE OLLMAN" T-shirts. An Austrian TV crew recorded the event for posterity.

In Boston, the *Real Paper* arranged a celebrity match of Class Struggle between three media personalities, the GOP candidate for governor of Massachusetts, the Democratic secretary of state for education, and Mortimer Zuckerman, one of Boston's leading capitalists, who has since become publisher of *Atlantic* magazine. Played in the office of David Rockefeller, Jr., publisher of the *Real Paper*, the game took on eerie overtones when Zuckerman, who played the Capitalists, tried his best to blow up the world just as he was about to lose. "Of course, capitalists would rather be dead than give up their wealth," Zuckerman said with the air of someone who knew what he was talking about.

A lot of products are also sold through testimonials by famous people. Why not Class Struggle? Amy Carter was one possibility. I sent a game to Zbigniew Brzezynski, whom I knew from a year spent at Columbia University, suggesting that he give it to Amy. My hope was that some reporter would find her playing with it, and she would tell him how much she was learning about what her daddy really does. We also sent games to Jane Fonda, Woody Allen, Bill Walton, Bill Lee, and Herbert Marcuse, all progressive celebrities. A blurb from any of them might have had a big impact on our sales. Marcuse was the only one who replied. He said it was a very good idea to promote socialism in this way, but felt that for him to say so publicly was "unbecoming." As someone who has the greatest admiration for Marcuse's work and life, a life that gloried in unbecoming causes, I was deeply disappointed by his reticence. Here I was sticking my neck out professionally and financially, as well as politically, and I felt that comrades who liked what I was doing owed me more than backroom support. Why such reticence?

I also tried to get a favorable blurb on the game from Sid Sackson, who is a kind of Babe Ruth of the games world. Sid is the creator of Acquire and about 40 other games. Anyone who knows games knows Sid, at least by reputation. If he liked it, really liked it, news of it would get out to games people everywhere. My opportunity came when Sid, whom I had talked to a few times on the phone, invited me to inspect the vast collection of vintage board games he kept in his home. "And yes, there will be time to play Class Struggle."

Grasping the importance of the occasion, Paule agreed to come along. She was also curious to meet someone whom her husband kept referring to as "a giant in the industry." Well, giants today come in all sizes. Sid is a shortish, retiring man in his mid-50s, who lives in a modest frame house in a suburban corner of the Bronx. After giving us a tour of board-game heaven, Sid, his wife, Paule, and I—like middle-aged couples all over America—sat down to play Class Struggle.

Sid examined the pieces of the game with the same meticulousness and serious concentration that a vulture shows before its prey. He was an expert on gaming mechanisms, but what did he think about political spoofs or capitalism? It was a tense moment. I reacted by talking too long about the simple rules, never arriving at the complex ones, and Paule by laughing wildly at every Chance Card. Paule is the most honest person I know, but that evening she acted her heart out. The necessities of business had claimed still another victim. To no avail. Even the dice balked at setting up interesting confrontations. Occasionally, Sid would ask a question, or his wife would smile weakly. But for the most part, they sat impassively through the ordeal. When it was all over, Sid confessed that he really preferred mathematical games. "I don't much like role-playing games." Neither do Paule or I, especially when they're carried over into real life. To this day, we cannot think of that evening without wincing in pain, not so much for the opportunity lost as for what it cost in personal integrity.

As a Marxist, I did not need to be instructed that truth is one of the first casualties of doing business—that honesty is the best policy only when it pays, which is not that often. But I was still surprised to feel myself the immense pressures that drive businesspeople to lie. In the case of Class struggle, Inc., we had the momentum, and it was important to go with it, to see how far it would carry us, and not be deterred—or allow potential customers to be deterred—by the few roadblocks that had been thrown across our path. So we took on the air of an unqualified success. The game, we claimed, was selling great all over the country (conveniently dismissing the thin strip of America between New York and Los Angeles); the media, we usually said, were unanimous in their praise of the game (store buyers had to be convinced that the game was respectable); and we denied that the stores that sold Class Struggle had received any complaints (even the few we heard about would be enough to scare off many timid buyers). Businesses generally don't complain, because it is bad for business. Success sells. Failure and belly-aching generate sympathy cards.

As business falsehoods go, Class Struggle, Inc., got back much bigger than we gave, the most frequent lies being—"I'll send you an order next week," "We'll call you back," "The boss stepped out for a moment," "We never received your bill," and, of course, the corker, "The check is in the mail" (which mixes lying with stealing). One of the most puzzling paradoxes of our times is how businesspeople, for whom lying is standard operating procedure, manage to retain the respect of a society based on a Judeo-Christian morality that condemns all lying as sinful. Would a society of vegetarians respect a ruling elite who practiced cannibalism? Only if the meat-eating rulers succeeded in mislabeling their actions as effectively as have our capitalists, who have gotten most of the public to view lying in business as "bluffing," "exaggeration," "sharp practice," "excerpting," "selective remembering," "neglecting to mention," and just plain "advertising," not forgetting "public relations" (where lying becomes a tax-deductible expense).

Capitalists have to condemn lying in general in order to get away with doing it in their particular sphere. Among themselves, however, capitalists and their spokespersons can be refreshingly honest about their dishonesty. At the Harvard Business School, for example, Professor Howard Raiffa teaches a course called "Competitive Decision Making" where students get credit for lying effectively. Most buying and selling involve negotiation, a give and take of one kind or another, and those who lie better do better.

While my own experience in business confirmed me in these views, I also found myself developing—much to my surprise—considerable sympathy for capitalists as human beings. For only the least sensitive of them/us can be comfortable with the knowledge that they are moral pariahs. Witness the increasing number of businesspeople who have joined Bible classes as a way of easing their bad consciences. When individual solutions to the problem of business immorality are as simple as choosing to go bust, the great majority will make the necessary compromises and bear the moral and emotional consequences.

For all the cushy extras they obtain just by being in business, in the last analysis, capitalists, too, are victims of the system that carries their name. Caught up in the short-term chase after profits, this is not something most businesspeople can see, let alone admit. I began to feel sorry for them, but in the same way that I feel sorry for the Hulk or Frankenstein. It's not really their fault, but—I had to force myself to remember—their pain doesn't make them any less dangerous to the rest of us.

My growing sympathy for capitalists as human beings was also a byproduct of my unsuccessful efforts to find money to pay Finn. Is this what the ancient Phoenician merchants, and my grandfather, who owned a corner grocery in Milwaukee, and all the small businesspeople I met at trade shows felt when they couldn't pay their bills? Recognizing our increasingly desperate situation, Nat Levine took me to see a factor with whom he had once done some business. Factors are legal Shylocks, hucksters operating halfway between banks and Mafia loan sharks, who lend businesses money and take their receivables as collateral. For small businesspeople who are owed a lot of money and who need a quick cash fix, it offers a short-term solution—at 24 percent interest (now close to 30 percent). Many factoring companies are owned by banks, who in this way circumvent the legal ceiling on interest rates allowed to banks. If we were lucky, Class Struggle, Inc., would now have the chance of joining many other small businesses "working for the factor."

The factor spent a day at the Class Struggle office reviewing our receivables to determine what kind of accounts they were, how long they owed us money, their credit ratings, and so on. His conclusion: There were too many small, oddball accounts— "What kind of business is Revolution Now Bookstore?"—and too many who owed us money for over three months. He would have to think it over. But if even the factor turned us down, what was left?

The Mafia was left. Loan sharking abounds in New York City, and I knew people who knew people who ... Of course, the rate of interest goes through the ceiling and if you don't pay on time they break your legs. It would be easier all around, I thought, if they simply took my business. The idea of the Mafia owning Class Struggle, Inc., tickled my fancy. They already run a lot of businesses on the other side of the class struggle, so why not a socialist business? They could then go around to stores that had refused to order Class Struggle making them an offer they couldn't refuse. Is the mob too patriotic to sell a socialist game? Al Capone said he ran all his rackets "along American lines."

Still, the lure of a fast buck might get even the Mafia to sacrifice some of their high ideals.

I mentioned the Mafia as a possible source of money at one of our board meetings. Milt and Ed smiled at my black humor. No one seemed to take the suggestion seriously. Maybe I didn't either. Or maybe I was testing their reaction to see how far I should go. All I knew was that the walls of our commercial empire had already fallen on three sides and that the fourth wall was starting to sway. My waking life had become a beggar's nightmare, more persistently painful than any of my colleagues on the Class Struggle board knew. And my sleeping life was interrupted by a constant flow of scheming. The nights left me as exhausted as a hard day's work. I had already thumbed my way through my address book, calling friends I hadn't seen in years with "the offer of a lifetime." Refusals were never as funny. Whatever humor there may have been in our situation had given way to a bitter aftertaste. The zest and conviction and fun had dissolved into sulfuric anxiety.

Was I ready to see the Mafia for a loan? I think I know what people who go to them feel like. What was left?

FOURTEEN:
JUST ANOTHER SMALL BUSINESS ABOUT TO GO BROKE

When the factor decided that our accounts receivable did not warrant a loan of the size that we needed, our space for maneuver had dwindled down to nothing. Nat Levine's $15,000 ($12,000 of which I had passed on to Finn) enabled us to buy a little more time, but now that, too, was gone. That same week, Bloomingdale's decided not to feature Class Struggle; the 10,000 games order we had been anticipating shrank to 500. And the customer in Holland who had asked for 5,000 games changed his mind. Odysseus had his Sirens; we had Bloomingdale's and Holland. Nat's warning to plug our ears against their sweet voices had come too late. We had bought 50,000 games we didn't need, not right now anyway, with money we didn't have. It was truth and consequences time. This was one game I didn't want to play. A class to teach? Another dentist appointment? How about a funeral? Where there's a will, there's usually an excuse. But not when THE * GAME * IS * UP.

Paul called to say that he had something very important to tell me. "Busy," I told him. "Save it for the board meeting tonight." I wasn't busy, just too depressed. In a few hours, I would have to confess to the board that except for Nat's loan, all my efforts to find money to pay Finn had failed. I had spoken to Finn the day before I heard from the factor and he was already quite angry and threatening a suit. There was no sense putting up an optimistic front, and I don't think I could have managed it even if I wanted to. The whole business was about to come crashing down on our heads. Class Struggle was on the verge of bankruptcy.

I could hardly get myself to say the word, but I would have to say it. What else could we do? I dreaded Howard's look. Going bankrupt is a lot like dying, with as much fright and ignorance attached to the results and as many mystifying tales told about what happens afterward. The debtors' prison has been closed, but what has replaced it? As the end approached, I began to feel cold in my extremities, a pervasive listlessness and a kind of dullness that I recognized as a defense against fear.

How had we come to this impasse? Christmas sales did not soar as we had confidently predicted, but we were still selling a lot of games. How does a business that sells 25,000 games in its first six months go bankrupt? Now, the answer was obvious—six months ago, even two months ago, we didn't have a clue: first, overexpansion—by ordering too many games too soon; second, because stores were scandalously lax in paying us for games already bought; and third, because we spent over $30,000 on wages, promotion, and advertising. (Neither I nor any other member of the board received this money.)

Yet if we had been able to get adequate financing, we could have made it over the hump, one of the many ships we had out looking for gold would have returned—Mandadori, French and Spanish editions for which contracts were about to be signed, money from stores that promised to pay us after Christmas; and maybe one of the dozen people who were considering whether to invest would finally see the dollars that were to be made selling revolution. All this money was close enough to see, almost to smell, but still too far away to be touched, counted, and handed over to Finn. Like the invalid who dies in his bed just as dawn approaches, our business seemed doomed just as it was about to become successful.

This is not what the script of the American dream calls for. It says right there in black and white that if you have a good idea, invest your whole kitty in it, and work like a demon, you too can get rich. Hardly a day goes by without *The National Enquirer* or *The Star* telling us about the man who made a million selling baseball hats with horns, prospecting in sewers for silver, or inventing a game. It's a great country out there. All people have to do is try. And try they do, or want to. A poll of workers on an automobile assembly line in Detroit showed that over 80 percent of them had either been in business or were planning to start one. Horatio Alger lives on in people's consciousness as a final and desperate hope, the only way of moving up in a society that insists that we march through life in single file (collective solutions *Verboten*).

Poor Horatio. If he was really a typical small businessman, he probably went bust, strangled his cat or his kid, and finished his life in a factory (if he was lucky) or sponging on the Bowery. Bankruptcy, as we learned, is as American as apple pie, and Class Struggle, Inc., was about to help itself to a large slice.

The time for the meeting of the board had come. I stayed in my bedroom "preparing papers" until everyone had arrived. When I came into the living room, I noticed that my somber mood had preceded me. No one spoke. Howard and Izzy were staring fixedly at the floor. The moment of truth—I don't know why it's called that—could not be put off any longer. "Well, guys," I said.

But before I could continue, Paul interrupted. "Not yet. First, take a look at this." With that, he opened up a Class Struggle game box he was carrying, and took out two game boards. He pointed to the low ridge that followed the fold in the middle of the board. "These are the new boards. I picked them up in the factory today. The ridge in the middle is so high it disfigures the board. I also think these boards are a little lighter than the ones we got last time. Wasn't Finn supposed to give us the same board?"

We took out some boards from the last edition of the game and began comparing. Everyone took part. Paul's anger—I had never seen him like that—began to build. "Jesus Christ, if we pay Finn $160,000, he ought to give us what we asked for."

"How many of the games are like this?" Ed wanted to know.

"There is no way of telling," Paul replied. "These are just the first samples, but they are probably all like this."

"Are they really that bad?" I asked. I could see what Paul was talking about, but the difference between the boards seemed to be very slight.

"I think so," Howard said angrily. "If I was a customer, I wouldn't buy a board like this."

"No, the real problem is not with customers," Paul corrected him, "but with store buyers. Some of them look the game over very carefully. They may be indifferent to its politics, but they want it to be well made. This sloppy manufacturing is going to turn them off." Paul spoke with great certainty, and then more tentatively. "A few of them, anyway."

"But they're already made, all 50,000 of them." Ed shook his head in disgust.

"And we haven't paid for them." Howard finally spoke the words that we had all begun to think. "Izzy, what does our agreement with Finn say, I mean about this new edition?"

"That he produce the same game he did last time. Yes," Izzy specified, noting the question in our eyes, "that means exactly the same."

"And if he doesn't?" Milt broke in before Izzy had a chance to finish.

"If he doesn't," Izzy continued, "I guess that means he is in breach of contract."

"Finn's about to sue us for the $95,000 we still owe him," I interjected. "That's the good news I was saving for tonight's meeting."

"Sue us? Sue us?" Howard shouted. "That bastard has just about destroyed our business by giving us a shoddy game. We should sue him for ... for a million dollars."

At this point, everyone began talking at once. Howard's indignation seemed to know no bounds, but Ed and Milton were exchanging gleeful cries. Izzy, knowing that his legal acumen was about to be tested, stayed as sober as the situation allowed.

It was as if a great natural force, a hurricane or a river of lava, that was about to engulf us all had been stopped dead by Howard's words, and had now begun to recede. My tiredness, the tiredness of months, had given way to an energy, indeed an exhilaration, I thought I'd lost. This was, as they say, a new ball game. Finn had outsmarted himself. In an effort to squeeze another half-percent of profit out of our hides, he had scrimped too much in manufacturing the game. We were now the aggrieved party. Rather than humbling ourselves once again to get another extension on the money we owed him, rather than going bankrupt because he refused to grant it, we could now take the offensive. He had given us something other than what we had contracted for. Whether customers were actually pressing us for games at this time was irrelevant. He had our $65,000, and we had received nothing.

After a brief discussion, we decided to sue Finn for the return of our money and $1,000,000 in damages. He could keep the games. In reality, we knew that he had no use for the games and that we would never get much in damages. Our fallback position, therefore, was to accept the games at a much reduced price, and a price that we could pay later when we had some money. Finn would only accept the latter deal if he were convinced that we were serious about a suit.

Only yesterday, I was desperately looking for money to pay Finn. Not finding any had been felt as a disaster, the worst possible thing that could have happened to the business. That was yesterday. Today, it seemed that not finding the money was our real success. We would have paid Finn and been stuck with damaged games and an even bigger debt than we already had. In retrospect, all the suffering of the previous months took on the guise of misunderstood happiness (easily and painfully misunderstood, to be sure). All the people I had cursed for not lending us money had their curses removed. And I had gained the invaluable lesson never to count misfortunes before they hatched.

The next day, Howard and I went to see Finn. Thinking that we had come to ask for more time to play our debt, he greeted us with barely concealed hostility. To Finn's puzzlement, I began by asking him to examine the difference between two game boards.

"This one comes from the last edition of the game, Bill. This is one of the new ones. Do you see any difference?"

Finn ran his finger over the little ridge in the middle of the new game board. "Well, I suppose this shouldn't be like this. Sometimes that happens. It's because ... In any case, it makes no difference."

"We think it makes a difference," Howard said in almost funereal tones. "Our manager, Paul Gullen, has told us that some buyers for big stores are very finicky about the appearance and manufacturing quality of the game."

"That's nonsense," Finn insisted. "I tell you nobody who isn't looking for this will notice it."

Not wanting to lose the initiative, I added, "The board also weighs less than the one you made for us last time."

"What?" Finn affected genuine surprise. He went out immediately for a scale. When he came back, he also had several copies of the new game board. He proceeded to weigh all the boards and carefully mark down their weights. Sure enough the boards all weighed between 1.4 and 1.6 ounces. The old board, which he also verified by weighing several examples, weighed between 1.7 and 1.9 ounces.

When the results of Finn's little experiment had become quite clear, Howard said, as funereal as before, "Bill, we take this matter very seriously."

"Look, Howard," Finn shot back. "I've been making game boards for twenty years. I'm telling you there is nothing wrong with this board,"

"The feel of a game, how heavy it is-and that includes how heavy the board is-all enter into the consciousness of a buyer," I said. "It's related to quality. The buyer for Toys-R-Us made a big point of this."

Finn's original defensiveness was now turning into annoyance. "This board is no lighter than the boards I make for Scrabble."

"Maybe So," Howard replied. "Butas you can see, it is light than the board you made for the last edition of Class Struggle, and therefore it is lighter than the board you contracted to make this time."

With the mention of our contract, Finn flushed, stopped all movement, and looked at us long and hard.

Howard was the first to break to break the silence, but Finn had already understood. "As it stands, we don't think we can use these games. So ..."

"You guys are really something. You can't pay for what you ordered, so you decide after they're made that you don't want them. It isn't my fault that you're having a lousy Christmas.

Where did you professors learn how to do business?" His face had turned deep red.

Finn's barbs contained enough half-truths to hurt. "Look, Bill, it's nobody's fault," I intoned without much conviction. "And business isn't bad-we really could use the games. But if we feel we can't sell them or that selling them will damage our reputation, then we have to take some action to protect ourselves. We want new game boards, just like the ones we had last time, just like the ones we ordered this time."

"There is also the matter of the damage done to our business," Howard added gravely, "due to the delay this will cause in getting games with acceptable boards. We will probably lose a lot of orders."

Finn had heard enough. The lines were now drawn. He would sue us for the money we owed him "and collect to the last penny," he promised, hissing the words out between his teeth. Straining to keep our cool, we replied that we would be suing him for breach of contract, asking for our sixty-five thousand dollars back and damages.

On leaving his office, something in me rebelled against the strictures of my new role. Finn wasn't a bad sort. We had shared some hopes and laughs together about his business as well as mine. On my last visit, he had talked about a daughter who was having a serious operation. "I hope your daughter recovers quickly, Bill," I said, turning toward him. I don't know why but I held out my hand. No, I do know why, but it made no difference. Finn put his hands behind his back and just glared at me.

Business. Wasn't I just being a good businessman? We had to protect our investment. Finn, too, was just trying to be a good businessman. I mustn't let any human feelings interfere with what business required. Unless those human feelings clear the way for more and better business, and that was not the case here. If you're a businessman, that comes first and everything else follows, serves the business. Business hours last twenty-four hours a day, seven days a week, and everything and everyone, slowly but surely, gets tied up with business, somehow.

We received court papers announcing Finn's suit, and sent him court papers announcing ours. But Finn knew that suing us would take years, during which he would be struck with a lot of games he couldn't use or sell, and that even if he won his suit, all that would happen was that he would force us into bankruptcy. Only a quick settlement offered him any hope of recuperating part of his investment. A few weeks went by when his lawyer, Herbert Jason, Jr., called our lawyer, Izzy, and asked whether something couldn't be worked out. "Like what?" Izzy asked. After several more calls, an appointment was made for Izzy and me to meet with Finn and Jason at the latter's office.

The evening before, the board met to hammer out a bargaining position. We had practically run out of games. If we were to stay in business, we needed more and we needed them quickly. We also reached an uneasy consensus that we could sell the new games despite the inferior board. Paul was unhappy with this decision, but eventually he, too, agreed. We would conduct business as usual, but if a customer complained, we would refund his or her money. Before he halted production, Finn had finished twenty-two thousand games, and he had the parts on hand to produce another twenty-eight thousand. The key question was how much was all this worth above the sixty-five thousand dollars we had already paid.

Izzy met me at Jason's plush Park Avenue office wearing the kind of three-piece tailored suit he puts aside for occasions such as this. "Did you bring your little tape recorder?" I asked. According to his lawyer, Finn denied admitting to Howard and me that there were any differences in the two game boards, and we decided that this time we wanted to have solid evidence of what he said.

Izzy patted his vest pocket. The recorder was so small it could not be seen. "It has been giving me a little trouble lately, but it should be all right," Izzy assured me.

Finn was already in the inner office with Jason. When we entered, Finn made it a point not to shake my hand. For the rest of the meeting, he tried as best he could to ignore my presence, casting only two or three glances in my direction.

Izzy and I sat down next to each other on an overstuffed couch facing Jason, while Finn sat, like a distracted Hamlet, in a swivel chair next to the window. Jason began by announcing rather formally that Mr. Finn wanted ninety-five thousand dollars that was owned to him for producing fifty thousand games for Class Struggle, Inc. Whereupon, Izzy responded just as formally that Class Struggle, Inc., wanted its sixty-five thousand dollars back, as well as a half-million dollars for damages to our business from Mr. Finn. He could keep the damaged games. Then, less formally, Jason said, "But there does seem to be some room for a compromise." When Izzy asked what he suggested, Jason responded that Mr. Finn would kindly extend the length of time for paying the money which we owed. Jason then asked Izzy what we had in mind, to which Izzy responded that we might consider dropping our suit for damages to the business if Mr. Finn returned our sixty-five thousand dollars and gave us all the finished games. This was one of the occasions on which Finn shot me a particularly hostile glance.

From these two extreme positions, both lawyers began to edge toward a common center. Each lawyer would introduce his "last best offer" by turning to his client to make sure he had not gone too far. Every now and then Finn would put on a show of total opposition, and once he even stalked from the room. Each time Jason would soothe him, saying that such an act of generosity and statesmanship on his part would surely bring Class Struggle to settle the matter right here. After witnessing this imaginative charade a couple of times, I decided to include it in my own act. Feigning outrage at their offer, I blew up. Izzy caught on, and gave me a chance to appear as the generous statesman. Business has provided me with the occasion for many kinds of acting—comedy, farce, adventure—but this was my first essay into Shakespearean tragedy.

After an hour and a half, we had crawled to offering them $15,000 on top of the $65,000 they had for the games already produced and all the raw materials (estimating it would take another $15,000 to $20,000 to produce 28,000 more games from these materials); and Finn had reduced his demand to $30,000 for everything. But I had already gone higher than I had been authorized by the board to go, and Finn had been more conciliatory than he had expected to be. Finn's temper was flaring more frequently now. No further progress could be made today. I had received his very last offer, and he took note of mine. The lawyers agreed to keep in touch. We said good-bye and turned to go. Izzy put his coat across his arm. It must have been the coat that jostled the tape recorder.

" ...such an act of generosity and statesmanship ..."

"What's that noise?" Finn asked Jason just as Izzy and I were passing through the door. I turned around and said as casually as I could, "The secretary has the radio on." Izzy, who was beating on his chest like a man in the middle of a heart attack, had managed to silence the recorder. As we continued to walk slowly toward the door of the outer office, Izzy looked at me sheepishly and whispered, "I told you it wasn't working too well.

FIFTEEN:
ENTER WARNER BROTHERS

Class Struggle's first Christmas season came and went without any substantial improvement in our financial situation. The stand-off with Finn did not save our life but only prolonged it. And you can't pay bills with bills. Too bad, because otherwise we could have climbed out of the soup. As it was, most of the stores, including Brentano's, which promised to pay us right after Christmas, continued to pay us with promises. This is, as I was beginning to learn, capitalism's version of the water torture, designed specifically for small businesspeople. Even these promises were hard to get, required a couple of letters and as many phone calls. Stores that paid us usually did so with an air of having done us a great favor. As in a minuet, we had to bow low and spin around a couple of times before we held out our hand, and again before they put anything in it. Protocol also required that they let us know in gesture and word who needed whom and who didn't.

Even the radical bookstores, who were in solidarity with our political aims, put the bill from Class Struggle at the bottom of the pile. As a comrade from a bookstore in New York explained, "We have to pay our bills from other publishers first or they won't send us any more books and we'd have to close down." Being socialist businessmen, we were expected to understand, and wait. As if we weren't being clobbered from the other end by our own creditors.

The one positive benefit of hearing so many different excuses from our customers was that it gave us a lot to choose from in responding to the people to whom we owed money. Except the bank refused to beg. So did the shippers and the utility companies: "Do you want to use the phone (or put on a light, or ship a game) next week? Then you better ..." No matter what the excuse, we generally ended up begging them for more time. What kind of crazy world had we entered? We were

155

a legitimate business, not a pack of bums. Yet it was always we who had to beg. Whether we were the creditor or the debtor didn't seem to make any difference. Being small and vulnerable was all that counted.

In the midst of all the juggling, the promotion, and the deflation, with Finn still holding out for $5,000 more, on March 25, I received a fateful call. "Hello. This is Louis Allen. I'm a movie producer. I very much liked your piece in *The New York Times*. It tells a fascinating story, and I would like to talk to you about the possibility of making a movie out of it."

The day before, *The New York Times* had published an Op-Ed article of mine that they entitled "A Marxist Turned Capitalist Finds Bottom Line Too Low." In it, I sketched how going into business had affected my health, sleep, food, family, friendships, and conversation, and expressed sympathy for other people caught up in the capitalist role. My conclusion was that a society that was no longer dominated by the search for profits could not help but benefit capitalists, as human beings, as well as workers. I said I intended to carry this message of hope to the next meeting of my Chamber of Commerce (something I did three months later: see the Introduction).

Several people had called to tell me how much they enjoyed the piece, but this ... There was a pause while I tried to figure out which of my friends was pulling my leg. Ira? He had already called up one day as Señor de Cuña and ordered 1,000 games for his store in the Amazon. But try as I did, I couldn't recognize the voice. "A movie?" I asked. I've got it now, I thought, It was probably a small radical filmmaker who wanted to do a 10-minute documentary on the game. Well, why not?

"Yes," the voice replied. "I'd like to do a full-length feature film on your story. You probably know some of my other films. I produced *Fahrenheit 451* and *Lord of the Flies*."

"Is this for real? Are you serious?" I couldn't keep my doubts from spilling over into the telephone.

"May I come over right now to talk to you, to show you just how serious I am?" All doubt about the authenticity of the call vanished when Louis Allen turned up in my NYU office an hour later. Directors and actors wear funky clothes. Producers dress in the most expensive garments money can buy. It helps set the tone: business, big business, serious big business, but business with a flair, an artistic flair that hovers somewhere between genius and grand Guignol.

Louis got right to the point. There has never been a movie about a Marxist game inventor, or a Marxist business man for that matter. What an unexpected contradiction, so full of possibilities for humor and insight. He considered it a great challenge, one he would like to take up. He asked me to tell him more about the story.

I related why I invented the game, how I got into business, about Finn, the banks, the Brentano strike, selling the game at Macy's. The more he heard, the more excited he became. "If we could only capture its essentials in a film!" he exclaimed.

Louis's call was quite a shock, and like all shocks, it dulled the functioning of some senses and heightened that of others. His enthusiasm for the story was infectious (or was my enthusiasm infecting him?). I had never in my wildest fantasies—and I yield to no one as a fantasist—imagined that Hollywood might do a movie on the Class Struggle story. Hollywood is the American dream factory. It's there to keep us all laughing and singing happily off the point while our whole society goes drip, dripping down the tubes. No, I had no illusions about Hollywood or the people who work there.

But movies are also a business, and businesses try to make money however they can. Capitalism is full of contradictions that offer some space for maneuver. Isn't Class Struggle, Inc., itself evidence of this? Hollywood, too, has its contradictions that offer some space for maneuver. And amid all the pressures to conform and to trivialize, opportunities occasionally arise for genuinely creative and critical work. Was this such an opportunity? And a movie would certainly sell a lot of games. My head was spinning. Things were moving too fast. I took Louis home for coffee, but really to have Paule meet him, listen to him, look him over.

When we got to my apartment, Louis addressed himself to my still unspoken fears. "The film would have to be a comedy—the subject is too serious not to be—but not a farce. It should be a satire with the comedy coming out of your impossible situation as a Marxist businessman. It is only natural," he went on, "that you are worried about how you would be portrayed. But if this film made you look ridiculous or evil, it would be a bad film. The fun comes from the way you've chosen to take the mickey out of the system, and from what you've learned about the problems of being a capitalist in the process. For this to work in a film, you have to be presented as sincere and well meaning, even likeable."

"I have no doubt that a good film could be made from our story," I replied, "especially if it stuck pretty close to what really happened. But I also know that the material lends itself to being distorted into a tale about nutty professor who exchanges his Marxist ideals for the greed of the marketplace, and finds happiness in becoming a millionaire."

"Look at the kind of films I've made," Louis shot back. "I'm not interested in doing anti-socialist propaganda, never have been. What I see here is a chance to make a film about a unique subject, and, yes, a unique character. You could probably help us by co-writing the film script. This way you'll have an important input in the final product."

At about this point in the conversation, Louis began, casually at first, to drop sums: "helping to write the film should net you about $30,000"; "about $15,000 or $20,000 for the option"; "the story itself is worth $50,000 to $60,000." The addition I did at the time gave me a total of just over $100,000.

I explained to Louis that Class Struggle, Inc., was run by a board of directors and that I would have to consult with them, and also that I needed a little time to digest all that he had told me. He would have his answer in a week. On leaving, he explained that he intended to co-produce this movie with his wife, Jay Presson Allen, who is better known as the scriptwriter of such films as *Cabaret* and *The Prime of Miss Jean Brodie*, but is now producing films as well.

The reaction of my Class Struggle colleagues to Allen's offer was one of overwhelming delight: "unbelievable, unbelievably wonderful! Why does fate always wait until we are just about to go over the edge before throwing us a rope? If Allen really means it, what do we lose?" Only Paule and Ed suggested that what could be lost was my reputation, but this had to be balanced against the chance to carry the same message that is in the game (or some part of it) to untold millions who would see the movie. Even more than our deteriorating financial situation, it was this that dictated my own increasingly favorable reaction to Allen's proposal.

Only Paule dissented. As it turned out, she had less trust in Hollywood and in anyone associated with it than the rest of us. "No good will come of this," she warned. "They're a bunch of unscrupulous crooks—'anything for a laugh' means what it says. They will try to make us look foolish, and once they begin, we won't be able to stop them." As always, Paule's worries left deep traces in my own thinking. Could she be right? There were still a few days before I had to give Louis an answer. I would think the matter through just one more time.

The next day, we had a visit from Mike Albert, an editor at South End Press, which had just published my book *Social and Sexual Revolution: Essays on Marx and Reich*. As a friend and political comrade, Mike considered it his duty to tell me what some people in the Movement were saying about my involvement with Class Struggle. "Not everyone grasps the education import of the game. Marketing Marx. It reeks of rip-off, of someone trying to make money out of the Movement's blood, sweat, and tears." That very week, I had read the same sentiment on the wall in one of the toilets at NYU: "Down with capitalism—don't buy Class Struggle—steal it."

"In the eyes of some," Mike went on, "Class Struggle just provides another occasion for the bourgeois media to ridicule the Left. 'Everyone just wants to get rich' is how the press interprets what you're doing."

Mike's remarks cut deep, not only because I respect his

judgment but because he knew that I hadn't made a cent on Class Struggle, that we still owed a fortune. "Not important," he said. "People perceive that you've made a bundle." As Mike spoke, I was reminded of an antiwar march in which someone was ejected from our ranks when it was discovered that he was selling "Vietnam Wins" T-shirts as a money-making gig. Mike's own sensitivity to mixing politics and business was such that he had refused to sell South End's book *No Nukes* at a Harrisburg rally protesting nuclear power.

When I told Mike about the movie offer and that I was leaning toward accepting it, he redoubled his efforts to save me from myself. "Radical ideas come out of Hollywood as mush or worse." Then, looking from me to Paule and back to me for effect, he continued, "You've also got to consider your reputation. After the game, this could destroy what's left of your credibility. Do you want people to think of you as another Eldridge Cleaver or a turncoat like Rennie Davis?"

"I am not indifferent to what people I respect think of me," I replied, "but in this matter I have to follow my political instincts. Will the film continue the educational work of the game? The game is socialist, but I have no illusions that the film will be. It will, however, highlight the game and increase people's familiarity with the concept of 'class struggle'. This can be done to some degree even when the context is unfavorable. After all, people's lives provide them with the raw material with which to fill in the meaning of 'class struggle'. What is missing for most Americans is the concept itself."

"Aren't you overdoing the importance of learning the meaning of one concept?" Mike asked.

"Not when that concept is 'class struggle'," I insisted. "Many on the Left mistake anger and frustration and a knowing nod of the head for a shared outlook. There are different ways to be angry, even at the same person or group. Who is the real enemy? Yes, I know it's that man over there, but in which of his capacities? Organized along what lines? In the service of what interests? Allied with what other people and institutions? Unless these questions are answered, many peace demonstrators will feel satisfied when Johnson is replaced by Nixon or Carter, and protests by blacks and feminists will begin to slacken when white male capitalists are joined by a few token blacks and women. Missing is the category of 'class struggle.' It is the single, indispensable key to the whole capitalist puzzle, giving all the other pieces their proper proportions and showing how they link up.

"Take the movie *Nine to Five*," I went on. "It contains a lot of class struggle, but it doesn't use the concept. This leaves workers fighting against a bad boss and hoping for a good one. Only when the concept of 'class struggle', which plays down this distinction in favor of the more fundamental one between *all* bosses and *all* workers, has entered the minds of America's workers, will socialism become a possibility."

"And you think the game and the movie can do that?" Mike asked, a little overcome—I suspect—by what he considered my naiveté.

"No, of course not, not by themselves," I said. "But at this juncture in American politics, with no mass socialist party or press, they can play a useful role. Add to the game and film the hundreds of media stories they have and will provoke." I handed Mike a two-inch-thick packet of press clippings on the game. "If the game has introduced the idea of class struggle to a few hundred thousand people, these stories have been read by millions."

Mike paused to examine the one piece about which I feel the most pride. The large headline in *The New York Times* read "Class Struggle Is the Rage in Washington." Under it is a cartoon of a worker and a capitalist arm-wrestling. The story that follows is not about the game at all, but about some union leaders who have accused the National Association of Manufacturers of engaging in one-sided class struggle. In its choice of a headline and accompanying cartoon—and even to an extent in how the story was written—*The New York Times* had been influenced by the three pieces it had already published on the Class Struggle game. The game was helping to make it possible for the capitalist press to write more freely about class struggle. The game, as window dressing, was helping to get the real thing put into the window.

I'm afraid Mike left my home that evening only partially convinced, but my discussion with him greatly clarified my own thinking about the movie. If I had any doubts before, I knew now that the same logic that had carried me into the Class Struggle business required that I take this next step.

Having made the decision to accept Louis Allen's offer, the question was how to get the best possible contract. Everyone I consulted, including Sol Yurick, who had sold his novel *The Warriors* to Hollywood (Paule winced at the thought of what Hollywood had done to that book), advised me to get an agent who specialized in movie deals. The William Morris Agency has the reputation of being the country's top movie agency, so I called them, and a week later signed a contract with Fred Millstein of William Morris to negotiate with Louis Allen on my behalf.

I knew Rodney Sokol, Class Struggle's agent for the sale of foreign rights, would not be pleased when I told him the news, but I was unprepared for the hyperbole: "I took you guys out of the gutter, made you a household name, and this is the thanks I get." After negotiating the Mondadori contract, Sokol's main achievement was to share his work with Simon and Schuster, burdening us with another 25 percent commission on everything we earned overseas. This unusual arrangement with a major publisher brought us a certain amount of publicity, one new licensing contract (Spain), but so far no new cash. For eight months he had been treating my Class Struggle colleagues—it seemed to us—with the contempt a harsh schoolmaster reserves for naughty children, and bending my ear about big deals that never came off (except—if this is an exception—in the case of Simon and Schuster). The guy traded only in superlatives. Now he was acting like the proverbial Jewish mother who had put her son through medical school and wasn't invited to the graduation. For Class Struggle, Inc., it was one more business connection terminated in a burst of fireworks.

Fred Millstein's and my first meeting with Louis Allen to discuss the movie contract took place in Jay Allen's spacious art-deco office suite overlooking the Broadway theater district. Louis began by telling us that Jay was going to produce the film on her own. Noting my hesitancy, he quickly added that she shared all our ideas about the importance of sticking as close to the facts as possible, that this is what made the story both funny and significant. From there, Jay took over. Jay is a very handsome woman in her early 60s, intense, very take-charge, apparently struggling hard to make people forget she is a woman while never missing an opportunity to make them aware of it.

Jay was very businesslike. "I have a contract to produce five films for Warner Brothers, and I intend to make the Class Struggle one of them. Though Louis suggested that you help write the script, I would prefer if you simply consulted on it. I have a couple of professional writers in mind. You would tell them what happened and they would do the rest."

The rest of what? I thought. Co-authoring the script would give me some measure of control over what was finally produced. What influence could I have over the final product as a consultant?

Jay was forthright. "This is 5- to 10-million-dollar project. You can't expect that we are going to allow you a veto power over what we do. It comes down to a matter of trust. Take a look at the kind of movies I've done, and then decide whether you can trust me with the story."

I felt very uncomfortable with the reduction of my role to consultant. Everything now depended on whom Jay would get as writer and on how much I could influence him. Jay was right about it all coming down to a matter of trust, but Jay was an offshoot of Hollywood, and Hollywood is a business. How much trust could I have in decisions made on the basis of the criteria that operate in business? Still, Jay's own track record as a film writer was impressive: *Cabaret, The Prime of Miss Jean Brodie, Funny Lady.* No *schlock* here. Was I already too sold on the idea of a film? Was I building up Jay's credentials because it was too late to back down? Howard, Izzy, and the other members of the Class Struggle board were already celebrating the movie contract as an accomplished fact. I remembered that in my discussion with Mike Albert, I said introducing more people to the notion of class struggle was sufficient for doing the movie. That remained the bottom line.

I gave Fred the green light to start the negotiations. Our strategy was simple. Louis had talked vaguely about $100,000. We would come in asking for $200,000, and expect to compromise at around $150,000. It was not to be. At their first meeting, Jay's offer rounded off at about $70,000. Fred told me that Jay has a reputation as someone who gets her kicks out of hard bargaining. We would have to drop our demand to $150,000. Fred returned from his next bargaining session with Jay to report that something very strange was happening. Her offer had dropped to around $50,000. Instead of moving toward the acceptable middle ground, as typically happens, Jay was beating a retreat, and he found himself running after. Was she losing interest?

Fred contacted a couple of producers he knew to see what they thought was happening. They told him, first, they were surprised that any Hollywood type wanted to do a movie on such a controversial topic. And second, since the story was not written down in a book, it is always possible to rip-off the essentials and wait for the injured party to sue. Some such thing happened with the movie *Norma Rae*. In their view, by offering me anything for the story, Jay Allen was mainly interested in buying insurance against a lawsuit. Their advice: Take whatever Allen offers—quick. After two more weeks of peering into tea leaves, I decided to accept their advice.

All the reasons for and against making the film remained as before. Only the money had now dipped to $40,000. I signed. Of the $40,000, I got only $5,000 on signing—that was for a one-year option on the story. Another $5,000 applied to my work as a consultant and would be paid after I told my story to the scriptwriter. If and when the script was officially accepted by

Warner's for production, I would receive another $20,000. The last $10,000 would be paid when shooting on the movie began. Fred fought hard to secure two and then one percent of the movie's gross profits—to no avail. As a sop, Jay agreed to give me 1 percent of her producer's net profits; that is, after all expenses and taxes were paid. Given the kind of games played by accountants, only the biggest blockbuster films show any net profit for producers, so this was no gain at all.

According to my agreement with Class Struggle, Inc., one half of everything I got for the film would go to the company. Of the $5,000 initial payment, the agent took $500, Class struggle got $2,250, and I got $2,250. When news of the Class Struggle movie hit the press, everyone was convinced—and quite concerned—that I had made a financial killing. My NYU colleague Frank Moreno came into my office and said he would be satisfied if I would just tell him the ballpark figure: "Was it more than a quarter of a million bucks?"

Frank was one of the people who had turned down a chance to invest in the game earlier. There had to be some tangible benefits to this movie thing. "Yeah, Frank," I said. "A lot more."

A few weeks later, Fred, a lawyer for William Morris, Izzy, and I met with three lawyers for Warner Brothers to go over some riders to the contract that remained unresolved. In particular, there was the question of who would get the profits from possible spin-offs of the movie, such as TV sitcoms, coloring books, T-shirts, pencils, and, yes, Ping-Pong balls. Fred explained that the film companies were all suffering from *Star Wars* syndrome. *Star Wars*, it seems, made more money from all the junk that was piled on afterward than from rentals on the film, and some of this money managed to slip through the fingers of its producers. Never again. Since there was no way of knowing what movie would produce spin-offs or what form they would take, the language in the contract was meant to cover every possibility. They were adamant. I was mostly amazed. Somehow I couldn't quite picture America's youth drinking "Class Struggle Cola," and the idea of the best legal talent in town spending an afternoon arguing about "Class Struggle Ping-Pong Balls" left me feeling like a guest at a mad tea party. I half-expected Jay to turn up dressed as the Queen of Hearts.

Fred Millstein brought me back to reality with a jolt when, in the course of bargaining, he referred to me with a casual sweep of his arm as "the property." Me? Had I sold something more than just a story? By going into business with the game, I learned what it felt like to be a capitalist. Was I now going to experience what it is like to be a commodity?

Warner Brothers got the Ping-Pong balls.

•••

Just as the game led to an offer to do a movie, the movie triggered off interest in a book. By confessing all in a book, I thought I could protect myself in part against the inevitable distortions of the film and carry further the same political work begun in the game. It was also a welcome opportunity to reflect on what I had actually done and what had been done to me. In July, with the help of John Brockman, another agent (I now had more agents this year than hair cuts), I signed a contract to write this book on the still-unfinished story of the game (and now the movie) with William Morrow publishers, and received a $4,000 advance, half of which went to Class Struggle, Inc. I bought a pocket-sized notebook, which I carried with me at all times, and tried to write down whatever I was feeling or could remember of what seemed like the already-distant past.

"No, not such long sentences, too theoretical, aim for the guts. It is important to find just the right voice to tell my tale" (from my notebook). After 20 years of academes, this was not going to be easy.

GREGOR

What is that lisping, selling sound, that tentacle creeping from behind the door? Nothing to worry, it is only Gregor. And what is that whiney, bossy bleep, the oozing yellow slime on the floor? Nothing to worry, it is only Gregor. Marx may have known what businessmen do, but Kafka understood better what they become. Gregor Samsa went to bed one evening a hard-working salesman, and woke up the next morning a giant cockroach.

Even shrunk to the size of her finger, Alice remained whole and healthy when compared to Gregor. Bad posture, worse vibes, waving a balance sheet to make a point—the signs of a metamorphosis had been there for some time; but I had been avoiding them, disbelieving them, treating them like a joke: "Hey, I'm getting to sound just like a businessman."

I decided to observe these strange thoughts and feelings more carefully, to be both germ culture and scientist. Like Freud, who slowly watched himself become a cocaine addict only to discover that he had lost control over the process, I followed my descent into Gregor with the bemused self-confidence of someone who knows better.

And then it was too late.

SIXTEEN:
THE GRAND TOUR: SELLING GAMES OR
CARRYING THE WORD?

In May 1979, the letter from Ediciones Grijalbo finally arrived. Grijalbo, Spain's largest radical publisher, had agreed to do a Spanish edition of Class struggle several months before, but kept putting off sending us the $15,000 advance called for in the contract. Now, at last, I thought, we will have enough money to pay for the settlement we had just reached with Finn. My joy was stillborn. Instead of a check, I found a brief note canceling the contract—"problems of distribution."

Overcome by a sudden wave of exhaustion, I had to sit down. Shock therapy works. My mind was wiped clean of thoughts. I couldn't lift a finger or raise an eyelid; yet I was awake, even oddly alert. I could feel the corners of my mouth turn down, making a horrible grimace of my face, but I was powerless to change it. A student called to ask how I treat late term papers. She had to be kidding. Here the world was collapsing, my world of business, and she wanted advice from a professor. Lips that have to bend in order to form words did what they have always done. I even managed to sound normal. Maybe collapse is normal.

What the business was doing to me now shouldn't happen— you'll forgive the expression—to a businessman. Is it possible that I once found some excitement in this runaround? The constant, unremitting pressure, the deadlines that could never be met, the crescendo of questions that had no answers, the little jobs that didn't get done until I did them (small businessman's megalomania?), the steady parade of people to whom I could never say what I really thought, and, most of all, the 180-degree turns in our fortune started to take a heavy toll on me, physically and emotionally. Where I once bounced, I now began to drag. Yet I couldn't sit still. I bitched whenever the phone rang, but found that I was even more nervous when it didn't. I was becoming a junkie, a phone junkie, needing interruptions like a fix. Concentrating on anything for more than 10, 15 minutes was impossible.

At night, I ground my teeth so badly that four of them broke. I put on pounds, developed bad breath, stomach cramps, and a smile that stayed on long after I had stopped smiling. The business became an obsession. Conversations on other subjects began to bore me, and just as surely I began to bore people who hoped to talk to me about other subjects. Fun was something I packaged in a box and sold (now) for $12.

I couldn't pass a book or game store without going in to check on the sales of Class Struggle, and if the salesperson wasn't looking, moving the game into a better position on the shelf. No question about it—I was becoming a pain in the ass. But more could always be done, and if not me, who would do it, who would push others to do it? I rationalized that this was what Howard and the others wanted me to do, but my behavior was becoming more and more compulsive.

When the Gullens asked about taking a couple of weeks paid vacation, I responded, "Of course you can go, and August is a good time for us. Enjoy yourselves." Inside, I felt a twinge of pain. Didn't they know we had a million things to do? How could we afford to pay them for not working? Biting my tongue, I said nothing. Again, I blushed at having such capitalist thoughts, but they came with the situation, the squeeze Class Struggle was in, and my position as boss. As a businessman, I didn't so much originate these thoughts, as receive them and pass them along.

Even my political commitment was beginning to fray at the edges. I had always been delighted by each downturn of sales reported in the marketplace—"People buying less junk," I thought. Now, the same news appeared somehow threatening. I caught myself thinking, "If the collapse of capitalism could wait just a little longer, until we got our business on its feet." A bolt of lightning would not have produced a greater shock. Slowly, I was getting drawn in and becoming part of the mechanism that I was trying to expose and explode. How I spent my days was beginning to take its toll on what went on inside my head—a good Marxist lesson, but one from which I thought I was exempt by virtue of my socialist ideas. No such luck. Material conditions, where one fits into society and the interests and problems this brings in its wake, affect everyone's thinking. No exceptions. I was finally learning what it means to become what Marx calls an "embodiment" of my function, of capital. The battle for my soul was on in earnest, and I was just becoming aware that it had begun.

Outwardly, I joked about really becoming a businessman, but inwardly I began to get afraid, spooky afraid, about what was happening to me. I hesitated to share these fears with anyone, even Paule. Why? To do so would be bad for business. Just a little more time, I told myself, and Class Struggle, Inc., will be able to take care of itself, but the bends in the road seemed to multiply and become sharper, and my efforts at the wheel were more necessary than ever.

It's also bad for business to spend too much time wallowing in self-pity. Have to act fast, take up the slack, maximize the chances. I wrote to Grijalbo telling them how they could solve their distribution problem and predicting what great things the movie would do for international sales. Just in case. I also intensified our efforts to get another bank loan from Citibank to pay Finn the $20,000 we owed him as part of the settlement of our two lawsuits. For this, he agreed to hand over 22,000 finished games and the parts for 28,000 others.

Where was the great thrill in besting a business opponent that Monopoly had led me to expect I would feel? Instead, I felt very sorry for Finn ... and myself. Perhaps it was because I really wasn't sure who had won. The rules for the business game had forced us to battle toe-to-toe like two gladiators until one of us was bloodied. Inflicting financial pain and enjoying it was not in my character, not yet. Would that, too, change?

In early June, I went to Los Angeles to the American Booksellers Association Convention, where Class Struggle, Inc., shared a large booth with Monthly Review Press, South End Press, and Larry Hill Publishers, America's three largest radical publishers. Politically speaking, we had arrived. Along with Volume I of *Capital* and a subscription to at least one socialist newspaper, Class Struggle had become a staple in the household of any self-respecting radical. Commercially speaking, our success was as tenuous as ever, with promises of various degrees of certainty outpacing actual sales by about five to one.

Shortly after my return to New York, I received another letter from Ediciones Grijalbo. They had changed their minds! Again! My letter had convinced them they could deal with the problems of distribution. They also found the movie very exciting. Work on the Spanish translation would begin at once. Still no money—the $15,000 advance was "on its way"—but this time how could I doubt them? The same week, Dargeaud, a French publisher best known for its Asterix comic books, made us an offer to do a French edition of the game. That night it seemed as if the stars shone more brightly than they had for a very long time. Had our fortunes finally turned? I wanted desperately to think so. To compound our joy, Citibank chose this moment to lend us the $20,000 we needed to pay Finn. We had already paid them back close to $15,000 on their initial loan of $30,000, so this was more a matter of refinancing an old commitment than making a new one.

The warmth of the summer had come, and with it a little bit of stability had entered my life as a businessman. For the first time in almost a year, I was not out pounding the pavements in search of loans and investments. For the first time in almost seven months, we were not on the verge of bankruptcy. The loan had given us a little breathing space. How good it was to breathe!

Getting 22,000 games all at once from Finn meant that we had to find some place to put them. Game boxes had already spread through all the rooms in my apartment, and Paule and Raoul were desperate to bring this "temporary" arrangement, which had already lasted over six months, to an end. Running out of alternatives, we decided to rent a larger office with some warehouse space attached on Twenty-third Street just across from the Toy Building. Was the address only a coincidence, or a sign of our full entry into the industry?

Another consideration was that the room in Ed's loft that had been serving us as an office had become much too cramped and noisy with Ed's two little girls and Chi Chi, his barky terrier, playing hide-and-seek under the desks and behind the boxes. The heat was irregular, the elevator only slightly less so—how could people work in these conditions? That was the socialist speaking. But we can't afford anything better. That was the capitalist. I was glad when the necessity of finding more space to store our new games finally resolved this uncomfortable contradiction.

Life in our new office started out like a TV soap opera. The phone didn't work for a week—a business like ours lives on the telephone—and it was only after I screamed for the president of the phone company that they sent someone out to fix it. Back from delivering Class Struggle games on a hand truck, John Mason, our crackerjack part-time salesman, fell one floor down the elevator shaft, receiving the fright of his life and badly wrinkling the three-piece suit he always wore to work. While Bobbi, our Iranian trucker, set fire to a rented truck by overloading it with games and game parts (it puzzled me, as well). With each new near-disaster, I kept reminding myself, "But at least we can pay our bills," and to a small businessperson, nothing is more important.

Relieved of the necessity to scrounge for money for Class Struggle, I could also teach a double load in summer school to refurbish my personal finances, to the puzzlement of my NYU colleagues, who couldn't understand why someone who had just made a killing in business would want to take on so much teaching. Then, in July, I received an invitation from Mondadori to come to Milan for a September press conference to kick off the appearance of *Lotta di Classe*. Though the Spanish and French translations were far from ready, the companies that were to do them agreed to pay a share of my costs, and a grand tour of Europe to promote the game was quickly arranged.

When the time came to leave, I got a worried call from my parents, who warned me as usual to be very, very careful, but this time there was a special request. Frightened by a TV special on the Red Brigades, my mother wanted me to promise her that while I was in Italy I wouldn't talk to any Communists: "Do you want me to die of a heart attack? Please, Bertell, promise."

My first stop was Barcelona, Grijalbo publishes a lot of Marxist literature, but what caught my eye was their series of political comic books by the Mexican cartoonist Rius—*The Communist Manifesto Comic Book*, *Capital for Beginners*, *Mao*, and about a dozen others. Rius has done more to popularize socialist ideas in the Spanish speaking countries than any other person, and I felt honored to share the same publisher. Juan Grijalbo, the elderly owner of the company, seemed very enthusiastic about the potential of Class Struggle in Spain. Their earlier cancellation of the contract had been a mistake and he apologized. Since this was their first game, they had had some doubts on how to produce and distribute it, but this was all cleared up, and he, personally, was convinced that this was something they had to do. Grijalbo's general manager and son-in-law was more subdued, very businesslike, but this didn't seem to matter. They then surprised me by presenting me with an already finished Spanish translation of the game, and asked me to check it for accuracy.

Most of the next day was devoted to giving interviews to journalists from a half-dozen newspapers. "Is this a joke?" "Are you for real (or the Spanish equivalent thereof)?" "Class Struggle—a game?" "How much money have you made?" "What do your students think? Your university? Your government?" "How can such an idea come from America?"

Before leaving Barcelona the next morning, I stopped off to say good-bye to Señor Grijalbo and his associates. I found them all looking very worried. They had just received a call from someone who said he had the Spanish rights to Class Struggle and offered to sell them to Grijalbo. Did I know anything about this? Of course not, I assured them. We had the worldwide copyright for the game and for "Class Struggle" when used as the name of a game, and we had not sold the license to anyone else. Actually, the surprise was such that I couldn't remember what Izzy and Simon and Schuster had actually done, but I assumed the best to put them—and myself—at ease (Izzy, don't fail me now). Señor Grijalbo said it was not uncommon for someone to claim the Spanish copyright on a foreign product in order to make an undeserved commission on the sale of the copyright to the company that hoped to use it. We decided to treat the call as an inept attempt at blackmail. Apparently, Grijalbo smiled, Class Struggle's success is such that it is attracting crooks and kooks just like any other capitalist success story. And the $15,000 advance? Still not ready, but it would be waiting for me, Grijalbo promised, when I got back to New York.

In the departure lounge of the airport, I picked up copies of Barcelona's three daily newspapers and found full-page accounts of the interviews I had given in two of them (three more equally long and equally favorable stories on Class Struggle appeared in Barcelona and Madrid papers in the next few days). Just before my plane was due to leave for Paris, I decided to call the people at Dargeaud to let them know I would be arriving at their office about 2 P.M. that afternoon.

"Sorry. Didn't you get our telegram?" The voice on the other end of the line seemed decidedly uncomfortable.

"What telegram?" I asked.

"There is a squeeze on our financial resources, and we have had to cancel our plans to produce Class Struggle."

I went cold. How? When? No, the voice insisted, there was no sense in coming to discuss it. It was beyond their control. I was still trying to get further clarification, looking for an angle, a crack in his rejection, when my plane for Paris was announced over the loudspeaker. I had already bought my ticket, my suitcase was aboard the plane, but now what reason did I have to go? Nor did I have any reason to stay in Barcelona. Too numb to decide, I let myself be carried by the crowd that was moving toward the plane. Licking one's wounds among the ivory-colored monuments of Paris is no less painful than anywhere else, but it is more genteel, more literary.

Still somewhat in a daze, I took my seat on the plane. It seemed like a good time to take stock. I took out my notebook and began to write: "Hard to write when one is feeling strong emotions. If they're positive, I am too busy enjoying them. If negative, like now, I just feel numb. Except for my chest, on which someone has dropped a heavy barbell. Hell of a thing to do. I can see Howard's bent-over head. Think of something else. I never liked roller coasters—up, down, down, up, up, and now down, more down it seems than ever. But maybe it's because I'm alone and so far from home. Dargeaud had promised to chip in $400 toward my trip. I suppose that's off, too. Or is there a sense of honor in business?" (Later insert: "There isn't.")

"We are now high over the red and brown checkered fields outside of Barcelona. Beautiful sight. Why can't I enjoy it? Where would I put the enjoyment? My inner space is taken up with emptiness. Why am I here? There has to be a very good reason for why my feet are so high off the ground, my heart so far from its hearth." I recited all the reasons I could remember for inventing Class Struggle, and going into business to produce and market it. "At a bare minimum," I wrote, "the repetition of the word in the mass media is political, makes a criticism, provides a tool, sets up sides, and helps unify different kinds of workers as fighters on the same side—against the capitalists.

"So I continue my one-man journey to carry the word, 'class struggle.' Yes, that's it." I was starting to feel better. "I'm not selling games but carrying the word, a word that explodes in the head and rearranges people's thinking, a word disguised, denied, hidden. I am carrying it up front and in the open. I get it through customs by holding it in my hand and pointing to it with a smile. The thought police are used to finding it well hidden at the bottom of a suitcase. So they laugh. We laugh together. It couldn't be more unexpected if I held my pipi in my hand.

It's naughty, naughty-funny, a kind of joke. And who wants to look like a jerk who can't take a joke?

"Like the prophets of old (ouch! Dangerous analogy/good thing no one reads this), I am carrying the word, word of the imminent destruction of the old life and word of the new life which will follow. In its nature, this is not the kind of job that can be done by a mass of people. Looks too political. Wouldn't get by the thought police. One eccentric, hard to classify—a little this, a little that—whistling 'Yankee Doodle Dandy' could probably get into Fort Knox. I've done better. I have toyed my way into Fort Consciousness.

"But I must get over this feeling that when I'm not selling games I'm not doing anything. To play my Class Struggle card I had to become a businessman. This function required that I act like a capitalist, which in turn gave rise to certain petty emotions. But I have to be careful not to let these emotions get the best of me. I can't let myself react like a little capitalist who has just lost some business—though this is what I am, and I have just lost some business ... and it does hurt something awful."

While in Paris, I decided to visit our few customers to ask them who they thought might be interested in producing a French version of the game. Au Nain Bleu ordered a dozen games airmail. It must have cost them a fortune! I couldn't help wondering what they were charging for the game. I found the shop in one of the swankiest commercial quarters of Paris. Blue, it seems, is the toy and game store for the super rich, with $1,000 stuffed pandas in the windows and sales clerks who wear white gloves and stovepipe hats.

The manager was pleased to meet the American who invented this "exotic" game. There had been any number of raised eyebrows, and at least one customer had registered an angry complaint. "You see, Professor Ollman, most of our customers are, well—how do you say?—capitalists. Class struggle is not a joking matter in France as it is in America." I hastened to assure him that class struggle is not a joking matter in the

United States either, or not yet (or was it not anymore?). No matter. The game was selling, and he said that was all he cared about, though I detected that he would have liked me to say it was all a big put-on.

I also visited Jeux Descartes, an adult game store in the Latin Quarter, which is owned by a self-made English entrepreneur, Peter Watts. Class Struggle, he said, could sell over 1,000 copies in France if we could only produce it very cheaply. How about packaging it in a bag or a plastic sack instead of a box? An intriguing idea. I remained a little skeptical, but Watts said once he finished his calculations he would make us a bid to do the French edition of Class Struggle in this format. The trip to Paris seemed to have paid off after all. I left for Milan in high spirits.

My greeting in Milan by Mr. Giovanni Hausmann, the cultured general manager of Auguri Mondadori, was warm but a little strained. Just the week before, the Italian journal *L'Espresso* had published an article listing me as one of the Americans who signed a petition on behalf of Paolo Negri, an Italian professor who was jailed on suspicion of having ties with the Red Brigades.

"Yes, of course, I signed the petition," I said. "There doesn't seem to be any evidence of wrongdoing. As far as I can see, the Italian government has arrested Negri because of his writings, and not because of anything he did. No doubt you signed the petition as well."

Hausmann tried hard to smile, but he was visibly worried. "Italian journalists," he explained, "like to see plots everywhere." I assured him that I didn't belong to any plot, and that I have signed petitions in support of political prisoners in many countries, most recently in East Germany, Argentina, Iran, Chile, the U.S., and Italy. But until the Italian government provided a satisfactory explanation for why it arrested Negri, I told him, in my eyes it was the government that was on trial and not Negri.

Hausmann was decidedly unimpressed. His sole concern, he said, was for the game. It was controversial enough as it was.

"If somehow it gets connected to the Negri case, then ..."

"I didn't come to Milan to campaign for Negri," I tried to reassure him, "but to give a press conference on Class Struggle. However, if the press asks me why I signed the petition, I will have to tell them what I've just told you. Democracy is seldom lost all at one time, but rather in bits and pieces. Those of us who believe in civil liberties ..." But Hausmann had already stopped listening.

Once again, a choice to make between business and politics. Could I say my piece on Negri without embarrassing my business associates at Mondadori and possibly ruining the sales of Class Struggle? Could I stick to business without losing my soul? Should I come on strong against the Italian government and make a big international incident? Would the press play it up if I did? Would it really help Negri? I slept very badly that night.

The next morning, the first thing I did was to arrange with my old friend Pino Cimo, who had come from Rome to cover the press conference for *Il Messaggero*, to ask me a question on the Negri petition if the other reporters failed to do so. The press conference was scheduled for 10:30 A.M. in the Hall of Congresses of the extremely posh Hotel Milan. Mondadori had never held a press conference for a game inventor and they were not sure what to do. Did they really need pretty girls handing out copies of the game at the door and simultaneous translation in four languages? A hall for 200 people looked huge and cavernous, all the more so at 10:30 when only three or four reporters were present. I tried hard not to think of the obvious parallel. Hausmann looked very glum.

A company of bartenders arrived to serve drinks for the expected army. Then, in ones, twos and fives, the Italian press arrived, filling up the front half of the room. By 10:50, every major paper and magazine in the country was present. Class Struggle had come a long way since our first press conference in Ed's loft. Hausmann's gamble seemed to have paid off. If only Ed, Howard, and the others were here to share this moment.

In his introduction, Hausmann emphasized that Class Struggle could only have been invented in America, and that I was more an American than a Marxist. Mondadori agreed to produce the game, he said, because it was a good game, a timely one, and a humorous one. He concluded that, in his eyes, it was a mark of capitalism's strength and tolerance that it could sell a game of this kind.

This is only one side of the story, I thought to myself as I listened to Hausmann talk, but in this situation it is the right side to emphasize. Mondadori was walking a tightrope. They had invested a lot of money and prestige in buying the Italian rights to Class Struggle. How would the Italian political parties, Left and Right, consumers, the game industry, and others respond to their act of bravado? They had to be worried and careful.

The first questions were the ones I had heard many times before. Then—"Why didn't you sell the game to a Communist publisher?" It was the reporter from the Communist paper *L'Unità* who wanted to know. "If you had found me one earlier," I replied, "maybe I would have."

"Will Class Struggle really get people to change their political attitudes?" asked a noticeably worried member of the conservative press. "I don't know," I answered. "Play it and find out."

And always and again, the concern about how I was going to spend all the money I was supposed to be making.

It was around this point that I noticed that the man who was translating my English into Italian was having a difficult time with it. I began my next answer by quoting the comment in the *National Star* that "next to smoking marijuana, Class Struggle is the biggest hit on college campuses. Sex, apparently, was in third place." I was told later that the translation of this came out: "With its discussion of sex, Class Struggle is a big hit with college students!"

No one had asked me about Negri. Sensing that the press conference was almost over, Pino raised his hand and asked why I signed my name to the Negri petition. Ready and relaxed, I spoke for a full five minutes, firmly concluding that in the eyes of world opinion it was the Italian government that was on trial in this case. The translator, who had been taking notes during this time, stumbled even more than before and finished his remarks in less than a minute. Before I could react, Hausmann was on his feet thanking the reporters for attending and declaring the conference over. Later, Pino confirmed my suspicion that the translator left out most of what I said and rendered the rest innocuous.

"The Italian press learned that you are a good American liberal who is against putting people in prison," Pino joked. I was furious, but there was nothing to be done. The choice of how to mix business and politics, it turned out, was not always mine to make.

Before I left Italy, Hausmann introduced me to Ulrich Roder, the general manager of Heye Company, the largest publishers of calendars in Germany, who was paying him a friendly visit. Roder expressed great confidence in Hausmann's business instincts. The fact that Mondadori was producing an Italian edition of Class Struggle, he said, was good evidence that the game would sell well in Italy and probably elsewhere. Would he take a chance with a German edition, not a chance but—as he himself said—a sure thing? Roder smiled. Hausmann did most of the selling. I don't think he enjoyed being off on the end of a limb all alone with this unpredictable Marxist professor. Roder finally agreed that it would be a good idea for Heye to do a German edition, but he had to consult with colleagues before making a definite offer. He promised to call me in New York in a week with their decision.

England was my next and last stop. Two days visiting newspapers and publishers produced five stories on Class Struggle and a couple expressions of interest in producing a British edition of the game (or was this simply good English manners?). The final afternoon in England was mine and mine alone. I chose to spend it with Isaiah Berlin in Oxford. I needed a strong potion to help me recover from the emotional traumas of the last couple of weeks. I needed to talk to someone without thinking of how I could sell him a dozen games.

Conversations with Berlin have a way of taking off from wherever they begin and quickly spanning the centuries. Political humor reminded Isaiah of Voltaire, whose biting satire, he claimed, did more damage to the Catholic Church than the attacks of any other critic. But for humor to have this effect, the position against which it is aimed has to be "sacred" and its defenders pompous. Humor, Isaiah pointed out, is especially effective in destroying exaggerated feelings of self-importance. But capitalists are not particularly pompous, not in the way that the Church Fathers and aristocrats were. Did this mean that humor had more political potential in the hands of liberal critics of religious and aristocratic absolutism than it does now in the hands of socialists who wish to use it against capitalism? I shall have to think more about this. It would certainly help to explain why there has been so little socialist humor in the current class struggle.

We also speculated on what it meant for young people to laugh at those in authority. By itself, knowing that the present order makes no sense, laughing at it, usually leads to cynicism and pessimism, as one recognizes that nothing can be done. Humor can help to destroy an edifice, Isaiah said, but how does it help to build one? But there are kinds of humor, I argued, that also point the way, where revealing what is absurdly wrong is only part of the message. Class Struggle is an example of this. In part, it criticizes the unfair advantages of the capitalist class. In part, it tells workers where, how, and above all with whom to struggle in order to overcome this situation. Putting this serious message in the uniform of a clown is funny.

"You really owe it to yourself, if not to the rest of the world, to play Class Struggle," I told Isaiah. "Yes, with Ayer and Hampshire and a few other Oxford philosophers, I'll tape the session and play it on the radio." I said it half in jest. The other half, I guess, was my way of trying to sell Isaiah a dozen games. Whether to humor me or because it appealed to one of the most wicked funny bones in the British Isles, Isaiah agreed.

SEVENTEEN:
THE MARXIST MILLIONAIRE

"They laughed some, but winced a lot more." Luis Gonzales-Cruz, a recycled Mexican bullfighter who is now an international banker by day and one of my better graduate students by night, was telling me about the evening he spent playing Class Struggle with a few banker friends. We were coming down the rickety elevator from my NYU office. A little white-haired old man who was riding down with us noticed the copy of Class Struggle I was carrying and interrupted to ask, "Is it true that the professor who invented this game teaches here at NYU?" Without waiting for an answer, the stranger nodded sagely and told us that he had read all about this fellow. It seemed he was a Marxist and that he had made a million dollars from this game. "Isn't America something?" the old man asked, with a nod that indicated we didn't have to answer this question either.

Luis smiled broadly. I forced myself to smile, too, but inside I really wanted to cry. Class Struggle, Inc., was once again teetering on the brink of bankruptcy. Yet everyone was sure we had made a bundle. One Italian news story had referred to me as "the Marxist millionaire." My favorite Left causes were no longer satisfied with $10 and $20 donations. A couple of publications even sent me their annual financial statement along with letters recounting all the wonderful things they could do with $5,000. Where there was so much smoke (press), people figured there had to be fire (money).

Class Struggle, Inc., had made money for designers, manufacturers, bankers, distributors, jobbers, store owners, trade shows, shippers, landlords, photographers, accountants, the telephone and electric companies, newspapers where we placed ads, Uncle Sam (taxes), our workers (wages), and even a SoHo bum who regularly wore a Class Struggle button because it earned him an extra dollar a day in handouts. I was beginning to feel like a big teat on which everyone was sucking, voraciously, unappreciatively. Is this, too, what other small businessmen feel?

I made nothing. Worse, at this point I was out over $3,000 in unpaid expenses. When I told people that Class Struggle, Inc., still owed a lot of money, all I usually got for my candor was a disbelieving smile or a wink and the assurance, "Bertell, you can tell *me*." Why so much concern about all the money I was supposed to be making? Jealousy? A belief that socialists have to be poor? Fear that General Motors might soon fall to a socialist takeover? Being broke is bad enough. Being broke and mistaken for a millionaire—by everyone but the bank, that is— is about as funny as coughing up blood. Not my idea of hilarity. For all the media excitement, my European trip did not generate one American dollar. Neither the Heye Company nor Jeux Descartes ever called with offers to do foreign-language editions. No letters, no explanations, nothing. The $9,000 we got as advanced on the movie and the book helped keep us afloat over the summer, but this was the fall. Besides the monthly payment due on our bank loan, the rent, a huge trucking bill for moving Finn's stock of games, and miscellaneous expenses connected with running a business, we found ourselves owing an additional $20,000 to Long Island Packaging Company for putting together 28,000 finished games from the small mountain of spare parts bequeathed to us by Finn. Half of this money was due immediately.

Before my incipient ulcer could break loose from its moorings, Simon and Schuster received a check from Ediciones Grijalbo for $15,000, of which our share was a little less than $10,000. At last. Pull, pull, pull, and the tooth had come out. The joy I felt in getting paid for the Spanish license lasted no longer than the 24-hours it took to transfer this money to Long Island Packaging. The rest of what we owed them would have to come from our receivables, now close to $100,000, but few of our customers seemed to be in any hurry to pay. One major New York bookstore, we learned rather late, stays in business by refusing to pay its suppliers, selling stolen books, and going in and out of bankruptcy. Other, less proficient businessmen simply stalled, with the implicit threat that if we continued to bother them, they would take their orders elsewhere.

Do we contact a collection agency? This is a question we had been consciously avoiding for several months. Images of a long-mustachioed Simon Legree driving some poor family out of their coldwater flat for nonpayment of rent flashed before my eyes. The ultimate symbol of capitalist oppression, the professional bill collector. Could we stoop so low?

A capitalist fable recounted by the Marxist economist Howard Sherman offered some guidance: "Suppose a landlord decided to be kind to a poor tenant and collect no rent. The landlord would be unable to pay the mortgage and the bank would take over. Suppose the director of the bank that owned the mortgage decided to be kind to the kind landlord and not replace him. In that case, profits would fall and the bank director would be replaced. Suppose by the furthest stretch of the imagination that the stockholders in the banking firm decided to be kind and not fire the kind director. Then the bank would eventually go bankrupt, and a new bank would take over the mortgage and fire all the kind people."

Of course, there is something rotten with a system that penalizes kindness, but while we were operating inside it, we couldn't make believe it didn't exist. Customers who hadn't paid their bills for over a year—with the exception of a couple of radical bookstores with whom I had developed close personal ties—were handed over to the Dun and Bradstreet collection agency.

"But no strong-arm stuff, please."

Despite our mounting problems with getting paid, expanding sales remained our top priority. A little more push, a jot more luck, we reasoned, and the game might yet go off the charts. Practically, this meant breaking big into the market outside New York. All our visits and calls to the major chain stores only yielded gigantic telephone bills and a carload of delays and excuses, until Penney's, one of the largest department-store chains in America (1,200 stores), decided to test-sell the game.

The breakthrough took place two weeks before I left for Europe, when I convinced Writing Sales, the Milwaukee-based wholesaler that sells games to Penney's, Sears, and Montgomery Ward, that Class Struggle's extraordinary media coverage justified its promotion into the big time. Given the risky nature of his gamble, Mike Newsome of Writing Sales thought it wise if I joined him when he presented Class Struggle to the Penney's buyer. The meeting which was only a couple of days away, was scheduled for the Sheraton Hotel at the O'Hare Airport in Chicago.

The morning opened with a smooth-as-silver sale of 500 games to Chicago's Marshall Field Department Store. Arriving for my appointment at the hotel, I began to feel that this had all the makings of a historic day—for Class Struggle, Inc., for the gaming industry, for America. The big sell was already underway when someone's junior assistant let me into the living room of the hotel's presidential suite. Holding forth from the wooden, thronelike chair in the center of the room was the Penney's buyer. He had his jacket off and spoke more softly than the half-dozen jacketed men sitting with open order books on their laps on the three over-stuffed sofas that surrounded him. "Start slow," King Penney's was speaking. "50,000 will do for now, and if things pick up, we'll order 100,000 more later."

Noticing my entry, Mike waved me over and introduced me to the assembly. "This is the professor who invented that crazy game I told you about. I've never seen so much press on any game in my whole life. The guy's been on the 'Today' and 'Tomorrow' shows, and ..." I handed a copy of Class Struggle over to the buyer, looking eagerly for some sign of interest on his face. The future of Class Struggle, Inc., could be decided in the next five minutes. I forced myself to stay cool. Play it like a businessman, I told myself.

The buyer turned the game over in his hands to get the feel of it, weighed it, and then, looking carefully at the cover, asked, "Marx, huh?"

"Well, at least it isn't Lenin," I joked, or tried to. Yes, I thought, biting my lip. Just like a big-time businessman.

"Well, I can't see how we can put Marx's picture in Penny stores," the buyer responded, but in a tone that seemed to leave the question open.

"It's a very small picture ... not at all threatening," I shot back. "Look how he's holding hands with Rockefeller, all set for a friendly game of Class Struggle. Media throughout the country have praised it as a good and humorous game. Most Penney customers will already know about Class Struggle and feel favorably disposed toward it."

"That's right, Harry," Mike chimed in. "I think it's worth taking a chance on—in a small way."

"There's even going to be a Warner Brothers movie on the story behind the game. How's that for acceptance?" Noticing that the buyer's eyes picked up at my mention of the movie, I handed him a couple of press stories on the subject. As he began to read, I raced through my head looking for other ways to convince him. I just couldn't let this fish get away. What could I promise him? Should I threaten his life?

"Well ... maybe in a small way." The buyer's words sent a torrent of blood rushing to my head. "I can't see our selling any of these in the 'better dead than red' towns of the South." The remark brought an uncomfortable laugh from the salesmen in the room. "Put some games in a dozen stores in the North, and if they do well," the buyer concluded, "we can get several thousand more for Christmas."

At the time, it sounded like we had scored a touchdown. I could barely restrain myself from giving my college yell. Not yet. Mike said he would send in a smallish order, probably a gross (144), and distribute the games among a dozen typical Penney stores. If they sold quickly, he would order a lot more, and not just for Penney's but for Sears and Montgomery Ward as well. All this happened at the end of August.

When I returned from my European trip at the end of September, I learned that a gross of games had been shipped to Writing Sales two weeks before. Mike had said it would take a couple of weeks from the time they received the games to distribute them to the different stores, and another two to four weeks to know the result of the test. What could we do now besides chew on our collective fingernails awaiting the result? We discussed the matter at a meeting of the board and quickly agreed that we would deal with this important business matter like good businessmen. We would cheat. We would buy the games ourselves to give the impression that Class Struggle was the most popular toy item since the hoola hoop. It wasn't that we didn't have confidence in the game's appeal, but why take unnecessary chances, especially when something so important is at stake.

The problem was to find the Penney stores where the games were selling, and to recruit people nearby to go in and buy them. We approached the problem like an army getting ready for battle. Friends and relatives in 20 major northern cities were contacted and primed to act when we gave the signal. It was important not to strike before the games were in place. We would wait another week, and then ...

The month of September also saw another breakthrough of sorts. Do Something for Jesus (DSJ), a group that distributes board games as part of its effort to raise the moral level of the American people, decided to include Class Struggle among its offerings. "Educational and inspiring" is how the president of DSJ, Tom Abbry, described Class Struggle. The initial order was for a modest 144 games, but great things—we were promised—lay ahead. DSJ had just signed contracts with the Girl Scouts and the Little League to have its games sold door-to-door all over America. When a 12-year-old girl walks into a home in Tuscaloosa, Alabama, with a box of cookies in one hand and a copy of Class Struggle in the other, it is a sure sign that either the apocalypse or the revolution is just around the corner.

Then, a day before the DSJ brochure—half born-again exhortation, half advertisements for games, including Class Struggle—was to go to press, Abbry called up quite agitated from his HQ in Wisconsin to relate that a colleague in

California had just told him that Ollman is the leader of an international communist conspiracy to overthrow the American way of life, and that he may even be the antichrist. "Tell me, Paul," he asked our manager, to whom he had spoken several times on the phone but had never met, "is Ollman the antichrist? Tell me the truth. I can take it."

Paul spent the next half-hour reassuring Abbry about both my humanness and my patriotism: "Ollman has said again and again that socialism is as American as apple pie." Apparently, that and similar aphorisms struck just the right note, because Class Struggle retained its two pages in the DSJ brochure. Visions of millions of Girl Scouts on the march!

On the promotional front, media interest in Class Struggle began to lag just as we were approaching the Christmas season. An ominous sign. Without the TV ads that sold most games, Class Struggle had to reach people's consciousness in other ways. The papers that were attracted by the film had already written about it or asked to be notified when production on the film began, something that was still far in the future. We badly needed to come up with a new wrinkle in the Class Struggle story. Mulling over our problem at a board meeting, Milt noted that the film offer was a hard act to follow. Then with his customary zest—"Hey, how about sponsoring a 'Marxathon'? We can get hundreds, maybe thousands of people to run from Rockefeller Plaza to the New York Marxist School on Nineteenth Street."

"If you want to run, try running for President," Ed suggested, and we all laughed. I stopped laughing sooner than the others, feeling goose pimples of excitement sprouting along my arms.

"Why not?" I said. "Presidential elections have done a lousy job of choosing Presidents. Maybe we can put them to good use helping us sell a socialist game." Class Struggle speaks of elections between our two capitalist parties, the TWEEDLE DEEmocrats and the TWEEDLE DUMlicans, as elections in which the workers can only lose.

"What are you going to offer people?" Milt asked. "Fun and games?"

"No, that's what they're getting now, and the games aren't much fun." My mind was off and running. "Give 'em what they deserve—that's the platform—free heating fuel to the poor, unrecalled Pinto cars to Ford Motor Company executives. The possibilities are endless." The balance of political forces in America being what they are, Left electoral strategy is essentially educational, but how educational can it be when radical candidates are almost completely ignored by the capitalist media? But reporters are always looking for a new angle and something humorous. The prickly barbs tossed off by the candidate from Class Struggle would not be ignored.

Once their surprise had subsided, the reaction of the Class Struggle board was positive, but except for Ed, whose political instincts are most in tune with my own, hardly enthusiastic. Still, I resolved to push ahead, but before declaring my candidacy, I sounded out several friends whose political judgment I trusted. The consensus was that most radicals would not understand my gesture. The ambiguity that surrounded selling games to promote socialism would be compounded, and many would conclude that I was an opportunist, in it for the money and the glory.

"The Left parties will not appreciate this attempt to upstage them," Ira Shor argued. "And what of the comrades who mistake you for a serious candidate?" Mike Brown asked. "They would be left in the lurch."

There was obviously something in these complaints, but I couldn't help feeling that they missed the point. Here was a chance to introduce more socialist content into the public debate, to help delegitimate the election process itself as a fair way to choose our government (it could be fair, but cannot be as long as money talks so loudly) and to sell more Class Struggle games. After all, capitalism is all about selling. Who understands this better than us Marxists? Nothing is holy, nothing is left out. Why not play the capitalist game out to the end? They sell presidential candidates like toothpaste. Let's sell toothpaste, or a game in this case, like a presidential candidate.

Could it be done? Could one run an ad campaign like a presidential election, make friends, win laughs, promote sales, and keep one's political soul? There was something wonderfully out of whack (frighteningly, Paule thought) in all this. Inventing a game to promote socialist ideas had led to going into business, which led to media notoriety, which led to movie and book contracts, which was about to lead to running for President. What next?

Welcome to the shortest election campaign on record. The Class Struggle candidate retrieved his hat from the ring after a talk with his lawyers from Arnold and Porter: "We're trying to portray you to the judge as a serious scholar and an ideal department chairman for the University of Maryland. It's bad enough that you spend so much time these days selling games. But running a humorous campaign for President would be the final straw. If you want to have any chance of winning this case, drop this idea immediately."

There was still the Marxathon. Maybe next spring.

The tension generated by our precarious financial position was beginning to take its toll on the *bonhomie* which, along with Camembert, had been a staple at Class Struggle board meetings. While all the world admired or hated us for the fortune we were supposed to have made, every session now opened with Howard complaining about all the money he had "thrown away" on the game and how broke he was. The crowning blow came when he needed money for his son's schooling and found that the bank would not lend him any more because of the loans he had co-signed for Class Struggle, Inc. None of us were any better off, but Howard had fallen from higher up. Our sympathy for him was genuine, but nerves were frayed. What could we do that we were not doing already?

Howard consistently complained that our expenses were too high, but he could never give concrete examples of where we could save money. He kept asking for detailed figures on everything, and more and more time was spent by our limited work force preparing financial statements for our meetings. Our move into a larger office a few months back provided us with much-needed space, but it also meant a larger rent. Money for trade shows and publicity had already been cut to the bone. There were no frills.

"Why did I do it? I must have been crazy." Sitting in the large easy chair in the corner of my living room, with his head buried in his huge hands, Howard was the picture of despair. What had begun as a comedy might yet end up as tragedy. A Christian might have tried to bring relief by attesting that money isn't everything, but a Marxist knows better. In capitalism, money stands for comfort, power, status, security, and all the advantages these things confer. Losing one's life savings is to die a little.

My heart went out to my old friend completely, but my head struggled to stay in control, to continue planning and pushing forward. It was our only hope to get back on top. I consoled Howard, I tried to reassure him (the movie, the book, foreign rights—the big break had to come somewhere), I provided all the figures he asked for, I worked all the harder on my own. To no avail. Our once-warm exchanges became curt and businesslike, sour businesslike. Paule and I became very worried about Howard's health. How much longer could he continue like this before cracking up—or making us crack up? Apparently, helping corporate managers deal with the tensions of their job—Howard's consulting work—offers little relief when the pinch is on the other foot. "Physician, heal thyself!" was never a practical demand.

Howard opined that no one cared, really cared, about his suffering. Where there had been laughter at our board meetings, there were now only taut lips and a controlled gnashing of teeth. Pushed beyond his emotional limits one evening, Ed reminded Howard that after our initial success it was he who insisted that present investors be given an opportunity to buy all remaining shares. "Like any other businessman," Ed said, "you gambled so much because you wanted to make more. So, if you lose your money ..." There are times when truth should only be given out in small doses. Besides, the last $20,000 of Howard's $90,000 commitment had come in the form of a loan when our company was desperate, so Ed's remark was not completely accurate.

With our ultimate fate now clearly outside our control, there began a search for scapegoats. In his anguish, Howard found an easy target: If Paul could only sell more games and work harder, faster. Our chief problem, according to Howard, was that Paul was not cut out for this kind of work. "How could we have hired a poet to mind the store? He's too slow, too deliberate, too gentle, doesn't have enough hustle. He should get out into the Toy Building, like we did, and make contacts. Everything in this business is a matter of connections, and he is too shy to make them."

Howard had been telling me this for some months, and I had always responded that it wasn't true, that Paul's laid-back, literary style was effective, especially with the bigger buyers. I also reminded my major partner that he was one of those who urged Paul to quit his job and become our full-time manager, a post we guaranteed him for a year, and that was only six months ago. We should also remember, I said, that it was Paul who saved our collective skins by noting the deficiencies in the boards Finn made for the third edition of the game.

Nothing helped, and little by little, Howard began to go public with his criticisms. At each board meeting, he would urge Paul to make more contacts, visits, calls—"Then, call them again," he would say. And Paul would respond that he had made this or that connection, then—increasingly—that such connections were not very fruitful. Witness Howard's friendship with the president of Pathmark Stores, Paul said, which had yet to produce an order (they did later order a gross).

While I strongly defended Paul against Howard's misdirected criticisms, I cannot say that I was altogether satisfied with his work. Paul lived far away from the office and often came to work late. When we had a big order to get out, he would complain about all the heavy work he had to do. Lifting isn't fun, especially when it's 50 cumbersome boxes of games, but it was a part of the job. He waited for me to tell him when to call particular customers much more than I would have liked. And his home phone was always off the hook—sometimes the business *couldn't* wait—which drove me up the wall. One day when I came into the office, Paul showed me some wooden blocks he had just made for his little son. On company time? I thought.

I didn't say this. I didn't say any of this to Paul or to Howard. In the case of Paul, I felt ashamed for having such capitalist thoughts, shocked and deeply ashamed. But this didn't keep them from continuing to gnaw at me, undermining the respect I had for Paul and eventually my own self-respect. Like any other capitalist, I resented my workers for complaining and not working hard enough. This may have been the most bitter pill of all for me to swallow. In the case of Howard, I hesitated to provide fuel for his already raging fires, convinced as I was that the main reason for our financial plight lay outside the Class Struggle office.

Finally, at a board meeting in November, Howard blew up at Paul—accusing him of not really understanding how desperate we were and not keeping a firm enough hand on expenditures. This time, Paul answered in kind, and stormed out of the room. He wouldn't be attending any more board meetings, he said. We had traveled a long way from the high-spirited outings with which we had begun our enterprise a year-and-a-half before. The ties of trust and affection that had bound us together in a common project were being eaten away by the most corrosive of social acids, business failure.

Even today, as I write these lines, I can't think of Howard without considerable pain. Paule has just asked me whether it is pain for the suffering he went through or for that which he caused us. Honestly, I guess I must say that it starts out as one and finishes as the other. Howard remains a dear friend and, as I've told him a hundred times, Class Struggle, Inc., owes him its very existence, but his unremitting despair became such a drag on my own emotions that I began to resent him for his suffering. I take no pride in this admission, but as a matter of simple self-defense I could do nothing else.

With the ship of state in danger of going under, our citizen-workers had to scramble to save themselves. Paul and our three part-time workers, Jo Ann, Paul Gettman, and John Mason formed a union and asked to affiliate with District 65, a progressive, general purpose union in New York City. Their main aim, they said, was to get covered by the generous medical plan that District 65 offers to its members, so generous that it continues to operate even after the worker's original place of employment goes out of business, but Paul's conflict with Howard probably contributed to their dissatisfaction. Even though the worker's made no new demands regarding wages and conditions, the simple fact of joining a union and affiliating with District 65 would cost us several hundred dollars in fees and contributions over the next few months.

It seemed like a very good deal for our workers. Besides, as socialists, we all favored unions. I didn't think anyone on the board would oppose this move. "But don't they see we're broke?" Howard said. "How can we afford it, even this relatively small sum? What happened to all this talk about our being a political group?"

"We are engaged in political activity," I responded, "but we are also a business, and in any business workers have different interests than their bosses. What our workers are telling us with this action is that we have to give a higher priority to their interests even if the business is going down the tubes. No, especially at such a time, because as workers they have so little to fall back on."

"If we don't permit them to form a union," Ed continued, "they'll go on strike. I can just see the picket signs—'Class Struggle: Unfair to Workers.' What a turnabout that would be. On the other hand, if our workers went on strike, it might be the most powerful statement we could make on the incompatibility between the interests of bosses, any bosses, and their workers."

So completely had Howard taken on the capitalist's role

that he saw no humor or danger or wisdom in Ed's remarks. The politics involved in forcing a strike did not seem to frighten him. As a failing business, he said, we had no money to pay into a union fund, and that was that.

"We'll just have to find the money somewhere," I said. "It isn't so much. And we can't afford a strike. Politically, it would be a disaster, and in dollars and cents probably unprofitable." I looked over to Howard. He didn't seem at all convinced. Was it just that I could afford to think of something other than money? All of a sudden, I felt extremely lucky not to have any of my own money tied up in the business. In that instant, I caught a glimpse of the fact that it might have been Howard's largesse even more than my Marxist views that had kept me from completing my descent into capitalist ways and mores. My debt to Howard was even greater than I had realized.

A week later, I visited the headquarters of District 65 and signed a contract with the workers of Class Struggle, Inc. Joe Kavenaugh, the union organizer with whom I dealt, said he had never met an employer who agreed so quickly to everything his workers asked for. He showed his appreciation by making me the first "capitalist" to receive a guided tour of the union building. "Hey Louie, come meet this boss who is on the side of the workers. He has even invented a game about it."

Our long stretch of the blues came to an end when Jay Allen called to say that she had finally found a writer for the movie. Six months had passed since I signed the contract, during which time three writers had turned down Jay's proposal—too unstructured and, according to one English writer, too American. It seems that writing a script from scratch is too much work for a mere $300,000, the sum Jay said she would have to pay for a good scriptwriter.

The wheel of fortune had finally come to a stop at Roger Simon—no, not the same fellow who did one of the first stories about the game for the *Chicago Sun-Times*. Roger Simon II wrote *The Big Fix*, both book and film, about an ex-radical detective who tries to make a life for himself after the demonstrations of the '60s have subsided. Starring Richard Dreyfuss (coincidentally enough, practically everybody's first choice to play me in *The Class Struggle Story*), the film avoided the worst caricatures of the genre and was moderately successful at the box office. Roger and his wife had just returned from a visit to Cuba—a good credential in my book—and Jay wanted me to meet them.

A couple of nights later, Paule and I found ourselves at One Fifth Avenue, a Village restaurant famous for its millionaire punk, as guests of Roger and Dyanne Simon. "Don't look at the prices. Eat, enjoy—it's all on Warner Brothers." Roger was a very boyish 40, short, with balding blond hair, a nervous staccato laugh, and an endless series of long Havana cigars, the most precious acquisitions of his recent trip. Dyanne, who is also a scriptwriter, was quiet and painfully sincere.

They informed me immediately that they had bought Class Struggle over a year ago and had enjoyed playing it with their two kids. Some of my story they had already read in the press and some they heard from Jay. What seemed to interest them more than anything else was what I felt about the movie. How did I see it? Before I could even mention it, Roger addressed my fear of having my socialist ideas caricatured. "Jay and I agree that any film that caricatured you or your ideas would be a bad film. That's not what makes the story worth doing."

Roger was a good audience for my game anecdotes and lost few opportunities to let me know how much he agreed with what I was trying to do. He particularly liked the story of my visit to the New York Chamber of Commerce that had taken place a couple of months before (recounted in the Introduction to this book), which reminded me that I had a lunch date at the Chamber for the following Monday. Progressive? Yes, and he even regularly read *In These Times*, one of my favorite socialist publications.

"What are your fantasies?" Dyanne wanted to know. I must have looked puzzled, because Roger went on: "You know, writers are always digging around for an angle, an inspiration. The film won't be completely true to life. We'll probably have to fictionalize your personal life, for example, to jazz things up. That's the price we all have to pay to move out of the small radical boutiques into the supermarket."

"What other kinds of changes do you foresee having to make?" I asked, feeling slightly queasy. The food was also too rich.

"Hard to say," Roger answered. "But I guess dramatic reasons might require that you really make it big at one point in the story, even if you haven't."

I left Roger that evening with generally positive feelings—overall, he seemed to be on our side in the class struggle—but I couldn't help wondering what other changes might be required for the sake of drama. Paule felt less comfortable with the Simons, less sure of their intentions, more suspicious of dramatic requirements, but she hesitated to throw more than a dash of cold water on my heightened spirits.

On Monday, I found myself again at the New York Chamber of Commerce, this time as the luncheon guest of Mortimer Gettman, the legislative vice-president of the Chamber. He had also invited my two business friends from the collection agency, who had approved of my speech at the annual meeting, so that we could tell him our complaints. Recently, the three of us had ruffled a lot of expensive feathers by requesting a copy of the membership list in order to call a meeting of small business-people to discuss ways of making the chamber more democratic. Though small businesses make up over 80 percent of the members, leadership is almost completely in the hands of big business.

"Surely there is a less confrontational way of settling our differences," Gettman said in a tone that was every bit as syrupy as our over-sweetened desert. "What do you fellows *really* want?"

Next to my reply that it was time for the Chamber to investigate the human costs on businesspeople of doing business, their demand to be put onto standing committees seemed easy to satisfy. "How else am I going to become president of this outfit," Bill, the angrier of my two colleagues, said, only half jokingly, "if you guys don't let me start at the bottom?"

"Consider it done," replied Gettman, complimenting Bill on "the reasonableness" of his request. A few more gentle strokes to Bill's ego, and our radical caucus had split in two. Like most small businesspeople, Bill really didn't want to believe that the wheel is fixed. Just give him a chance to place his bet, and he would show us. Another case of someone who played too much Monopoly as a kid. The Chamber of Commerce was safe from a socialist takeover, at least for the time being.

EIGHTEEN:
CLASS STRUGGLE BECOMES A WAR GAME .

The test with the Penney stores came to naught. With all our military planning, we never did find out where Writing Sales placed the games. Early in November, we were simply notified that the results did not warrant a larger order this Christmas. Lord and Taylor, which had ordered 500 games for their 30 stores, had the order canceled at the last minute by their merchandise manager. No explanation. Toys-R-Us, which had been promising us an order for over six months, never came through. Nor did Saks Fifth Avenue, nor did Filene's (Boston's largest department store), which kept insisting their order was in the mail, nor did ... nor did ...

How different our second Christmas season was from our first can be seen in the fate of the Class Struggle Santa Claus. It was Milton who had the idea of sending a Santa Claus with a bag full of Class Struggles to the Christmas-tree-lighting ceremony that takes place every Thanksgiving at Rockefeller Center. With radio mikes and TV cameras coming out of the cracks in the sidewalk, we were sure that a Santa handing out Class Struggle games and hollering appropriate slogans would steal the show. We rented a Santa costume, hired and primed an actor, and sent him on his way. The first Christmas, he got to Rockefeller Center a few minutes before the ceremony was to begin, but the huge crowd kept him from getting within a block of the event. We promised ourselves that next year we would do better.

Milton refused to let the Santa costume go to waste and wore it to another Christmas-tree lighting in Washington Square Park, across from NYU. The following day, NYU's student newspaper ran a front-page picture of Santa holding Class Struggle standing next to a noticeably ill-at-ease John Sawhill, president of NYU. Except the caption on the photo said that Santa had a remarkable resemblance to NYU

Professor Bertell Ollman.

The next Thanksgiving, we sent the same actor dressed as Santa to Rockefeller Center, and made sure that he got there an hour early. There would be no slip-ups this time. What we hadn't counted on was that a Santa with a bag full of games hanging around a still-empty Rockefeller Center looks kind of suspicious. Anyway, that's what the cops must have thought when they arrested our Santa for loitering, only to let him go on the promise that he would leave and not come back. Milton's reaction to the news? "Well, we'll just have to figure out a new way to attack the tree next year."

One of the modest pluses of our second Christmas season was that we finally landed a Canadian distributor. Beadie and Church, a small but efficient book distributor, ordered 3,000 games on the condition that I come to Toronto to do some promotional work. I arrived in Toronto on November 20 and spent four hectic days giving 16 different interviews. What Canadian newsperson could resist an invasion of Class Struggle launched from the bastion of capitalism?

A couple of socialist friends from Toronto advised me not to give an interview to the *Toronto Sun*. It is their city's equivalent of the *New York Post*, which is to say, read by most of the city's workers and reactionary as hell. In the words of one friend, "The paper never mentions 'socialism' without putting the word 'gulag' into the same sentence." The *Sun* would only use the occasion to mock socialism, they assured me. But I had been getting positive stories from such a wide range of papers that I thought I would take a chance. The reporter for the *Sun* was no less friendly than the other reporters I met, but I knew that this was no sure sign of what to expect. I recalled the friendly reporter for a Cincinnati paper who built his whole story around one buyer's refusal to stock the game and my off-the-cuff remark that "Marx never expected the revolution to break out in a department store."

It was with a slightly nervous stomach, then, that I picked up the next day's edition of the *Sun*. There, spread across an entire page, was a picture of the game and me, and a story that ran under the headline, "Socialism Is Fun." The entire story spoke of socialism and its connections with fun, freedom, and democracy. The word "gulag" did not appear anywhere. My Canadian friends were amazed that the reactionary owners of the *Sun* would allow such a positive view of socialism to go out to their million working-class readers.

At the beginning, I viewed media stories as a simple means to an end, which was to sell more socialist games, which in turn publicized socialist ideas. Could it be that the truth was just the opposite, that it was the game that served as the occasion for numerous media stories (now over 300) on the real class struggle, spreading socialist ideas to a much wider audience than could ever be reached by the game?

A few days after returning to New York from Toronto, I got a call from Thad McIlroy of Beadie and Church saying that the game had taken off in stores all over the country, but that Eaton's chain of department stores, Canada's largest, had refused to reorder because of a customer's complaint that the game was "subversive." This was not the first time that a store had tucked its tail between its legs and run for cover on hearing that terrible word. Should we hush it up as we did in the case of the Hunter College Bookstore (where the manager returned an order because a professor complained about the "Commie game") or Abraham and Strauss Department Store, also in New York (where a new buyer refused to reorder our fast-selling game when he discovered it promoted revolution)? If we once feared the effect of such news on our more timid customers, we decided the time had come to meet this censorship head on, and Toronto might be the place to start.

Meanwhile, Kristen Monroe, an NYU colleague who had a charge account at Eaton's from her days teaching in Canada, had written a letter to the store complaining about their action. Just days later, a response came from Mr. Fred Eaton, the president himself, who said that, from what he knew of the inventor, Class Struggle was designed "to subtly indicate that capitalists are vicious, fire-branding dragons," something he could not accept. No, he had not actually seen the game, but that wasn't important. Need he remind Professor Monroe that "the free world is shrinking day by day?" He was clear as to what he had to do. So, now, were we.

Copies of the letter were sent to media throughout Canada, triggering another dozen stories on Class Struggle, led by an editorial in Toronto's *Globe and Mail*, their *New York Times*, which asked, "How is Canada ever going to arrive at the necessary revolutionary action to bring the working class to power and create a truly classless society, if the T. Eaton Company refuses to pull its weight?"

Eaton's never rescinded their decision. However, the publicity they helped us generate for the game—"the subversive game, too hot for Eaton's"—made Class Struggle the hottest-selling new game in Canada that Christmas (according to *MacLeans Magazine*). When their Conservative government fell a few weeks later, Class Struggle, Inc., was quick to take credit for it. The word went out throughout Canada that this was but a small example of what subversive games can do. More, we promised, lay ahead.

Despite our success in Canada and increased sales in England and Scandinavia, our failure to break into the big chains in the U.S. made it clear to all of us that, as far as Class Struggle, Inc., was concerned, the game was up. Expenses, as Howard pointed out ever more insistently, were killing us. The promise of a film held out some hope for the future if we went into a kind of cold-storage arrangement, dispensing with our office and employees, and simply shipping the games we had left to stores that ordered without any prompting.

Still better, of course, would be selling the game to another company, but who would buy it? A couple of months before we had sent out a form letter to 60 game companies asking if they were interested in acquiring "the most publicized game since Monopoly." There were no replies.

Then, on December 10, I got a call from Eric Dott, the president of the Avalon Hill Game Company of Baltimore,

Maryland, announcing that he was interested in buying the U.S. license for Class Struggle. A bite, a big one! "And why didn't you return my call?" he asked, somewhat peeved. It seemed that he had telephoned the office a couple of weeks before and left a message on the recorder, but Paul never picked it up. Thank God Dott persisted. Avalon Hill specialized in war games—Battle of the Bulge, Stalingrad—and now, for purely business reasons, they wished to add to their list the biggest war of all, the war between workers and bosses.

Eric Dott invited me to come down to his office in Baltimore on Christmas Day to negotiate a deal. The idea of finally signing off on Class Struggle left me feeling numb and a little afraid to breathe, lest I discover it was only a dream. I wanted out so badly, but how does one get out of quicksand? My experience had been that the more I tried to extricate myself, the deeper I plunged. Anxiety over lack of money and missed sales had come to dominate my waking life. The weekend before Christmas, I went into Barnes and Noble and learned that the 500 games we had sent them a month before had not arrived at the store: "Still in the warehouse." I had gone there to buy a book, but all of a sudden I could hardly focus. "Yes, lots of people have been asking for Class Struggle," the manager said. "Too bad it's not here." Weak knees, weak bladder, dizzy, I could no longer control my feelings, the feelings of a failing businessman. My perspective had expired. Gregor had triumphed.

The offer by Avalon Hill actually intensified my anxiety. The little ray of hope that it offered threw a light on a spreading sickness that I had begun to hide even from myself in fear for my own sanity. This had to work. If Dott's offer gave us any chance of getting out of the hole, we would grab it. Everyone agreed.

Howard and Izzy accompanied me to Baltimore. Howard's stepfather was dying at that very moment in Miami, and Izzy's wife was one day late in giving birth to their first child. Yet I didn't think twice about asking either of them to come along. I needed their advice on financial and legal matters and their help in making a decision. Given his wife's condition, Paule said, if she were in Izzy's shoes she wouldn't go. I'm glad Izzy was in his own shoes that day and that he understood that duty to business came first. "Business is business" translated into American means "everything human comes second." The people at Avalon Hill obviously held the same credo, since they, too, gave up a holiday to meet with us.

On the trip down to Baltimore, we decided that our top priority had to be to sell Avalon Hill our stock of approximately 30,000 finished and partly finished games at the $3.20 price Finn had quoted us for each unit. With that we could pay our bank debts, which—if we included the $20,000 Howard borrowed on our behalf—came to over $50,000, and the $15,000 we owed to Nat Levine. Given our weak position, everything else was up for grabs. Necessity, as Izzy reminded us, is the mother of desperation. There was no money due on either the movie or foreign rights in the next few months. Before us stretched another spring and possibly summer of borrowing from Peter to pay Paul, and it was unclear that Peter would have any more to lend us.

Eric Dott and Tom Shaw, his managing director, met us in their huge, single-story factory, which houses all the components that go into Avalon Hill's 100-plus games. Eric was typical of the self-made, joking, Jewish executive we had encountered so often in the toy industry. His chief weaponry consisted of bluster, anecdotes, and gifts—mine was a pair of tennis shoes donated by another client. Tom was the shorter, more serious Gentile (or "redneck," as Eric good-naturedly called him). He saved most of his words for the bargaining session. While Eric waved his cigar in an "I don't give a good goddam one way or another" pose, Tom made sure that Avalon Hill's interests came out on top. We had seen the Mutt and Jeff routine (one tough, one yielding) before, but never done so well.

It took only two or three puffs of Eric's cigar to discover that Avalon Hill was as interested in obtaining our successful game as we were in dumping it on them. And why not? For them, it was so much gravy off the top. With a business infrastructure already in place, adding another game to their list did not cost them anything in operating expenses. Class Struggle was widely known and already selling in hundreds of stores. All that might have held them back was the politics of the game, but Eric assured us he wasn't frightened by the politics. He found the game very funny. If there were people who wouldn't buy it because they didn't like its politics, that was their loss. He was in business to make money, and he was convinced that this game would make him a bundle. (Much later, I learned that all of Eric's associates had argued against acquiring Class Struggle, going so far as to say that this would get Avalon Hill into trouble with the government.)

On the main point of buying up all our games at cost there was quick agreement, though they insisted on paying for them when the games were sold and not before. An exception was made for the first 5,000, which Avalon Hill agreed to pay for on delivery, which would give us $16,000 to pay our most pressing bills. After all the games we had on hand were sold, Avalon Hill undertook to produce a new edition of Class Struggle, leaving us with final control over its content. We accepted a royalty arrangement of 2.5 percent on the retail price of each game, which would increase to a hefty (for the game industry) 5 percent on the appearance of the Class Struggle movie. Money made on the future sale of foreign rights would be divided on a 50-50 basis. In an hour-and-a-half, it was all over, and sealed with a couple of knowing nods and handshakes all around. Eric and Tom said they would come to New York in 10 days to sign a contract and to work out the details of the transition.

Driving back to New York, I was still unsure about what we had done, and whether we had really done it. Was it a birth I had just witnessed, or another stage in our labor pains? No money had changed hands. Nothing was in writing. Yet the deal was in the bag, no? It was too soon to celebrate—I didn't want to jinx anything. With the sale of the game, I had also bought a new personal freedom. A creeping lightheartedness began to remind me what that was like. Eric's penchant for giving gifts reminded Izzy of a story about his uncle Abe who gave away everything that wasn't nailed to the floor. Howard and I laughed raucously. Pausing for an instant to exchange guilty glances, we continued laughing until it hurt.

The day before the Avalon Hill people were due to arrive in New York to finalize the deal, I got a call from Baltimore. It was Eric Dott. "Is it true what some people have been telling me, Professor Ollman" (all of a sudden he had become very formal), "that you preach the violent overthrow of the government in your class?" I swallowed hard—not because I hadn't heard this before but because this time it sounded like the swish of a guillotine. It seemed that my hopes were about to fall along with my head into the wastebasket.

With all the casualness I could muster, I tried to reassure Eric that I believed in the democratic process so much that I want to see it applied to all walks of our society, including the economy, something that will only happen when the majority of people want it. What's so violent about that? Eric didn't answer. Sweetly, calmly, I continued to pour democratic balm over Eric's worries, insistently, like there was no tomorrow, thinking—if I didn't succeed—there may not be. "Okay. Sounds like you were slandered again," Eric finally said, and he rang off, adding that he would see me at 10 A.M. the next morning. I couldn't help but think that if this was how he reacted to criticisms of me now, what would he do when the hate mail started pouring in? I spent the night worrying afresh whether a capitalist company could ever produce a socialist game.

The next day, Eric arrived in New York with Tom Shaw and Steve Nelson, a cigar-chomping Gypsy who serves as Avalon Hill's production manager. They all seemed very amused by the rickety elevator and other primitive work conditions in our windowless office/warehouse. "Our workers don't belong to a union, but they wouldn't work in these conditions," Eric kidded me, pleased at the chance to dig a capitalist poker in my ribs. I smiled. All I could think about was that they had actually come. Where was Izzy with the contract? At 10:30, Izzy, who had been kept up all night by his newborn infant, finally

arrived. Didn't Izzy's kid know the importance of this moment?
Didn't Izzy? Eric skimmed the contract, and signed it once,
twice, thrice. I signed. Bells, deep, drowning church bells, like
those signaling the liberation of occupied Paris, rang out from
the depths of my bourgeoisified soul. Did the others hear them?
People would soon be dancing in the streets, and I with them.
But not yet.

We still had to travel out to the Long Island Packaging
plant to decide how best to assemble over 20,000 unfinished
games and to arrange to ship the finished ones to Baltimore. On
the ride out to Long Island, the talk turned to Maryland. My
life as a professor had come to be dominated by my case against
the University of Maryland, which was slowly wending its way
around innumberable legal complications toward my day in
court. And now, my life as a Marxist businessman was going to
depend on the operations of a Baltimore, Maryland, company.
Coincidence or plot?

Eric also asked me how I, as a Marxist, felt being bought
out by a nonunionized firm—Long Island, which was then producing the game, is unionized. "Like a drowning person," I
answered, "who is thankful to whoever throws him a line. Why
do people expect Marxists to sacrifice their own interests for
those of others? It is Christians who are supposed to act like
this, though they seldom do. Marxism is something else. As a
Marxist, I understand that workers have an interest in forming
unions and, beyond that, in taking decision-making power into
their own hands and making things to serve people rather than
amass profits. If enough workers come to see this, given their
absolute numbers, they can win a new life for all of us. The
actions of a few well-meaning capitalists can do nothing to further this process.

"No, I'm not happy to sell Class Struggle to a firm that
employs nonunionized workers—or specializes in war games,
for that matter—just as I'm sure other capitalists are unhappy
to burn sulfurous fuels, contaminate streams, cheat on weights,
and defraud consumers. We do these terrible things to stay
alive and to succeed, where succeeding is the only way to stay

alive. From our point of view, that is caught up in the owning function, these appear as rational and even necessary ways of acting. People who object to what capitalists do should spend less time attacking us as individuals and more time trying to help us as a group by replacing the system of rewards and punishments that determine our antisocial behavior."

Turning to Eric's workers, Tom and Steve, I asked, "Is there a capitalist you know and like? Do him a real favor—get rid of capitalism." Tom and Steve found this very funny, while Eric, who of the three had the best sense of humor, didn't seem to laugh quite so hard.

A couple of days later, a truck came and picked up 5,000 games. Then three weeks passed and still no check from Avalon Hill. *The New York Times*, with its uncanny ability to feed my worst anxieties, ran a story on a big corporate merger that had fallen through at the last moment, just before the money changed hands. Meanwhile, Long Island was shrilly demanding what we owed them for completing the games. Our once-friendly landlord declared that breaking the lease would cost us six months extra rent (I recalled the bent smile on the autographed picture of Spiro Agnew that hung behind his desk—again Maryland). The bank sent us a curt reminder that we had fallen two months behind on our loan payments. Drews Department Store in Milwaukee chose this moment to return 60 partly damaged games.

In the midst of so much bad news, it was no surprise to learn that the Lanzer Company, which had agreed to do a small printing job for us, wanted the entire payment up front. Not only was our credit nil, but—according to Parker Ullger, the president of Lanzer—I had a reputation as a "ball-buster." "Me? A what?" And while his tone suggested that as a fellow businessman he admired someone who could be so tough, he also knew he had to be very careful in dealing with me. So that's what happens, I thought with some sadness, to nice Marxist professors who go into business.

Straining mightily at the bit, I finally called Avalon Hill— "Well?"—and was told "the check is in the mail." Happy, yet dreaded words. Another week passed, during which each new caller added a complaint, a problem, a demand that was supposed to take precedence over everything else and usually cost a lot of money we didn't have. Juggle, juggle. Everything seemed to be in the air at once. "Soon," I kept saying, "just as soon as we get the check." No human being should have to suffer through the speed-up of worries that strikes every small businessperson in time of crisis. Walking through a minefield or listening to buzz bombs while huddling in a London cellar must have been something like this. Except there the tension ended a lot sooner, one way or another.

Then, on February 27, having drunk the small businessman's poison to the dregs, drained of most human sentiments, fidgety, and emotionally frazzled, I opened the mail and found a check from Avalon Hill for $16,000.

PHOENIX

Not every cancer kills. Floods recede. Volcanoes cool. Maybe one day I, too, will recover from the ravages of business. In the meantime, I pass my days trying to put Gregor to bed while he continues to haunt my restless nights.

The Phoenix is a large, bespeckled bird with bright red plumage that lives in the deserts of Arabia. Every 500 to 600 years, it douses its feathers with holy oil and sets itself on fire, only to emerge newborn from its ashes. Since May 1978, I have wandered for what seems like 500 years in the deserts of business, and if my plumage is pale white, my politics are bright red. Muhammad Ali won back his boxing crown twice, Jesus returned from the dead, Solzhenitsyn from Siberia. Can I be reborn from the ashes of Gregor?

But how does one rebuild the teeth that have been ground down by anxiety over going broke, or recast a sensibility that has come to appreciate advertising jingles, or reestablish friendships that were used to bolster a sales organization, or remove the slight odor of shysterism that hovers over my scholarly reputation? The game is not over yet.

NINETEEN:
FROM THE RUSSIAN TEA ROOM TO THE FRANKFURT BOOK FAIR: CLASS STRUGGLE LURCHES FORWARD

The pressure eased off immediately, but "calm" remained a forbidden four-letter word. The Avalon Hill check kept the wolf from the door, but he set up camp where we could still see him, and threatened to return. There simply weren't enough funds to go around. Long Island wouldn't release more games unless they were paid and the banks were about to foreclose on our loan, so these two got top priority. Everyone else got an extra dose of promises.

Meanwhile, Roger Simon II arrived from Hollywood to begin research for his script on the Class Struggle story. The Toy Fair was on, and Roger asked me to join him in exploring this foreign terrain. He came dressed for the occasion with a 40-pound movie camera on one shoulder ("something with which to take a few notes"), and a big Warner Brothers badge on the opposite lapel. In the toy industry, magic and media go together like lox and bagels. Our entrance was pure Hollywood, with heads turning faster than the revolving door through which we entered the building. Roger couldn't have attracted more respectful stares if he'd had a giant boa constrictor draped around his neck.

First stop was the Avalon Hill showroom, where Tom Shaw was busy explaining Class struggle to a couple of store buyers: "It's a new game that ridicules the Establishment, any Establishment." So that's how a capitalist company sells a socialist game, I thought. Roger was a big hit with Tom and the half-dozen Avalon Hill salesmen gathered in the room, who finally had it confirmed for them that Class Struggle was not like any of their other games. Roger took some pictures of Class Struggle sandwiched on the wall between Panzer Attack and Waterloo, and asked people how they felt about selling such a controversial item. Nods, smiles, "as long as it sells"—all predictable answers, until an older sales representative from the

211

Southwest replied, "Hell, I'll sell it, but I wouldn't buy it for my kids."

Parker Brothers' huge suite of rooms was filled with store buyers getting the 24-karat guided tour through Parkers' newest games. Roger and I walked into the front room just in time to hear the tour guide boast that Parkers had budgeted $1.2 million of TV advertising for Schlocko and Rip-Off, the two games on the center table. A large TV screen on the wall proceeded to give us a taste of what the American public had in store for it next Christmas season. How many store buyers had asked me if Class Struggle was going to advertise on TV? "It's on the 7 o'clock news all the time," I used to say, but somehow this never satisfied them.

Roger started taking pictures of the games, the people, the sales pitch. Everyone was a little taken aback when his camera began to roll. Why so nervous? Wasn't this all one big show? We drifted into the next room and he continued to take pictures. There, too, a tour guide was telling a group of buyers about TV advertising. No one was talking about contents, playability, fun, but why should they? Parker's and the store buyers all knew why people buy games. It's the sparkle, it's the repetition of the name, it's the *image* of people having fun with it, everything you throw onto a 30-second commercial and repeat again and again—if you have $1.2 million to spend.

A hand tapped me on the shoulder and I turned around to see a burly-looking executive fronting an older, emaciated boss-man who seemed to be giving the orders. "Who gave you fellows permission to take pictures here?"

"Oh, it's all right," Roger answered. "We're from Warner Brothers." The mention of Warner Brothers created a visible stir all around, which is, of course, just what Roger intended. The expression on the older man's face, however, was meant to convey that he would not be taken in so easily. What? Who? Why? And, of course, credentials.

Before Roger had a chance to answer any of these questions, the burly type made a grab for his camera. "We would like to have your film—until this is settled."

"Hey, what's going on here? What's all the fuss?" I addressed myself first to the manager and then to the little crowd that was beginning to gather.

"Game thieves," someone on the edge of the crowd whispered.

Despite the growing tension, I couldn't refrain from laughing. "Roger," I said, "they're afraid you're taking pictures of their new games so we can run off and produce them in Formosa." Struggling to keep this crazy New York mugger from taking his camera, Roger finally managed to extract a letter of introduction from his wallet. My NYU identification card, replete with photo, established my own bona fide. And, of course, they had all heard of Class Struggle.

With the tide turning in our favor, Roger took his most authoritative tone to announce: "Warners is making a movie about the Class Struggle game, and I'm here to pick up some local color. You didn't do yourselves any favor in treating us like thieves."

Suitably humbled, and afraid he might have caused his company some bad publicity, the showroom manager apologized profusely, " ... but in the game business, one can't be too careful. There are dangers everywhere."

"So we've noticed," Roger retorted, and with his head thrown back so far that he looked like the tallest man in the room, he made the most beautiful stage exit I have ever seen, with me trailing three or four steps behind.

Before leaving the Toy Building, Roger and I met briefly with Harvey Stern, editor of *Toy Industry News*, the main publication for both producers and store buyers of games. Roger said he had some basic questions to ask about the toy industry, and Tom Shaw steered him to Stern as the resident expert. For Stern, Warners coming to the Toy Fair was "news," and he intended to do a big story on it. For Avalon Hill, it would be the first important benefit from their association with Class Struggle. Roger didn't have time for a full interview now, so he made an appointment to see Stern in a couple of days.

The next morning, Roger met me in my office at NYU and,

camera on shoulder, followed me through a typical day in my life as college professor. "No, Ellyn, I can't promise that you will have a part in the movie." Extricating myself from the teasing of departmental secretaries had become a daily ritual. In class, I introduced Roger to my students and asked them if they had any objections to Roger shooting some footage. The students knew about the movie, so I didn't have to begin from scratch, but I felt self-conscious and a little silly asking them all the same. No one objected and, with a minimum of hamming and a maximum of hemming and hawing, we ran through the script of a regular seminar as though it were really happening.

During our week together, I asked Roger as many questions about his work and about Hollywood as he asked me about Class Struggle. All of the answers I gave him are found in one form or another in this book. A lot of his talk about Hollywood centered on Jay Allen, our producer, who intrigued Roger as much as she did me. Roger kept assuring me about Jay's connections: "She has all the big fish out there on a string. All she has to do is pull." He seemed very pleased to have become another fish on her string.

On Jay's talent, I needed no convincing. Movies like *Cabaret* and *The Prime of Miss Jean Brodie*, which Jay wrote, are among the finest films I've seen. I also very much enjoyed her latest film, *Just Tell Me What You Want*, which she both wrote and produced, though the message of this film—which I saw only a few months after signing over to her my life story—left my knees feeling a little wobbly. In this film, everyone has his price. Especially in the culture industry, no one can withstand the lure of money and commercial success. The heroes are those who are honest about their greed. The others, for all their moral bleating, are fools and hypocrites, who succumb to the same gods in the end. It is not only the harshest condemnation I have ever seen of life in Hollywood (whether meant as a condemnation or not), but also one of the bleakest visions of human nature that I know.

What view could the woman who wrote this movie have of

the motives of a Marxist professor who went into business to sell a socialist game? How would this extreme skepticism, her belief that Mammon conquers all, affect my movie? When I shared these worries with Roger, he was quick to reassure me that the views expressed in *Just Tell Me What You Want* were not Jay's real views, but he could not give me any good reasons for believing this. In any case, Roger said, he was writing the movie, and he knew this was not what the Class Struggle story is all about.

Roger also met individually with Paul and all the members of the board except Ed, who was out of the country, and then took us all out to an expensive French restaurant in Soho to observe our interaction (not quite the same as over cheese and coffee in my living room, but it would have to do). "This is our first dividend as investors," Izzy pointed out.

"And probably our last," Howard intoned, worried that Roger might take him for a foolish optimist.

"A toast," Milt proposed, "to Jay Allen and Warner Brothers, to you, too, Roger, for saving our little combine from going under water for a third and final time."

While lifting my glass, I couldn't help but reflect on all the small businesses that don't have Warner Brothers to pull their chestnuts out of the fire. "Other small businesses," I suggested, "need help as much as we do. Can't we do something to get them all movie contracts?"

The idea appealed to Milton's talent for titles: "I can see it now—*Rendezvous at Barbatto's Barber Shop*, starring Charles Bronson as the Yankee Clipper, or *Gruesome Goings On at Goldberg's Delicatessen* with ..."

"I get the general idea," Roger interjected. "After Warners cleans up on the Class Struggle story, a whole new genre of movies about other small businesses will get started."

"It's the wave of the future for Hollywood, and probably the last hope," I added, "for America's small businesses."

Most of our talk was directed to giving Roger a heroic/mock-heroic picture of our entire adventure; in short, in telling him the full truth and nothing but the truth. As we saw it, we had set out to feed a tiger its own tail, to push the contradictions of capitalism as far as they would go by using the market to sell a product that attacks the market. So much we knew at the start, so much we planned. But we were sitting on the back of the tiger, and we didn't sufficiently appreciate the degree to which we ourselves were in danger. Who (or what) eats what (or whom) first? That's the story. Everything else is filler. Roger seemed to agree.

We had all been trying for months to imagine what Roger's version of our story would look like. Castro had his speech, "History Will Absolve Us." We had Roger. Despite the constraints of Hollywood, we gradually began to believe that this sincere and talented writer would effectively translate our Marxmo-Busimo adventure saga into the filmic vernacular of the American people. Not too socialist, mind you, but fair, funny, and politically pointed enough to continue the consciousness-raising work we had begun in the game. Only Paule remained skeptical.

What was our biggest hope for the movie? Roger asked. Our biggest worry? That was easy. Our biggest hope was that soon we would be able to stop worrying, and our biggest worry was that this was just a hope. José Iturbi, I confessed, is another one of my worries. Iturbi was once one of the world's leading pianists, specializing in Mozart. He migrated to Hollywood, where he wrote the musical score for *Anchors Aweigh* and played the piano in a number of mediocre musicals, with the result that he completely lost his serious reputation and following. "Is there a lesson for me in that story?" I asked, only half in jest.

Izzy's quick response was hardly reassuring: "Nothing to worry. We're only selling your soul to Hollywood. The body we're keeping here."

I recalled that two weeks earlier I had badly flubbed a radio interview on Marx's theory of class consciousness, couldn't remember, just couldn't organize things right. Too much small talk/game talk/money talk. The fine-tuning of two decades had been shot to hell. It was not just my waist that was sagging. My jump shot was off, my back hurt when I bent, and whenever I read anything these days I looked for the dice. This would make a good player piece, that a good Chance Card. Aarrrgh!

If we sold my soul to Hollywood, it was only because it had already been separated from my body by two excruciating years in business. Hollywood only confirmed what the market rendered infirm. José Iturbi? That's when news of the disaster reaches the shore, fate ratified by reputation. I shuddered and solemnly vowed into my chocolate mousse to return to my book on dialectics before the body left behind in New York grew cold.

Roger also shared with us one of his main problems in writing the script. How do you make a Marxist professor who invents a game to help spread socialist ideas attractive to a typical American audience? The people who see the film have to like this guy at the start, they have to care what happens to him, they have to root for him. This is especially true of a comedy. But if the character is pushing ideas that the audience abhors, how can they side with him? It was a problem with no easy solutions.

Milt thought it might win some sympathy if Roger made the hero crippled or blind. Izzy suggested that the movie begin with a lot of small, everyday tasks, like brushing one's teeth and putting the kid to bed, which would show that Marxist professors are as human as everyone else. Paule argued for using film clips from newsreels of actual social struggles in order to provide a historical setting for the story; it would also help people to understand better what Marxism is all about. Roger listened patiently to all our suggestions. For the moment, he said, he was inclined to have the hero fired unfairly from his job—Maryland—on the assumption that most Americans believe even Marxists should be treated fairly. Unfortunately, this is not an assumption we all felt comfortable in making.

After the Toy Fair, I called Tom Shaw to ask how Class Struggle had done. He was extremely pleased. From the figures he had seen so far, Class Struggle led all Avalon Hill's 106 games at the Fair—maybe as many as 3,000 sold. Tom then asked me why Roger Simon didn't turn up for his appointment with Harvey Stern. And if he couldn't make it, why didn't he call? Stern, he reported, was as mad as hell, and had decided not to do the story on the game. The news shocked me, not only because of the missed publicity coup, but for what it said about Roger. I immediately called him in California, and discovered that he had forgotten, but also that he simply didn't think it very important. He could get the information he needed elsewhere. "What's the fuss?" he asked. "It happens all the time."

About two months later, Roger came to New York again, this time to consult with Jay. How would I like to have lunch with Jay and him? "Mark Rosenberg, vice-president of production at Warners, will also be there. This is the guy," Roger said, "who has his hand on the money spout. He and Jay want to talk to you about Class Struggle." I had already heard a lot about Rosenberg. He is one of the "Hollywood Left" written up in the book *Creative Differences*. Ten years ago, he was a student active in the SDS. Then, after a short apprenticeship as a writer's agent, he moved into Warner Brothers and on up the greasy pole almost as high as one can climb.

Jay sent a limousine to pick me up at my office and take me to the Russian Tea Room on Fifty-seventh Street, where we were to have lunch. Sitting in the back of this converted hearse, I couldn't help but wish that Jay had paid me more for the story and spent less on these unnecessary frills. I recalled my ride long ago in McCarthy's hearse. What was the symbolism here? Was this one taking me to a still bigger city ... or returning me to the cemetery?

The Russian Tea Room is frequented by the kind of Slavs who knew the Czar but, unlike him, got away clean with their booty. What better watering hole for Hollywood's beautiful people, a Fantasy Island home away from home. My hosts were already waiting for me when I arrived. Everyone in the place was overdressed in bright silks and pale velvets, everyone except Mark and me—even Roger wore a mohair jacket. Full bearded, slightly unkempt, wearing a rough woolen sweater and jeans, Mark looked just like the people I had left in Greenwich Village half an hour ago.

Through his sizable bulk and rough appearance, Mark dominated our large table, a table which itself seemed to dominate the entrance to the restaurant. Everyone who came in had to pass by, and many of them said "hello" or nodded to Jay or Mark, as if asking permission to enter. The pecking order could not have stood out more clearly if this had been a feudal manor. We were sitting at High Table, and Mark, with his back against the mirrored wall, occupied the throne. If I had any doubts about this last, Jay's schoolgirlish attempt to make Mark believe that everything he said was so terribly clever put them to rest.

What do the most creative people in Hollywood talk about at a business lunch? The early talk focused on food, the borscht and the blinis on the menu, other famous dishes near and far, all the way to Moscow where Jay found the Russian food very inferior: "Communists can't cook." Mark, who is on the chunky side, said he wanted to lose 60 pounds, but only for the pleasure of putting them back on. "Death is the ultimate diet," Jay volunteered, but she couldn't recommend it. About death, Mark admitted, he is quite irrational. He won't fly DC 10s—too many accidents. And the first thing he does when getting on any plane is to check if there are any famous people aboard. Only when he spots one does he begin to relax. His reasoning is that it would take up too much front-page space in newspapers if a famous person died in a crash, so someone up there (God? The Press Lords?) won't allow it to happen.

Really fat is James Cagney, Jay said, and terribly conservative. He wanted to walk out of *Hair*. The Academy Award Ceremonies would take place this year without Jay watching. She just couldn't bear the thought that Bob Fosse might win something for *All That Jazz*. Working with him on *Cabaret* was a nightmare: "That man really hates women." Everyone agreed that *Just Tell Me What You Want* was a good film. It bombed, Jay believes, because audiences didn't like the main actors.

Eleven million dollars down the drain, but the three films Jay now had in production—particularly *Prince of the City*—would more than make up for this.

The Class Struggle story, of course, was still some way off. First we needed to get a script from Roger, who smiled bashfully on hearing his name mentioned. I learned that Mark reviewed Roger's book *The Big Fix* back in 1970 for Rodney Sokol's *University Review*. Small, small world. And that it was Mark who recommended Roger to Jay. Everyone seemed to like my idea of using pictures of old board games for the credits at the start of the movie. That was the extent of our discussion of Class Struggle.

Mark made it a point to tell me, when we walked together under my umbrella after lunch, that he no longer had the politics of his SDS days. His first priority now was to make money for Warner Brothers, but if he could promote a progressive film like the Class Struggle story and still make money, then why not? I went away from our meeting thinking that apart from Jane Fonda, Mark, Jay, and Roger were probably as good a threesome as Class Struggle, Inc., could hope to find in Hollywood, but somehow this thought was not as comforting as it should have been.

The contract with Avalon Hill had left Class Struggle, Inc., and its agent, Simon and Schuster, in charge of selling foreign rights. Freed from the day-to-day overseeing of the business, I could devote more time to corresponding with foreign companies that had expressed an interest in the game. Simon and Schuster, whom we were paying a 25 percent commission to do just this, did not do anything, it seemed, that I didn't specifically instruct them to do. They even neglected to bring the game to the American Booksellers Association convention in Atlanta this year because I forgot to remind them.

The liveliest lead for several months now had been with Michael Bertram, a long time *apparatchik* of the German Social Democratic Party, for a German edition. Michael was intrigued with the potential of the game as an educational and propaganda aid in the internal struggle going on within the SPD over the viability of Marxism. Marx had been one of the founders of the SPD, but recent leaders have substituted class collaboration for class struggle and exchanged his goal of human liberation for a comfortable serfdom together with a chance to help administer it. There remains a healthy quarter of the party, however, generally younger, more idealistic (realistic?) types, who hunger after redder meat.

In early spring 1980, Michael and his partner, Martin Suskind—a journalist and former speechwriter for Willy Brandt—made us an offer to bring Class Struggle out in German, which included an advance of $22,500. I had done all the negotiating. For their 25 percent, Simon and Schuster had only to draw up the contract, an activity that took them about four months, including two false starts and interminable delays. Michael originally hoped to have the game ready for the German elections that were held in September, but this proved impossible. By late summer, the delay over the contract began to threaten our agreement and the receipt of the money that waited upon its signing.

Nothing in the world of business takes place as it is supposed to. Once again my stomach marched up to my throat, and this time it remained there for the entire summer. Only absolute disasters, like earthquakes, seem to happen decisively. Everything else drags out, dissipates, spills over drop by little drop, while its victims busy themselves gathering napkins to wipe it up. Let no one talk to me about the efficiency of big business. If government bureaucrats worked at this pace, there would be a capitalist revolution.

The contract was finally ready, delivered, and, on September 2, signed. To sustain Michael's interest over the long, hot summer, I had offered to come to the Frankfurt International Book Fair on October 8 to help publicize the German edition. But I made it clear that I couldn't come until we received the $22,500 advance. Now it was Michael's turn to delay. Was it too late to produce the game this year? Had he changed his mind? To have enough time to organize my trip, we needed to receive the money at once. Two trans-Atlantic telephone calls later, on October 1, the check finally arrived.

In our entire time in business, Class struggle, Inc., has never received a check for more than $1,000—whether from a bank, a store customer, Simon and Schuster, Avalon Hill, or a foreign licensee—that hasn't arrived weeks and usually months late. No one pays when they are supposed to, when they say they are going to, no one except such green businessmen as we were when we started. With Class Struggle, Inc.'s share of the $22,500, we were able to pay back the last of our loans, including the money Howard had borrowed on our behalf. People who heard of our German contract were convinced that we had struck it rich. The truth is that there was $75,000 of initial investment, mostly Howard's money, that still had to be returned.

I arrived in Frankfurt on Friday, October 9, at 11 A.M., and despite a sleepless night went directly to the Fair. The International Book Fair: 20 acres of books and posters promising the ultimate pleasure/adventure/debauchery/even wisdom, if one could only understand all the languages in which they are written; 2,500 publishers huddling together at their little tables, while many of the people depicted in their 8,500 new books wander by, occasionally peering in to see what all the fuss is about.

Class Struggle, or *Klassenkampf* as it was now called, took up practically half of the booth of the *Vorwarts* newspaper, the official organ of the German Social Democratic Party. (Michael's connections in Germany's ruling party were already producing results.) Before I could park my suitcase, Michael thrust at me the articles that Germany's two largest magazines, *Der Spiegel* and *Der Stern*, had just published on the game. *Der Spiegel*, Germany's equivalent of *Time*, featured *Klassenkampf* in its story on the Frankfurt Fair. "Book publishers must be furious," Michael chuckled.

With his easy smile, flushed face, and twinkling Santa Claus eyes, Michael is the kind of man who hugs and kisses all the women he meets both coming and going. I learned later from his friends that for the last year he had talked of nothing but Class Struggle. Watching Michael's enjoyment in explaining the game to people at a party, laughing over a Chance Card and proudly displaying his news clippings, I could see what I must have looked and sounded like at the start of my own adventure. The realization was both amusing and more than a little frightening. Everything had an edge of sell.

On the first day, my main contribution to promotion was to hand Helmut Kohl, chairman of the Christian Democratic Party (and now Chancellor of Germany), a copy of *Klassenkampf* as he passed in front of our booth: "a gift from the workers of the world." Press photographers had been primed to stand by. The next day, papers all over Germany featured pictures of a surprised Helmut Kohl holding a copy of *Klassenkampf*, with the caption, "Kohl plays Class Struggle."

Sitting in the *Vorwarts* booth during a pause in the action, I could not help thinking that this was the party that passed the infamous *Berufsverbot*, a law directed against disloyal subjects that makes it virtually impossible for someone with my ideas to teach at a German university, or haul garbage for that matter; no "reds" can work for the state. Everyone I talked to here told me he was against the law, but also that it was not as bad as it seemed, and, of course, that the Christian Democrats would have done worse. When I told them what the *Berufsverbot* had done to the reputation of the SPD in other countries, they quickly agreed, and changed the subject.

The situation reminded me of my ineffective attempt to protest Negri's arrest in Italy the year before. My heart and politics were with the handful of people who carried signs at the Fair protesting the law, while I continued to sit in the booth of the newspaper of the party that made the law. Again, hard choices. Do I work with existing channels or join in the effort to expose them? In fact, I try as best I can to do both. To sacrifice either would leave me with a means that leads nowhere, or an end that can never be reached. Easy to say. Hard and terribly painful to attempt.

Most of my free time was spent wandering among the maze

of books. I visited Margaret Bernay, Simon and Schuster's director of foreign rights, at her booth, and found the game peering out at me from a bottom shelf. At least it was here. Margaret gave me the calling card of a "publisher" who had asked about Class Struggle. She hadn't paid enough attention to notice that the card came from a small bookstore in Norway. Nothing. Nor could she recall what other publishers had expressed an interest in the game earlier, so that I might visit their booths while I was in Frankfurt. Low key? Margaret practically vanishes. She doesn't believe in Class Struggle as a game, as a political event, or as a commodity. To her, we are like a poor relative adrift in a large, drafty castle, who should be thankful that we were taken in out of the cold.

"Couldn't you take her out, John?" Howard had once asked our resident good looker, John Mason, out of desperation. "That's how it's done in business." But he dropped the idea once Mason laid out what kind of expenses this would involve.

To us, it was now clear that Simon and Schuster was nothing but an expensive albatross that the smooth-talking Rodney Sokol had hung around our neck. The only "big business clout" (Sokol's favorite phrase) we had seen from Simon and Schuster was the clout they used on us in getting 25 percent of everything we earn on foreign rights. The deal generated a few news stories, and then, apart from the Grijalbo contract, nothing.

It was two years since Grijalbo had agreed to do a Spanish edition of Class Struggle, 15 months since they canceled out, and a year since they revived the project and sent us $15,000 as an advance. Since then, we heard only of postponements. I decided to visit the Grijalbo booth at the Fair to find out their latest plans. With a face that seemed to stretch all the way down to his shoes, old Grijalbo's son-in-law and general manager greeted me with the news that they had decided once again to pull out of our contract, this time for good.

After much study, he said, they concluded that distribution would be an insurmountable problem. "We are a publisher, not a game producer"—he had used the same words the year before in Barcelona. I could see then that Old Man Grijalbo consid-

ered the game an important political event, but I never detected the same interest in the people around him. And over time,
they poured enough acid on his enthusiasm to eat away the
foundations of our agreement.

When Grijalbo canceled their contract last year, it was as if
the earth itself had opened up underneath me. With Finn suing
us for his money, Class Struggle, Inc., was in a desperate state
at the time. Because of our contracts with Avalon Hill and
Warner Brothers, and now with a German edition, we were in
a much stronger position. Looking outward from the eye of the
storm, I felt strangely calm and distant form the whole affair.
Knowing that we had their $15,000 no doubt also helped. How
Grijalbo's son-in-law, I thought, must have fought against
sending us that money! He interrupted my reverie just then to
say that they didn't expect us to return the advance now, but if
we made another Spanish contract they would like us to pay
some of it back. "That's only fair, no?" he asked.

"What about all the money we lost in the two years you
made us wait?" I replied. There was no answer. Before leaving,
I could not refrain from adding, "But my main disappointment
is not to be published by the same house that puts out Rius's
Marxist comic books." Looking at me as if I were crazy, son-in-
law assured me that Rius's work is not typical of the books
published by Grijalbo.

Back in the aisles of the Book Fair, I was surprised to find
that my head was clear and my stomach resting comfortably in
its abdominal cavity. My disappointment was real enough, but
balanced, nuanced, viewed in a global perspective. I was neither overwhelmed nor dominated by this new turn of events.
Checking my senses carefully one by one, I determined that I
was in full control of all my faculties. Once again, I was something more than my job, my function. Gregor had receded.
Something had unlocked the future, and all of a sudden it
seemed as if everything was possible. In losing the Spanish
contract, I had recovered myself. *Olé!* Thank you, Grijalbo! I
wanted to fly home at once and tell Paule the good news. At
last, her Marxist prayers answered! But the fair had two more

days to run, and—who knows?—I might find another publisher for the Spanish edition. Embodiments of capital, as I was to learn, do not disembody so quickly.

TWENTY:
IS IT TIME TO BURY KARL MARX?

Hollywood

Roger had promised to send me a copy of the script as soon as he finished it. A first draft was ready by the end of October, but before letting me see it, he said, he wanted to show it to Jay "to settle a couple of points." When I reminded him that I might have some useful suggestions to make, he quickly agreed, and said he would be sending me a copy very soon. Meanwhile, he urged me to keep sending him chapters of this book as I completed them. Not having heard anything further from him by Christmas, I called to see what had happened.

Jay, he said, had the script, so why didn't I get a copy from her. "She's in New York and "—I think I heard Roger correctly—"besides, I don't have any mailing facilities in my house." Obviously, Roger was in no hurry to show me his script. His reticence hit me like a punch in the stomach, but it was too late to sound an alarm, the horses having left the barn a long time ago. Roger added that a few Hollywood people who read the script liked it a lot, but some found it too "soft," by which he understood too "political."

After leaving three or four messages with her secretary, I was finally able to contact Jay. Of course, she was delighted to hear from me, but she would just as soon not show me the script until everything was settled. Then she leveled with me: "Everyone who has a movie made about them complains that that's not the way it really happened ... You'll probably hit the ceiling." I responded, and tried to show by example, that I was the most reasonable of men. In fact, I was now quite scared and angry, and trying my best to hide both. Jay finally relented and said that after preparing a list of needed changes, she would send me a copy of the script. What did she think of it? "Quite good," she said, "but it needs some work. As it stands, it is not terribly clear why anyone should want to make a film out of it. The hero's relationship with one of the women also needs to be made more exciting."

Two weeks passed, with me trying desperately to make sense out of all these conflicting messages, and on January 16, 1981, Roger Simon's script, *Class Struggle*, was hand-delivered to my office.

Class Struggle told the story of Marcel Gabrilov (!), a Marxist professor of politics at NYU, who invents a board game called Class Struggle, and together with some friends goes into business to produce and market it. Why? Because it was there, the game and the system, and one had to let people know you were alive.

Meanwhile, hovering in the background is an evil dean who has just turned Marcel down for tenure, and Marcel seems a little paranoid for thinking that politics had anything to do with it. The business goes gangbusters from the start—capitalists all have a great sense of humor. Everybody loves the game, especially the games buyer at Bloomingdale's, who also falls in love with Marcel. Dropping his on-again, off-again NYU faculty girlfriend, Marcel returns the favor, and the real class struggle in the movie gets underway between working-class Marcel and uppity Miss Bloomingdale's. Marcel makes a load of money, and begins to enjoy the good life.

The fly in the ointment is played by the Brentano strikers who ask Marcel not to sell Class Struggle to their store. Propelled solely by motives of friendship—his friend has all his money invested in the business—Marcel himself drives a truckload of games across the picket line. Bad conscience. Tears. Girl takes off—she can understand the class betrayal but not the tears. When all appears lost, the offer from Warner Brothers arrives to save the business and provide Marcel with a new girlfriend.

The film is a soft-core romance. Marcel's politics are mush. He is also a sexist. His friends are all idiots. The language is full of clichés. The humor is unfunny farce. Need I go on? Well, Millstein had referred to me as the "property," and now I knew,

knew in spades, what that felt like.

There was a need to remain reasonable, but I felt wildly unreasonable, outraged, betrayed, and not only by the dubious politics of the script, but also by its staggering mediocrity. Here I thought I was dealing with giants, only to stub my toe on a couple of midgets. Receipt of the script set off a tumultuous debate among Class Struggle insiders, except for Paul and Jo Ann, who considered Roger's masterpiece to be so much beneath contempt as to be unworthy of further comment.

As much as Howard wanted a movie, any movie, in order to sell games, he practically cried when he read the script: "Our whole adventure reduced to a cockamamie love story between a nutty Russian professor and the chief games buyer at Bloomingdale's."

"Boring, dull, reworking of old ideas," was Ed's judgment. "Americans don't need to be told that socialists are really suckers for money and the good life, and that they love humanity in general but can't cope with persons who are close to them."

Izzy and Milt objected strenuously to the 101 uninviting, reactionary, racist, and sexist innuendoes. "Except for all the allusions to Russia," Milt pointed out, "Archie Bunker would be very much at home with this guy Marcel."

Paule, who has contributed immeasurably to the stability of our marriage by foregoing all her chances to say "I told you so," noted that Roger had depoliticized the film by systematically removing all traces of our real opposition, the capitalists. Gone are the banks, the manufacturers, the Chamber of Commerce,, the big distributors, and the big storeowners. It is as if he sought to portray a duel by focusing on only one of the participants. What's left looks arbitrary and ridiculous.

All agreed that missing entirely is the dimension of our trying to use the market against capitalism, and being used and formed by it in turn. "What can I do to popularize socialism?" got transformed into "How many games can I sell?," which—under the gun of the market—soon became "How do I avoid bankruptcy?," which finally settled into "Will I lose my soul?" In personal terms, this meant a gradual metamorphosis from socialist to salesman to beggar to insect (albeit, one with an enhanced appreciation for what all businessmen suffer) to whatever happy (?) ending still awaited me. Business works on the human psyche like slash-and-burn agriculture, leaving behind a wasteland of frayed nerves, automatic smiles, and cost-effective answers—yes, even on socialists. This is the heart of our story, and the stuff of real satire. In its place, Simon offered up Cold War prejudices, pop psychology, and formula frolic.

Why was the script so bad, so wrong? Was it Roger or Hollywood, or a combination of the two? We had all been impressed by Roger. He had shown us that he could do better, and had convinced everybody that he wished to be fair to what we were doing and to what we believed. Was it Roger who deceived us and, if so, for what purpose? Just to get our cooperation? Or was it Jay or Mark Rosenberg, responding to the commercial requirements of Hollywood, who pressured him to write the retrograde farce that everyone had said they didn't want? The funny, politically progressive, mass-market film that we had envisioned seemed further away than ever.

If Hollywood wasn't yet ready for Class Struggle, was Class Struggle ready for Hollywood? Did we still want them to do the movie? The question was, as they say, "academic," since our contract with Warner Brothers gave them the right to make any movie they wished. As Jay had said so many months ago, it all came down to whether I trusted them to do a good job. And based on their earlier films and on our discussions, I had trusted them, Jay and Louis. So I signed the contract, and consulted to the best of my ability on the story. Having read Roger's trashy script, we could no longer look forward with any enthusiasm or pride to the film. But, perhaps, all was not lost.

A film that, taken on its own, has frayed or even poor politics may provide particular viewers with something they need to become radicalized. Could even a bad film, but one that made the concept of "class struggle" available for Americans to think with, work in this way? If so, the Class Struggle movie might do radical work even though it does not tell a radical story or adopt a radical outlook on the story it tells. And, of course, even a bad Class Struggle movie would sell a lot of our socialist games.

Were all such arguments simply rationalizations that we gave ourselves to justify an increasingly untenable situation? Paule thought so. I am less sure. In any case, having pawned our other options, we had to convince Jay that the script needed major revisions. Roger, we decided to write off completely.

What I recalled of our last conversation—where the need for a more exciting romantic connection was the only specific criticism Jay made of the script—was not encouraging. I knew that she had no interest in making a film that was absolutely true to life or "politically correct," so the approach would have to be one that emphasized the ways the product fell short as art and entertainment. If Jay went ahead and produced Roger's script in more or less its present form, I could always disassociate myself from the film and level a broadside at those who made it. Trying hard not to lose sight of any of these conflicting considerations, on January 31 I wrote Jay a long letter laying out my objections to Roger's script along with suggestions on how to improve it.

Given my view of the script, I hesitated showing it to people outside the board, but I did send a copy to my parents, who had been asking about it for several months, along with my summary judgment and a warning not to draw any conclusions about me or what really happened from this fictionalized account. Only a few days later, my dad, quite agitated, called to tell me that I should be ashamed of myself for behaving the way I do in the movie. When I reminded him that it was all made up, he replied, "Okay, but do you really have to swear so much? I sent you to college to become a gentleman, and here you go using every dirty word in the book. I never knew you talked like that."

"Dad," I assured him, "I don't talk like that. The writer put those words in my mouth."

"Okay, if you say so," my dad went on, "but I was very disappointed to learn how you run around with other women.

Does Paule know about that?"

"But Dad," I said, "in the movie, my wife has been dead for 10 years. You know that Paule is alive. This is not a true story. Please, repeat after me—Bertell did not write the movie. It is almost completely made up." He repeated the words. I thanked him, and was about to hang up, when he added, "You really should have told me, Bertell, about Billy—I mean Raoul—dropping out of school like that."

Here was something I had not counted on. Were people, even people who knew me well, going to treat the movie as giving them a glimpse into my secret and inner life? It was a chilling thought. I had better hurry up and finish these True Confessions.

Maryland

In the spring of 1981, events in my academic-freedom suit against the University of Maryland were rapidly moving to a head, leaving me little time to worry about Jay's tardiness in responding to my critique of the movie script. And on May 18, more than three years after I had been offered the position of chairman of the Department of Government and Politics at Maryland, the case finally arrived in U.S. District Court in Baltimore, Judge Alexander Harvey III presiding.

What we set out to show, in brief, was that the reasons University of Maryland president John Toll gave for rejecting my appointment were not the real ones, that—despite their denials—the defendants were disturbed by the fact that I am a Marxist, that considerable political pressure was exerted on former President Wilson Elkins, President Toll, and the Board of Regents to reject me, that Toll and Elkins consistently tried to minimize and even deny this pressure, and that neither Toll nor Elkins was indifferent to it.

The case began on a sour note with Judge Harvey declining to examine all evidence relating to Toll's appointment of chairmen and full professors after July 20, 1978, the date he rejected my appointment, on the grounds that whatever Toll did after the case began was irrelevant. David Bonderman, my lawyer, had argued that we needed to examine Toll's later decisions to see if he really raised his standards on the qualifications of candidates and on the procedures followed (as he maintained), or whether his extraordinarily high academic standards and ideal procedures were meant to apply only to Professor Ollman.

Dr. Robert Gluckstern, chancellor of the College Park Campus of the University of Maryland, who together with Provost Murray Polakoff had recommended my appointment to President Elkins, was the first witness. He reiterated his opinion, first expressed in the spring of 1978, that I would make a "very good, an excellent chairman."

Immediately after news of the appointment of a Marxist chairman hit the press, Gluckstern testified, he got a call from Governor Blair Lee, who said he had received many complaints and wanted to know what was going on: "Doctors, lawyers, merchants reacting unfavorably ... Senator Bishop irate" read Gluckstern's notes on the call, the first call he had ever received from the governor. In the period from late April to May 1978, Gluckstern also received "expressions of concern" on this subject from several state legislators.

Gluckstern sent the Ollman docket with his recommendation to President Elkins for his final approval on April 20. On May 1, Gluckstern met with Elkins to discuss the matter. Gluckstern testified he had never seen Elkins so angry. Elkins said Gluckstern "should have anticipated the public reaction" (from notes of Gluckstern). There were long silences during which the two men stared at the ceiling and at the floor. Elkins said that the Ollman appointment had stirred up more opposition than any other event in his 24 years as president and that he might have to take the whole matter to the Board of Regents.

Gluckstern also testified that Dr. Herbert Brown, then chairman of the Board of Regents, and Dr. Louis Kaplan, former chairman of the Board of Regents, both sought him out and urged that he withdraw his recommendation of my appointment. Dr. Kaplan stated that persisting in this matter was not in the best interests of the university nor—he made clear—in

Gluckstern's best interests.

Delegate John Hargraves, who had been chairman of the Appropriations Committee of the Maryland House of Representatives in 1978, was one of several state politicians who testified at the trial. He admitted telling both President Toll and University of Maryland Vice-President for Legislative Affairs Frank Benz of his "deep concern" over the Ollman appointment, a concern that he was loath to define until pressed to do so by my attorney: "No, it had nothing to do with Ollman's administrative experience ... I just don't think Marxism has a place in this country."

On May 25, claiming the case was still too broad, Judge Harvey disallowed all evidence relating to Toll's decisions on chairmen appointments during his 13 years as president of SUNY-Stony Brook, before coming to Maryland. My lawyers objected, asking if we could not point to the standards Toll used after he rejected me or to the standards he used before he rejected me, by what standards could one judge his claims that he treated Ollman no differently than any other candidate for a chairmanship? The objection was overruled.

On June 2, after three years of waiting, I finally learned what President John Toll found wanting in my qualifications. Though he was somewhat concerned with my tolerance as a teacher, Toll said he was unable to come to any conclusion on this matter. Toll admitted that he had made no effort to check out my tolerance with anyone at NYU, where I had taught for 11 years, because—as he put it—he did not know anyone there and had no confidence in their discretion.

On scholarship, Toll said he was also concerned with my "declining productivity" after publishing *Alienation: Marx's Conception of Man in Capitalist Society* in 1971. This was particularly evident, Toll said, when he compared my scholarly output with that of Professor Robert Holt, the other finalist for the Maryland job. When shown that Holt had published far less than I did in the 1970s, Toll expressed great surprise. In any case, Toll insisted scholarship was a minor factor in arriving at his decision.

What, then, were his main reasons for rejecting me? What were the chief qualifications that I lacked? Toll said one main reason for denying me the appointment was that I lacked "administrative experience and good administrative judgment," particularly the latter. Two instances were referred to in support of this conclusion: 1) my efforts in the spring of 1970 to secure the removal of Dr. Ivan Bennett, then dean of the Medical School and vice-president for medical affairs at NYU, for his continuing involvement in chemical-biological warfare research for the Department of Defense; and 2) my supposed participation, also in 1970, in a student occupation of the Courant Institute of Mathematics at NYU.

Toll admitted that his entire knowledge of the Bennett affair came from two documents: a letter from Dr. David Robinson, then vice-president at NYU, who defended my role as not exceeding normal academic bounds for disagreements of this kind, and my own account of what happened. These were the same two documents that had convinced Provost Polakoff and Chancellor Gluckstern that there was nothing disreputable about my conduct. Here, too, Toll made no effort to contact anyone at NYU, not even Dr. Bennett, who, he said, was an old friend of his.

On the Courant Institute matter, Toll admitted that he relied wholly on a letter sent to a professor at Maryland by NYU mathematician Peter Lax, in which I am referred to as "a ringleader of the takeover." Again, Toll made no effort to verify this charge. If he had, he would have learned—as did Provost Polakoff—that all the NYU administrators from that period believe it to be false.

Toll insisted that he was not concerned with the political aspects of the Bennett and Courant affairs, but for what they showed about my "poor administrative judgment." How one got from anti-Vietnam War activities, real and alleged, to "administrative judgment" was never clarified.

Besides my lack of "administrative experience and poor administrative judgment," the other major reason Toll gave for rejecting me was that I had no experience procuring large grants of money, with the implication (false) that department chairmen are responsible for the grants obtained by members of their department.

Did Toll know about all the state legislators who called or wrote in with their veiled threats on the Ollman appointment? Only vaguely, he said. In fact, he was so uninterested that he wasn't sure who among them opposed me and who supported me! When confronted with his own vice-president's testimony that he discussed these communications with a very interested President Toll as they came in, Toll professed not to remember; nor could he recall that he asked his secretary to keep a special file on letters and phone messages from politicians.

On June 8, former University of Maryland President Wilson Elkins took the stand. He testified that he talked with the governor at least once and to four or five state legislators on the Ollman appointment, and that he received letters and phone messages on this subject from about a dozen other politicians. In this group were all the key figures involved in determining the university's budget.

In April and May, Elkins noted, the governor dealt with the Ollman appointment in three different press conferences, the first two times to warn against possible financial repercussions to the university, and the third time—which occurred just after the two men had met—to assure Elkins that the decision was his and that the politicians would not interfere.

Elkins denied a comment attributed to him in the April 24, 1978, issue of the *Diamondback*, the University of Maryland student paper, that the possibility that some legislators disapproved of my appointment would have to be a factor in his decision. (It was three days later, on April 27, that Elkins began receiving legal counsel from the State Attorney General's Office.)

Despite the barrage of opposition to the appointment— from politicians, from half of the Regents, from a dozen conservative columnists, and from the general public (340 hostile letters were received)—Elkins testified that he did not know of anyone who criticized me on political grounds, "with one possible exception."

In his closing summation, Bonderman stated that from 1970 to 1978, seventy-one people were recommended to President Elkins for chairman or director of a department at the University of Maryland and all were approved (two with minor qualifications). Ollman's was the first recommendation to be rejected. If all 71 people whose appointments were approved were white, Bonderman said, and the first recommended candidate to be rejected—though he possessed the same general qualifications as the others—were black, no one would have any difficulty understanding the reason for his rejection. Given the public uproar about Ollman's Marxism and the extraordinary political pressure brought to bear on presidents Elkins and Toll, Bonderman said, there should be even less difficulty in understanding why Ollman was the first recommended candidate for a chairmanship at the University of Maryland to be rejected.

In his summation for the defense, Assistant Attorney General Paul Strain restated Toll's reasons for rejecting me, and then said that the case really rested on the credibility of the three main witnesses—Ollman, Elkins, and Toll. Whom could we believe? To help Judge Harvey answer this question, Strain concluded with a moving eulogy of Presidents Elkin and Toll. as dedicated educators, visionaries, and builders of a great university.

Overall, the trial went pretty much as we expected, though I became increasingly troubled by the numerous rulings, over 30 in all, that went against our side. Izzy tried to console me by pointing out that judges often lean one way to give themselves more freedom to make a decision that goes the other way. It makes them look less biased and reduces the likelihood of a successful appeal, he said. On the other hand, if all these rulings simply revealed a bias ... We didn't have long to wait to find out the answer. On July 27, Judge Harvey rendered his decision.

"For this Court to find in favor of the plaintiff, it would have to reject large portions of the testimony given under oath in open court by President Toll, by President Elkins, and by Vice-President Horbake [their closest adviser in the Ollman matter]. This the Court will not do." I lost!!! They won. But why?

Harvey explains: "This Court in viewing and hearing these three witnesses and in considering their many years of experience in the field of higher education, found each of the witnesses to be impressive in a distinctly different way. Dr. Toll impressed the Court as a man of great integrity ... Dr. Elkin had served this very large state university for 24 years before his retirement on June 30, 1978. He had been a Rhodes Scholar at Oxford, had presided over tremendous growth of the university since 1954, and was hardly the sort of man who would give sham reasons for acting as he did. Dr. Horbake had been academic vice-president for 18 years ... his calm and judicious demeanor in answering questions on both direct and cross examination was hardly that of a dissembling witness."

The judge was saying that he simply could not conceive that these men, really *such* men, men holding such positions, could lie. Then why had I begun a suit in the first place? What was the sense of spending a month in court addressing a judge who now told us he was deaf? Obviously, Judge Harvey had never heard of Watergate, or Brutus for that matter. Nor had he seen the Italian movie *Investigation of a Citizen Above Suspicion*, where the chief of police turns out to be the murderer. Taking one's cue from the *Social Directory* is a much easier way to decide cases than weighing the evidence, but it has little to do with most people's idea of justice. None of the misstatements, contradictions, nonsequiturs, lapses, and new incriminating evidence that we had brought out at the trial found their way into Judge Harvey's lengthy account of events, which was taken entirely from the testimony of the defendants.

A more sinister interpretation of the decision is suggested by glancing at Judge Harvey's own social background. The Harveys are one of the two richest families in Baltimore. One brother is chairman of the Maryland National Bank and serves as chairman of the Board of Trustees at Johns Hopkins University. Another brother is head of the largest brokerage firm in Baltimore. Judge Harvey himself was a contemporary of Toll's at Yale in 1944, though—as he jokingly remarked at the trial—the two did not know each other then.

What was I doing in allowing such a ruling-class type to sit in judgment over me anyway? Hadn't I read the square on the Class Struggle board that says "Capitalists control the courts"? Why didn't I opt for a jury trial, a choice one has in civil suits? One reason is that my lawyers convinced me that Harvey was a "maverick," that the typical Maryland jury would be very hostile to a Marxist and too favorably disposed to presidents of the state university (a poll had shown President Elkins the most popular man in the state), and that a jury trial would take much longer. My lawyers were wrong.

On another level, however, I had gambled on the contradiction within the ruling class between their need for legitimation (getting people to believe the rules are fair and apply to everybody) and their need for effective repression (keeping critics away from the microphone) being resolved in this case in favor of the former. By denying me the chairmanship that had been awarded me by my academic peers, Judge Harvey has made it more difficult for the University of Maryland (and, through extension in the public mind, for other universities) to function as *neutral* instructors and *scientific* evaluators of the social values and ideas required by capitalist society. The product has been tainted. This is a high price to pay, and I considered Harvey too smart in the way of ruling-class politics to accept to pay it.

I, too, was wrong. In retrospect, it is clear that whatever boost the legitimation function of the university might have received from an Ollman victory had to be balanced against the delegitimating effects of declaring two university presidents and a Board of Regents guilty of conspiracy and lying. Hence, Harvey's insistence that people in such positions don't lie. If I had won, the university might have added a highly placed critic to its faculty without scoring any appreciable gains on the legitimation scale. A poor bargain.

But the court, whose reputation for delivering equal justice for all also helps legitimate our capitalist system, would have come out of the affair smelling of roses. With Harvey's decision, on the other hand, the court takes its place alongside the University of Maryland in the docket, as a declared opponent of academic freedom, tolerance, honesty, and elementary fairness. As Judge Harvey may yet learn, this is an even higher price to pay than learning how to live with Professor Ollman.

Rome

"Is it time"—as William Buckley asks (*New York Daily News*, Dec. 12, 1980)—"to bury Karl Marx?" It really all depends on the position one takes on Cacus. Cacus was a Roman mythological figure who stole oxen by dragging them backward into his cave so that their footprints made it appear they had gone out from there. After quoting Luther's account of this story, Marx exclaims, "An excellent picture, it fits the capitalist in general, who pretends that what he has taken from others and brought back to his den emanates from him, and by causing it to go backward, he gives it the semblance of having come from his den."

From my perspective as principal owner of Class Struggle, Inc., everything seemed to revolve around me: buying, selling, hiring, promoting, the works. Nothing and no one in our business seemed to move until I said "go." It was easy to see how businessmen get the impression that they are gods and creators of the economic universe, providing jobs and products as well as ideas, and that anything they manage to retain for themselves as profits is their just and well-earned reward. Complaints could only be sour grapes or based on ignorance. Most people in our society accept this view, because it seems to accord with the evidence, with the "footprints" in the sand, with what is there for everyone to see.

But, as in the case of Cacus, this does not tell the whole story. To find out what really happened to the oxen, we would have to go back to the night before (do a little history) and poke our heads into the cave (examine the larger context). The full truth, when we discover it, is the exact opposite of the apparent truth. In the case of the capitalists, only by investigating how most businessmen have obtained their wealth from the surplus labor of previous generations of workers, and how the laws and customs of our society are biased in their favor, can we see that it is not the capitalists who are serving society (and, hence, deserving of a reward) but the rest of society that is serving them. The businessman's power to make important decisions is not denied—the "footprints" are there—but, by placing the exercise of this power within its social and historical contexts, what it all means gets turned around. In their different ways, all of Marx's theories perform this common work. So long as capitalism hides its real relations behind its appearances, its underlying processes behind its surface events, its basic structures behind its temporary forms, class struggle behind class collaboration, and its potential for an egalitarian democratic order behind the present inegalitarian one—so long will Marxism be needed to uncover the true situation.

And the capitalists and those Marx called their "ideological handmaidens," who protest that teaching Marxism constitutes "indoctrination," who would purge Marxist themes from Hollywood, who deny Marxists elementary justice in the courts, and who insist that "it's time to bury Karl Marx" ...? Well, Cacus, too, had an interest in keeping people from finding out what went on in his cave.

241

APPENDICES

I
LAST ROUNDUP

On August 27, 1981, I began an appeal in my case against the University of Maryland. Unfortunately, total bias on the part of the judge is not accepted as a legal ground for appeal. Fortunately, Judge Harvey made several bad judicial rulings, which even a conservative Court of Appeals and Supreme Court cannot completely ignore. My lawyers continue to work for free, but my bill for "incidentals" (postage stamps, telephone calls, deposition fees, etc.) has now reached $73,000. The Court has also decreed that I must pay $25,000 of the costs incurred by the University of Maryland (no doubt to discourage other frivolous discrimination suits).

Aside from working on this book and helping to organize the First Radical Humor Festival, my main "leisure" activity during the academic year 1981-82 has been sending letters, placing ads, and organizing benefits to raise money to fight the Maryland case. So far, we have netted $7,000, all of which went to pay for typing up the month-long trial proceedings in order to begin the process of appeal. Justice was always expensive; injustice came cheap. Now, you have to be rich to afford either. My libel suit against Evans and Novak, where Izzy is serving as my lawyer *gratis*, is likewise mired deep in the appeals process.

Jay Allen never responded to my letter on Roger's script, or to the reminder I sent her six weeks later. In July 1981, two years after I signed the movie contract, Warner's let their option for the Class Struggle story lapse. Cold feet? Cold hearts? Commercial pressures? I shall probably never know. (Psst, buddy. Want to buy a hot movie?)

Avalon Hill recently sold 500 copies of Class Struggle to the Defense Department for distribution to PX stores on U.S. bases around the world. In the words of the brigadier general who is in charge of ordering, "We like to buy Avalon Hill war games because they help build fighting spirit in our boys."

Avalon Hill also brought out a slightly revised fourth edition of Class Struggle (more strategy options) in their attractive bookcase format. AVAILABLE AT GOOD GAME STORES EVERYWHERE. And a computerized version of the game is due out shortly, also from Avalon Hill. In the new edition, minor classes are able to win on their own, not just in alliance with capitalists or workers. Will this compromise with reality in the interests of better gaming result in the same kind of deradicalization that befell Elizabeth Magie's the Landlord Game (later Monopoly)? A disturbing thought. But to carry the game to more players, the gamble had to be taken.

A contract for a French version of Class Struggle fell through at the last minute when—according to the president of the company that had undertaken to produce it—high leaders of the French Communist Party indicated their opposition to the game on the grounds that it is too radical. After a satirical article on this in *Le Nouvel Observateur*, the company changed its mind—"can't waste such good publicity"—and we now have a French contract.

In December, 1982, the numbers look like this: We have sold 85,000 units of the American version of Class Struggle, close to 80,000 of the Italian, and almost 15,000 of the German edition. Class Struggle, Inc.'s financial condition has eased to the point where we have only $19,000 to go to get us back to where we started four years ago. I have not earned a cent on the game. And we have been left holding the bag (empty) on over $30,000 worth of bad debts. Among the customers who have not paid us anything at all is "Do Something for Jesus."

With the help of special breathing exercises, I can now pass Brentano's without looking in the window to see how well the game is selling. And Raoul has stopped calling his father "Gregor."

Last word: The *International Herald Tribune* of March 9, 1983, reported that workers who have staged a six-week long sit-in at the elegant Café Biffi in Milan, Italy, "bide their time playing a board game called 'Class Struggle.' For the bartenders, waitresses, cooks, and stockroom attendants, it is more than a game." From such small beginnings ...

II
WHERE ARE THEY NOW?

Howard has just finished a self-help book on successful scheming called *Zen and the New York City Subway Rider*.

Milt has created a board game called the Acting Bug, and is trying to find a company to produce it.

Izzy is working on the definitive history of libel and writing satirical Op-Ed columns for *The New York Times*.

Ed continues to labor over the foundations of economic theory and is writing a socialist science-fiction novel.

Paul used his unemployment benefits to complete a novel based on his early life (pre-Class Struggle) experiences, and has returned to college teaching.

Jo Ann has started a daycare center to train future revolutionaries.

Paule, when not working on her doctoral thesis in French literature, can be seen dancing on the rooftops in celebration of the fact that her husband is no longer a businessman.

Her husband, Bertell, is no longer a businessman.

III
PROFESSOR'S EPILOGUE:
IN PRAISE OF SMALL BUSINESS II

Monopoly is a business; business is a game; and the game is class struggle played with loaded dice. No take-backs. We are the pieces as well as the players, and our life is the board on which the game is played. To this extent, my experience in business confirmed what I had already put into my game.

Unfortunately, the Class Struggle game, which focuses on the conflict between the two main classes in capitalist society, workers and capitalists, offers little insight into the special situation of small business—except to point out that it is a minor class unable to act alone, and that it can ally with either major class. The "Natural Alliance Rule," which doubles the assets of Small Business when it is allied to the Capitalists and the Professional Class at the same time, makes it appear that the greater advantage lies in tying its fate and fortune to that of the Capitalists. Certainly this is what most small businessmen believe and how they act, particularly in the United States.

The story of Class Struggle, Inc., as it emerges from this book, argues for another strategy. From our experience, it is clear that most of the oppressive conditions in which small businesspeople labor are determined by their relations with large suppliers, large distributors, large banks, large landlords, large competitors, and, occasionally, large customers. The vise in which small business finds itself is operated by—and for— big business.

In face of the capitalists, small business is somewhat in the position of a dinner guest who is shown to the table but given only crumbs to eat, and then unceremoniously shown the door, only to be invited back the next day for a replay of the same scene. So pleased are small businesspeople to be invited to the boss's home, artfully disguised as a Chamber of Commerce, that they are generally willing to suffer the inevitable frustrations and all the indignities that go along with it. Despite appearances, however, it is not small business that needs big business for its survival, but just the opposite. If the guests in our analogy stopped turning up for dinner, there would be nothing to put on the table. Yet the real nature of capitalism's dependence on small business has been hidden from the general public by a disinformation campaign of monumental proportions.

For example, among the facts one can learn about small business by opening up almost any economics textbook are the following:

You can borrow all you want at the going rate of interest. If markets are reasonably competitive, you can sell all you can make at the going price.

You can always sell more by cutting the price, never by raising it.

It is reasonable to assume that all buyers and sellers in a market are well informed.

Making a sale is the same thing as getting paid for it.

The net effect of all of the above is to give a sense that small businesspeople largely control their own destiny, that the competitive game they are playing is more or less fair, and therefore that they have a good chance of winning (being successful).

The experience of Class Struggle, Inc., has shown every one of these "facts" to be either wrong or in need of major qualification:

Promotion and especially distribution costs were an enormous drain on our resources.

We could not borrow what we needed no matter what we were willing to pay.

In a reasonably competitive market, we could not sell what we produced at any price, chiefly because of distribution bottlenecks beyond our control.

Cutting our price would have done no good; raising it—if this allowed a larger cut for various middlemen—might have helped.

Store buyers only know the price of the things they sell (and sometimes their weight and color), while most consumers are ignorant beyond belief.

And there is a world of difference between selling something and getting paid for it.

What emerges from the above is that the market is even more lopsided and small businesspeople have even less influence over their destiny than is generally believed, and consequently, that their chances for survival, let alone success, are very small indeed. When Jerry Rubin, the ex-Yippie leader, became a banker recently, he gave us his main purpose—to help small businesspeople: "Let's make capitalism work for everyone," he said. But that's just the point: It can't be done. At every turn, Class Struggle, Inc., was reminded of the inequality of power in the marketplace, and forced by our weaker position to do less and pay more. It's called "free enterprise": The enterprises with power are free to use it as they wish against those without power—consumers, workers, and small businesspeople alike.

Capitalism's way of solving problems is to pass them on to the next person, who—if he has the economic muscle—passes them on again until they arrive at those who are too weak to do anything but live with them. Or die from them. Squeezed on all sides by a variety of big neighbors, this is the lot of small business. The class struggle of small business, therefore, is first and foremost a struggle against big business, and only secondarily against the workers, who are its employees. Occasionally, this becomes evident to small businesspeople themselves when—as happened recently in Youngstown, Ohio—a large corporation closes its factory and delivers death notices to an entire community.

The mythology in which small business is swathed carries over to explanations for why businesses fail. According to a Dun and Bradstreet survey of "experts," most failures are due to "lack of business-management knowledge," and a whole new industry has gotten started to supply it—at a cost (still another cost to small business). But this is like saying that people on the *Titanic* drowned because they couldn't swim. The boat sank—remember? Likewise, with nine out of 10 small businesses failing within 10 years of getting started (U.S. government statistics) the odds of succeeding are very small even in good times. And right now things couldn't be worse, with small businesses going bankrupt at a faster rate than any time since the Great Depression of the '30s. No doubt being a good manager contributes to the success of those few who make it, but so do gross overwork, willingness to lie and exploit others (including one's spouse and kids), and simple good luck.

In the case of Class Struggle, Inc., we certainly made some managerial mistakes, the most serious of these being to order more games than we needed for our first Christmas. Our case is unusual, however, since we were always sales maximizers—trying to get our socialist game into as many hands as possible—rather than profit maximizers. Being caught short of games when people wanted them struck us as an unpardonable political sin, which—it seemed—we could only avoid by taking a big commercial gamble. We did, and lost. Still, most of the economic problems from which we suffered were not the result of confusing politics with commerce, but arose out of our situation as a small business in capitalist society.

From the statistics on business failure, it also appears that "life in business" occupies but a small part of the lives of most of the people who go into business. Rather than a *step up* to big business, small business usually functions as a *revolving door* back into the working class from which most failed entrepreneurs have started out. Choosing the right metaphor here is everything. Not only are most small businesspeople former workers, they are also future workers. For most of the people involved, small business functions as a transition class, taking them from where they started back to where they started, usually worse off than when they began. No other class can make this boast. Small businesspeople should ally themselves with the workers, then, because this is the way to put maximum pressure on their capitalist opponents today; and this is the way to secure maximum benefits for themselves, as workers, tomorrow.

Could capitalism survive the defection of small business to the side of the working class? Clearly not. At the same time that big capitalists are plowing under an ever-greater number of small businesses through heavy-handed competition and mergers, their need for their junior namesakes has never been greater. Politically, small businesspeople provide the shock troops for capitalism. They do the brunt of the fighting (organizing, propagandizing, voting), while the big capitalists, the corporate 500, like any general staff in time of war, stay safely out of the line of fire.

Ideologically, small business (more than the existence of "free land" in the nineteenth century, and the relatively easy access to higher education today) puts flesh on the idea of equality of opportunity, the core rationalization on which democratic capitalism stands or falls. It is only because people believe that they really have a chance to become rich, respected, and influential that they can view their present setbacks as temporary. No wonder most American workers cannot admit that they belong to the working class, that they have settled there for good. The guilt and despair with which most people respond to what they take to be a personal failure to "make it" would translate into rational anger and radical politics if they recognized the full range of disadvantages with which they have been forced to compete, if they realized that the game is not Monopoly but Class Struggle. Consequently, capitalism repeats the same lie in a thousand ways, lauds the "entrepreneurial spirit" without cessation, and pulls one unlikely small-business success story after another out of its media hat to show not only that it can be done but that "you" can do it. The message, the echo, and occasionally the title of the article itself (as in the case of *The New York Times*, December 6, 1981) is— "In Praise of Small Business."

What equality of opportunity actually amounts to today emerges more clearly—and truly—from the story of the young reporter who asked a leading capitalist how he made his fortune: "It was really quite simple," the capitalist answered. "I bought an apple for 5 cents, spent the evening polishing it, and sold it the next day for 10 cents. With this I bought two apples, spent the evening polishing them, and sold them for 20 cents.

And so it went until I amassed $1.60. It was at this point that my wife's father died and left us a million dollars."

Capitalism lives on a lie and a secret. The lie, most imaginatively expressed in the game Monopoly, is that everyone has an equal opportunity to become a capitalist. The secret is that there is another way, a different set of rules for organizing society. Like all truly great secrets, this one lies hidden in a dungeon guarded by a dragon. That dragon's name is "Red Scare." The secret is socialism. Class Struggle, anyone?

"These really are good times, but only a few know it."
—HENRY FORD 1931

EPILOGUE 2002

WHY "BALLBUSTER?""?

"Do you want to die ugly?". This was the arresting question posed by a leaflet I was handed in Washington Square Park, just blocks from my NYU office, early last year. It was Plastic Surgery Week (how could I have forgotten?), and I had just been singled out for a free consultation. No, I don't want to die ugly, but I didn't see what a face-lift could do, since the ugliness from which I suffer is all around me in society. The task is to make the world a more beautiful place in which to live and to enjoy life for everyone, and I have done (and will continue to do) all that I can to help. "Plastic surgery—no, Socialism—yes", you might say, is my motto.

Inspired by this motto, in 1978, I started a business to produce and market my board game, Class Struggle, and, in 1983, I recounted my "adventures" (sic, sick?) as a Marxist game inventor and businessman in *Class Struggle is the Name of the Game: True Confessions of a Marxist Businessman*. The book also told the story of my academic freedom controversy with the University of Maryland and the two law suits, which were still in the courts, that it occasioned. What has happened since?

THE GAME: Avalon Hill continued to produce the game until 1993, when it was taken over by Mattel, one of the giants in the industry. In 1985, Avalon Hill even came up with a computer version of CLASS STRUGGLE, which had little razmataz and no advertising, and bombed badly. Mattel could have taken up the baton—the game was still selling a few hundred a year—but decided not to (why sully, I suppose, their family-friendly reputation?), and not to answer any of my letters or calls asking them for information. People still contact me wanting to know where they can get the game, but basically it has been unavailable since 1993, though every now and then a copy shows up on e-bay.

The final figures for the game are these: over the fifteen

years of its existence, Class Struggle sold around 230,000 copies in five language editions—roughly, 95,000 in English, 95,000 in Italian, 20,000 in German, 10,000 in French and 10,000 in Spanish. That's pretty good for a game and excellent for a radical book, in this case one that is read by turning over Chance Cards rather than pages (it really was a "book in a box"), especially if one considers that every game was played by several people. There can't be many radical works that were read by over a million mostly young people.

THE BUSINESS: whenever I tell people that we sold about 230,000 games, the usual response is that we must have made a mint. As anyone who has read the previous pages knows, we didn't. In fact, over the whole period, we lost about $15,000, most of that being Howard's money. (So please, please comrades, stop asking me for large donations to your worthy causes—I never got rich.) How Class Struggle, Inc. could sell so many games and still lose money is, of course, one of the sadder stories told in this book. No, "Do Something for Jesus" and fifty plus radical book stores around the world and ... have still not paid us for the games they "bought".

Class Struggle, Inc., which began its life in 1978 and spent most of its existence on the verge of bankruptcy, disappeared for good in 1983, without ever having made it onto the Stock Exchange or into the black for that matter. And I lost one of the titles I wore with the greatest of pride, President of Class Struggle, Inc. The members of the Class Struggle board are all still alive and kicking, somewhere (and, I hope, someone), though our interaction has dwindled to next to nothing. It's been over ten years, for example, since I've seen Howard, though we've talked a few times over the phone. The strains brought about by our time in business have yet to dissipate. (I miss you, Howard.)

THE MOVIE: "The Class Struggle Story" remains the best movie Warner Brothers never made, and Paule still has to elbow me in movie theaters to interrupt my hissing whenever the Warner logo comes onto the screen. Given the disastrous script that Roger Simon wrote, I am delighted, of course, that the project was halted. But, given what they could have come up with had they stuck closer to the facts, I admit to feeling even now a gnawing disappointment in the outcome. In 1986, an English producer started out to do a documentary of the Class Struggle story for English T.V., but that too came to nothing.

ACADEMIC FREEDOM LAW SUIT: when the first edition of this book came out, my two court cases, one against the University of Maryland for firing me from an academic post for political reasons and the other against the newspaper columnists, Evans and Novack, for libel, were still pending. Having lost the former in District Court for what seemed to me (and my lawyers) absurd reasons (see chapter 20), I thought the appeal stood a decent chance of succeeding. But in ignoring all the evidence we brought forward and relying solely on his subjective judgement as to who was telling the truth (the principal defendants denied having any political motive in rejecting me for the job), Judge Alexander Harvey III knew exactly what he was doing. It didn't matter that his reason for believing them rather than me and the host of witnesses I had assembled came out of our respective standing in the Social Register. What counted is that he had made a judgement based on what he thought of us and not on the facts of the case (which allowed the facts to be dismissed or distorted in the most bizarre fashion), and higher courts do not like to second guess lower court judges who take this way out. In 1983, both the U.S Court of Appeals and the Supreme Court refused to hear the case.

The fund raising efforts to help pay my legal expenses peaked at $8,000. With a bill from my lawyers for $75,000 (the cost of "incidentals"; they estimated the full cost at $700,000) and a $25,000 fine levied by Judge Harvey (to discourage other "frivolous discrimination suits"), I was on the verge of personal bankruptcy. Not wishing to push me into bankruptcy by insisting that I pay for their *pro bono* help, the firm of Arnold and Porter cancelled my debt to them, with the understanding that if/when I make a million dollars from the Class Struggle game I will pay them what I owe. They really seemed to have more faith in the Soviet and Chinese markets for the game than I ever did. On appeal, the fine levied on me by Judge Harvey was reduced to $15,000, which I was allowed to pay over a period of years.

To conclude: the University of Maryland was put on the American Association of University Professors' (AAUP's) "blacklist" of schools that have infringed on the academic freedom of their faculty, and remained there for over a decade. While strenuously rejecting this charge, President Toll proceeded to freeze the salaries of my supporters in the University's Department of Government for several years, all the while defending his academic freedom to do as he wished to those under his authority. And ever since the controversy with Maryland began, I have never met anyone, either in or out of academia, who knew anything about the case (and the press coverage was extensive), who did not believe that my Marxist politics determined the outcome. So if Presidents Elkins and Toll won in the state court, I seem to have won in the court of public opinion. As a teacher, I'm pleased, of course, to have helped so many people understand how academic freedom really works in America, but I only wish that this lesson had been a little less expensive.

LIBEL SUIT: While the coffin was being nailed shut on my suit against the University of Maryland, in my libel case against Evans and Novack the hammer—at least for the moment—had been put in my hands. Evans and Novack were but "one" of about a dozen columnists who ranted against this "avowed Marxist" at the height of the Maryland controversy. But, where the others merely expressed their opinions, Evans and Novack introduced a number of factual claims that were false. For example, they referred to a "well known liberal professor" (unnamed and possibly non-existent), who is supposed to have said, "Ollman has no reputation as a scholar, only as a political activist". Now, if what one person thinks of another's scholarship is a matter of opinion, a report on what a group of people think of it is not. It is something that can be studied scientifically, even quantified. And a reputational poll taken by political scientists shortly before these events showed that my peers had a very high regard for my scholarship. Thus, a statement that seemed to provide crucial factual information in what was still an undecided dispute was simply false. Given the importance that the academy attaches to scholarly reputation, the intervention of these highly influential conservative columnists could not be ignored. The libel laws are supposed to protect people from such assaults, so I was stunned when, in 1979, the District Court judge saw only opinions in the Evans and Novack column and dismissed my suit.

With Izzy serving as my lawyer, we appealed to the Court of Appeals in Washington, and, in 1983, the three judge panel that heard the case decided *unanimously* in my favor. It felt really good to win one. Could our legal system work—sometimes—even for a Marxist? I was beginning to wonder. At this point, rather than appealing to the Supreme Court, as we expected, Evans and Novack asked the Court of Appeals to rehear the case *en bank* (that is, all twelve judges on the court together). When they agreed—a first for a libel case—the stage was set for several judges who were to become householde names in the next decade to strut their stuff.

In December, 1984, the Court of Appeals overturned the three to nothing vote of their panel by a vote of six to five. The majority opinion was written by Judge Kenneth Starr of Whitewater and Lewinsky fame, who demonstrated his commitment to principle by claiming that context (in my case, the appearance of the offending column on the opinion page of a newspaper) was the decisive factor in determining whether what was said could ever be taken as a fact, as opposed to an opinion. This was widely recognized at the time as greatly expanding the role that context plays in coming to any judicial decision. Yet, only a decade later, Starr was to insist that context (in this case, the desire to save a girl's reputation) was completely irrelevant in determining whether Bill Clinton had lied or not.

But the opinion that shocked and amused me most came from

Judge Robert Bork, the court's leading conservative, who had built an enviable reputation as a legal scholar arguing against judicial activism (judge-made law). Since sticking to the letter of the law in this case, however, meant giving the nod to a dreaded Marxist, Bork had no difficulty finding an exception to his general rule. The result was a new category in libel law that Bork called the "political person" (not "public person", a category already recognized by the law, where someone who is famous has to show intent to harm as well as the falsity of the offending claim). Instead, a "political person" is someone so involved in the politics of his country that "he must accept the banging and jostling of political debate in ways that a private person need not". What Bork seems to be saying is—if you come into the water, you should expect to get wet. So if the notion of "public person" makes it difficult for someone to whom it applies to use the libel law, the notion of "political person" would make it impossible for the person to whom it applies to do so.

When Bork penned these lines, General William Westmoreland and then General Ariel Sharon had big libel cases against U.S. media in our courts. They were not too political (both won their cases). Apparently, I was. Why? Bork gives two reasons: I ran for office in my professional association (the American Political Science Association) and, worse, I invented a political board game called "Class Struggle"—in which, he says, "Players representing workers move a little hammer around the board; those representing capitalists move a little top hat. At the end, players move to a final confrontation—revolution!". How's that for being up to my neck in the politics of my country? All I can surmise is that Bork read the quote from Plato on the grave danger game inventors pose for society (which precedes chapter one of this book), and decided that, whatever the cost to the law, Ollman had to be stopped. Judge Ruth Bader Ginsberg, since promoted to the Supreme Court, did not let her reputation as a "liberal" keep her, at least on this occasion, from agreeing with her famous conservative colleague.

The five judges who took my side in the case seemed to share some of my amazement at the majority's twisted reasoning.

Judge Antony Scalia, also promoted to the Supreme Court a few years later, described the Evans and Novack column as a "classic and cooly crafted libel". Bork's "political person" innovation was dismissed as a "strange notion" and "frightening". For Judge Wald, another who voted with the minority, Bork's was an "astonishing view" and "incomprehensible". For higher court judges, this is strong language. In my trek through the courts, I seemed to be collecting examples of particularly inept thinking, or was Bork just another case of an opponent acting stupid like a fox?

As I mentioned, the vote against me was six to five, but twelve judges heard the case. The missing ballot belonged to Abner Mikvah. According to a friend of his, who is a friend of a friend of mine, he agreed with my position in the case, but then at the last minute decided not to vote, because he feared that he would be accused of getting back at Evans and Novack for a critical column they wrote about him twenty years earlier when he was a Congressman from Illinois. Had Mikvah voted, the result would have been six to six, which would have left standing the three to nothing vote of the panel in my favor. Evans and Novack would have had as little success appealing the case to the Supreme Court as I did subsequently, and I would have been on my way to winning five million dollars (the amount we had asked for) in damages. It would have been nice to pay Izzy for his stellar work in representing me... and Howard. Losing big is easy, especially when one has as much experience of it as I do. Losing by a thread is a fish of another color. My imagination has never stopped churning over this one.

The Evans and Novack case held one further surprise for me, and that was the view expressed by some of our better known civil libertarians, like *New York Times* columnist Anthony Lewis, that the court majority led by Judges Starr and Bork had struck a major blow on behalf of freedom of the press. Rather than seeing my suit as someone with unpopular ideas seeking to obtain an honest, if not fair (that would be too much to ask), presentation of his qualifications for an academic job, it was treated as a misguided attempt to muzzle a free press. Missing completely in this broadside was any notion that the media not only presents news and criticisms but also suppresses both. The formal right to publish what one wishes on any subject is, of course, a great popular victory won after many years of struggle. But it is equally important to recognize that, in our capitalist society, what's called "freedom of the press" is largely a matter of the owners of the press publishing what they wish and keeping those who radically disagree with them from doing likewise. It was my ability to speak freely without losing my job and not Evans and Novack's freedom to lie about me in their column with the intention of depriving me of my job that needed to be defended. The question, after all, was not whether libel laws should exist. A good case, and one I am tempted to support, can be made against them. But they do exist, so the real question is— should they be applied equally to everyone? And the responsibility of every honest intellectual is to seek out where and why they don't.

A few years later, it was Bork's turn to be nominated to the Supreme Court, and the public debate over his qualifications raged on for months. When Bork complained bitterly—and again—that many of the things that were being written about him were untrue, I couldn't forebear writing a letter to the *New York Times* in which I reminded readers of his words in my case. Surely, if an obscure professor was too involved in the politics of his country to do anything about the lies people wrote about him, then surely someone at Bork's level of involvement should also grin and bear it when that happened to him. I don't think that showing Bork up as a hypocrit led the Senate to reject his nomination—there were too many other good reasons—but I must admit that in the absence of legal justice a little poetic justice tastes very sweet.

Finally, my whole experience with the courts raises at least three important questions that merit some attention in this Epilogue: Did I really expect to win? Them to play fair? And what does the outcome show about trying to use the courts (or any other part of the system) against the system? The truth is I thought I had a good chance to win when I started these suits. A typically naive American? I hope not, for the facts in both cases were overwhelmingly in my favor, and in the Maryland suit I had the support of most of the academic community throughout the country and even of a section of the press. I never believed, of course, in the "objectivity" of the courts, but I admit that I did underestimate how inventive a judge could be when his strongest biases were being tested, and, correspondingly, the crucial role of the courts as the last line of defense against any threat (even a minor one like a Marxist department chairman and game inventor) to the system. Caught in a contradiction between the rule of law (necessary if people are to believe our system is fair) and the biased interpretation and application of the laws (necessary if the system is to serve the special interests of the capitalist class), the courts swing uneasily between these two extremes. Still, the number of surprises, where important interests of the capitalists (or of the state, or schools, or media that serve them) are at stake, are very few. Alas, I was not to be one of them.

In such a world, the main job of the radical critic can only be to use this contradiction in the work of the courts to expose the biased rules of our political game for what they are. The temptation—and one to which I have sometimes fallen victim—is to believe we can do more, but we can't, that is in any but the most trivial matters, until enough people recognize their interests in replacing our profit oriented system with one directed toward serving human needs. This doesn't mean that the effort to do more—like taking the University of Maryland and Evans and Novack to court and even trying to sell socialist revolution across the counter in the form of a game—cannot on ocasion contribute to raising just such a consciousness.

THE BOOK: First, the good news, at least for the author, is that this book got excellent reviews (even in the business press), some of which you can read in the blurbs on the back cover of this volume. The heart-breakingly bad news is that the book was almost impossible to find, anywhere.

When Wm. Morrow, then America's sixth biggest publisher,

offered to publish my business autobiograhy, I felt as if I had scored a coup. Morrow had money, clout, distribution—ah, distribution—all the things that Class Struggle, Inc. lacked. After all the distortions in the media, my version of the "Class Struggle" story was finally going to get a hearing. I also considered it a great advantage that most of what Morrow published was pure junk. Sandwiched between books by the Queen of England on horseback riding and Princess Grace on flower arrangements (really), I thought, my "True Confessions" could not fail to get by the thought police and land on the shelves of books stores everywhere.

Well, the chocolate coating provided by the Morrow imprimer turned out to be not quite thick enough to hide the acid thoughts that lay beneath. In 1983, Waldens and Daltons were the two biggest book store chains in America, with outlets in most of our shopping malls. They bought virtually everything that Morrow published, and, between them, accounted for about two thirds of Morrow's sales. Neither chain ordered my book. Since store buyers don't have the time to read the books that they order, I could only conclude that I was given away by the words "class struggle" in the title. Waldens and Daltons brushed aside my irony, and simply decided not to annoy (enlighten?) their largely middle class customers with another commy tract. That left only independents as outlets for my book, since—given the low-brow bent of its list—Morrow's sales representatives didn't even visit university book stores and Amazon.com and its various clones hadn't made their appearance yet. Morrow's reaction was to cancel its modest advertising budget and treat the book, whose official publication date was still a month away and before any of the reviews were in, as already dead in the water.

As calmly as I could, I pulled out the few hairs that were still on my head, and then organized a call-in of outraged customers at Waldens' and Daltons' stores in fifty cities requesting, demanding, pleading for the book. To no avail. Over the next year, as the mostly enthusiastic reviews started arriving (over 27, a goodly number) and people kept calling to complain that they couldn't find the book, I swore that if I ever had a chance to do a second edition there would be another title. If "class struggle" is an amusing name for a game, apparently much of the humor gets lost when it is used as the opening words in the title of a book. And to suggest, as my title did, that "class struggle" is also the name of an actual game only led many of the independent book stores that did order to bury the book in their game section. So when the good folks at Soft Skull Press contacted me to say that they would like to publish a second edition of this book, I was pleased to accept, insisting only that it carry another title. Maybe this time we can get it into places where the people who want it can find it.

This was not the first offer I had to do a second edition. That came from "The Third Force," a neo-fascist political group in England, who were extremely enthusiastic about my "defense of small business"!?!? Maybe I shouldn't have been so surprised, since fascists have always had a sweet tooth for small business (and vice versa). They didn't even mind that I was of Jewish origin. Hadn't they just sponsored a lecture tour of England by an orthodox rabbi from Brooklyn? Very impressed by Israel's treatment of the Palestinians, this time around, they assured me, they weren't going to be anti-semitic. All they asked from me was permission to write a brief Introduction of their own to correct, I expect, some of my socialist excesses. How could they have thought that I might agree? I never saw small business as a solution to anything, for the individual or for society. But just raising this question scared me into dropping everything and re-reading my book. Naw, I couldn't see it. Do you?

BALL BUSTER: Now you know why this second edition has a new title, but why *Ball Buster*? Readers will recall that near the end of the book a printer who had done some work for Class Struggle, Inc. told me that I had acquired a reputation as a ball buster. While his tone suggested that this was more compliment than insult—he only wished he could be so tough—the charge sent me into a tizzy of self-doubt and remorse. A "ball buster" is someone sitting on an upper rung who is pityless, unyielding, single minded, with all the social aplomb of a bulldozer, willing to smash anything (no matter how sensitive) or anyone (no matter how vulnerable) in pursuit of his goal. The term is often applied to the no-nonsense kind of woman who makes the men under her tremble. This has led some to consider it a sexist term. But a man can also "bust" other people's "balls", even women's. It is a person's behavior that counts, not his or her gender. Is this, I sadly thought, what happens to kindly Marxist professors who go into business?

Over the brief life span of Class Struggle, Inc., a variety of literary figures came to mind as representing who I was becoming as I moved through the different chapters of my story: most notably—Faust, Odysseus, Alice (from "Wonderland") and Greggor (from "Metamorphosis"). At the start of each section of this book, I tried to share with readers some of the emotions and fantasies that each succeeding figure triggered in me. But ball buster? This was never part of my self-image. Yet, I had to admit that I had acted tough, business-tough, on a few occasions— Gould, Finn, Brentano strikers, collection agency, Grijalbo (for readers with photographic memories)—when the very life of our enterprise was at stake. I had learned how to negotiate from the hip like other survivors. It's not pretty in the "trenches" (Paul Gullen's term for the world in which we operated), nor calm, nor safe, nor fair. There, showing too much concern for others equates with being a sucker, the harshest condemnation of all among people in business. Unless, of course, such concern burnishes one's reputation (and brings more business) or is tax deductible. Despite the enormous pressures to do so, I never wholly succombed to this business morality, though I can see why some might disagree and interpret my account of life in business as the "birth of a ball buster". Whence, the title.

My best attempt to summarize the story is that we went into business to use the market against the market, a version of feeding a tiger its own tail, and found ourselves being used and formed by the market in turn, for we were sitting on the tiger's back. The outcome as to who or what would eat what or whom first was never certain. Now, twenty years later, I think I can say that the result was a draw. Through the game but also through the book and the movie offer and the over 300 media stories that they occasioned, we helped teach millions of people something about the real class struggle. Capitalism remains standing, but, as much as any critical effort can, we gave it a black eye. Class Struggle, Inc. and its president, on the other hand, were knocked from one end of the ring to the other, but, despite all the bruises, we too were never knocked out. To achieve this draw, we had to play by their rules of the game, and I had to act like a business-man. Still, I struggled mightily not to lose my socialist soul in the role. Did I succeed? I guess you will have to judge. There is a question mark after *Ball Buster* in the title, because I believe that ultimately I did.

Even if I am left off the hook, however there is still a terrible ball buster in my story. It is capital itself with its imperative to maximize profits and the lavish rewards and dire penalities it sets up to insure compliance. Capital busts everyone's balls, the capitalists' included. Now planetary in scale, it is busy busting the balls of mother nature. It is so big and so powerful that most people view it as a natural phenomenon about which nothing can be done. But history demonstrates that different societies have used the surplus wealth available to them in a variety of ways: to serve God, or expand military or political power, or to attain glory or status. It is also possible for a society to use such wealth to satisfy social needs. Only in capitalism, is this surplus directed to self-expansion, to creating a still larger surplus. Only here is what was a means to other ends in every earlier civiliza-tion an end in itself. Only in capitalism is everything and every-one sacrificed so that capital can grow. This may, indeed, be the best short definition of capitalism. All the basic features of cap-italism—including the roles people acquire from their relation to the prevailing means of production, the objective interests that come with these roles, and the drive to serve their interests (and to consider any action that does so "rational" and "efficient")— emerge out of this historically specific dynamic. George W. Bush may have summed it up best when he described himself in his earlier incarnation as a businessman as a "pitbull on the pant-leg of opportunity".

GLOBALIZATION: There are many people who believe that our society has changed so much since Marx wrote (and, maybe, even since the first edition of this book) that any analysis of capitalism based on his theories cannot be very useful. My response is that the beginning of all wisdom about our society lies in recognizing that it has changed a great deal since the time of Marx, but also that it has changed not at all since then. How can this be so? It is so, because capitalism is made up of a number of relatively stable relations and processes that have existed for the whole of the capitalist era, and others—largely but not completely shaped by the former—that evolve over time. Among the first group of conditions we find the separation of control over the means of production from those who work with/in them (with the corresponding need of workers to sell their labor power in order to survive), the self-expanding quality of wealth as capital (with its corresponding imperative for capitalists to maximize their profits, as dealt with above), the commodification of more and more things that people use that were once free (with a corresponding growth in the power of money), and the spread of alienated social relations, especially of competition and mutual indifference, into all walks of life. This is also the dimension of capitalism with which Marx was chiefly concerned.

Within this underlying structure, hemmed in by it but also propelled by it, the many social and institutionl forms that give each capitalist society its concrete character have evolved through a series of stages into something that many people today refer to as "globalization". While there is little dispute over the changes that mark this new period, few recognize it as the most recent stage of capitalism, as the latest set of forms in which capitalism as such is embodied. If globalization is capitalism on a world scale, with fewer political impediments to its growth than in the past, then Marx's analysis of capitalism—as incomplete as it necessarily is—will be as useful as ever. So for those readers who want to know how with all the changes in society I can still be a Marxist, my answer is, that with our worst problems (economic crisis, unemployment and part-time employment, growing inequality, corporate thievery, imperialist wars, ecological destruction and degradation in the quality of life generally) all rooted in the capitalist character of our society despite and often through these changes, how can you *not* be a Marxist? Unless, of course, you have an interest in not doing anything about them.

How does the demise of the Soviet Union affect this conclusion? It doesn't at all, since I never considered the Soviet Union a model of socialism. Therefore, its collapse, whatever one takes to be the reasons for it, offers no evidence for why socialism can't work. Like Marx, I have always viewed socialism as a post-capitalist social formation, one that solves the problems that arise in capitalism making use of means—wealth, technology, educational levels, democratic tradition, organizational structures, corporate planning, work ethic, etc. (all weeded from their ties to profit)—that are largely supplied by capitalism itself. Perhaps the number one lesson of Marx's materialism is that you can't make something out of nothing—you really can't—and both Russia and China had nothing, or very close to that, when their governments set out to build socialism. What was impossible for them is possible for us. Will it happen? As we sink deeper and deeper into the present depression, capitalism's worsening problems and all the unnecessary waste of people and wealth that they bring in their wake will create enormous pressures on us to act. I also take it as a hopeful sign that 45% of high school students in a recent study claimed that the phrase, "from each according to his ability, to each according to his needs", came from the U.S. Constitution. They simply believed that anything that sounded so good had to be part of our founding document. It isn't, but with their help we may yet make it so.

If globalization and the demise of the Soviet Union have left my Marxist views intact, they do require some adjustments in my board game (should some socialist entrepreneur be interested in bringing out a new edition). For the most part, "Class Struggle" was meant to reflect the structural relations between workers and capitalists, or that dimension of the system that has undergone little change, though most of my concrete examples were drawn from the most recent period. Thus, I don't see the need for any important revisions in the rules of the game, but there are a number of new "players" and developments—such as Enron, Davos, free trade and the freer movement of capital across national borders, the spurt in financial speculation of all kinds, deregulation, privatization, the I.M.F. and the World Bank, neo-liberal ideology, the collapse of the Soviet Union and of European social democracy, and the ecological crisis -that cry out for their own Chance Cards and/or squares on the board. Instead of altering the fundamental capitalist nature of our society, however, most of these developments have simply removed the various blinders and disguises that have kept most people from seeing what that nature really is (a nature captured most graphically by the German philosopher Schopenhauer when he described capitalism as "aesthetically a tavern full of drunks, intellectually a madhouse and morally a den of thieves"). Hey, that's not a bad Chance Card.

PROFESSIONAL LIFE: By early 1983, with the business finally behind me, the autobiography written and the legal suits no longer requiring my active involvement, I could return full time to my work as a scholar and teacher. The problems that had always preoccupied me—particularly, dialectical method, ideology, class consciousness, the theory of the state, Marx's vision of communism and pedagogy—continued to do so. They became the subjects of several books: *Left Academy: Marxist Scholarship on American Campuses*, co-edited, vol. I (1983), vol. II (1984), vol. III (1986); *The U.S. Constitution: 200 Years of Anti-Federalist, Abolitionist, Progressive, Muckraking, Feminist and Especially Socialist Criticisms* (where the courts get their's), co-edited (1990); *Dialectical Investigations* (1993); *Market Socialism: the Debate Among Socialists*, co-authored (1998); *How to Take an Exam...and Remake the World* (which is written in the same style as *Ball Buster?*) (2001); and *Dance of the Dialectic: Steps in Marx's Method* (which brings together the best of my theoretical work) (2002).

Besides teaching at NYU, I also lectured widely on these topics in Australia, England, France, Sweden, Russia, New Zealand, Canada, Cuba, Mexico, Japan, India and China. The insights I acquired during my years in business travelled with me, so that in pouring cold water on my audience's temptation to take the "capitalist road"—as I did everywhere—I could draw not only from Marx but from Ollman.

The release from business also left me time to undertake a number of politico-educational initiatives. Among them was my appeal to the Canadian Government to invade the United States "to remove the mad clique who had just taken power in the country, who had many more arms than they needed and whose actions were threatening the peace of the world". Reagan had just used these words in justifying his invasion of little Grenada. The description didn't apply there, but it did here. So if this threatening situation called for foreign intervention, then—it seemed obvious to me—it was our country, and not Grenada, that should be invaded. After a number of Canadian newspapers printed my appeal, some of my compatriots denounced it as an act of treason (and I had one more title to go with my name).

NYU has also benefitted from my practical experience in the world of business. It is there that I learned that the people who work hardest earn the least. When NYU was casting about for ways to deal with a reoccurring financial crunch, I tried to bring this lesson home by suggesting that we should fire some of our highly paid administrators (whose numbers have rapidly prolif- erated throughout the academy), so that those who remain would have to work harder and we could pay them less. This one takes some unravelling, but who said learning is always easy?

So, yes Virginia, there is life after business, even integrity and other opportunities to spread the word and fun—and all without the debilitating anxiety that attaches to the bottom line. What I appreciate most is that there is no longer any need to twist my words and screw up my face to make a sale. I say what I want when I want, and smile only when the urge strikes. The main message, therefore, that I would like those I left behind in business to get from my autobiography is—YOU DON'T HAVE TO DIE UGLY. You would think these words would be enough to cause business-people to flock to the banner of revolution, but I won't hold my breath until it happens.

McCOY AWARD: In September, 2001, the New Political Science section of the American Political Science Association chose me as the first winner of its Charles McCoy Lifetime Achievement Award for Scholarship and Teaching. It's too bad that Messrs Toll, Elkins, Hoover, Harvey, Starr, Bork, Evans and Novack weren't there to hear my acceptance speech, for—with a few changes—it is the inaugural lecture they kept me from delivering at the University of Maryland. But you can hear/read it, because the confessions of a Marxist scholar and teacher provides an ideal conclusion to the Epilogue of this book on the confessions of a Marxist businessman.

SPEECH: "Thank you, Carl Boggs, for your kind introduction. When Jean-Paul Sartre won the Nobel Prize for literature, he turned it down. He didn't approve of where the money came from. The Nobel fortune, as most of you know, had its origins in the production of dynamite. I think Sartre would be proud to accept the McCoy Award, given the sterling progressive credentials of both Charles McCoy, after whom the award is named, and the Caucus for a New Political Science. I know I am, especially when I think of the wonderful socialist scholars and activists that I would have voted for had I been on the nominating committee—Michael Parenti, who is here this evening, Fran Piven and Howard Zinn for starters.

"Except as a Life Achievement Award, it set me thinking about what exactly I had achieved. And here I confess to feeling rather uncomfortable. After all, my main goal as a scholar, teacher and political activist has always been to help abolish capitalism, and, as you may have noticed, it hasn't happened. Not as of 8:00 pm this evening anyway. Still, I have done what I can, and I promise (or threaten) to continue to do so as long as I can.

"On this occasion, I would like to let you in on a little secret. Karl Marx is only one of my main influences. Equally important to me is the early 20th century American humorist, T-Bone Slim. It's Slim who said, 'Whenever you see an injustice, the only polite form of response is—attack'. If I have any religion, this is the whole Ten Commandments. Marx's writings have simply helped me understand where most of this injustice comes from, how best to attack it and what a better world might look like. Did I say 'simply'?

"Which still leaves the question, 'Why political science?'. Why choose political science as the main terrain on which to fight this battle? Here I can do no better than cite the words of the American sociologist and social philosopher, Barrington Moore. According to him, 'To maintain and transmit a value system, human beings are punched, bullied, bribed, made into heroes, encouraged to read newspapers, stood up against a wall and shot, and sometimes even taught sociology'. Or—he could have added—economics, or psychology, or political science. And he also neglected to mention that the most effective of these is teaching sociology and political science.

"But don't think that most of the professors who maintain and transmit capitalist views—not, for the most part, by extolling the virtues of private enterprise but chiefly by taking capitalism for granted and ignoring the big questions—don't think that most of these professors, that is, the majority of our colleagues, are comfortable in this task or even fully aware of what they are doing. They're not, which doesn't make what they do any less pernicious, or our work in combatting them less essential.

"What is it, then, that I (and I hope many of you) do in political science? Well, in his book, *In Praise of Folly*, the Dutch humanist Erasmus tells the story of a man watching a play who, all at once, leaps onto the stage and tears the masks off of the actors to reveal who they really are. With this breach, it is very difficult for the actors to go on as before. Now, if you think of Marx as the man in the story, and the capitalists and their ideological spokespersons as the actors, you can begin to understand both what Marx and Marxists do (or try to do) and why the capitalists and their academic and other allies are not too pleased with him (and us) for doing it.

"Unmasking capitalist serving lies and distortions is not an easy task. Success is uncertain; it is not well paid; and it can be very lonely. Here, I have been unusually lucky in being able to share my life with Paule, my wife, who has inspired me, educated and comforted me, and kept my feet to the revolutionary fire for the last forty-one years. Those who know her (and us) know that I could not have done any of the things you are honoring me for tonight without her. Our son, Raoul, who has designed the covers for my last three books, has also made a unique contribution to his father's modest success. Could Paule and Raoul please stand, so I can publicly declare my immense love and appreciation and thanks for who and what you both are?

"Finally, before departing, I would like to lead all of you in a special Pledge of Allegiance that I prepared just for this occasion. So please raise your right hand and repeat after me:

'I pledge allegiance to the struggle
Of one species, indivisible,
To rid the earth of capitalism
Before it rids the earth of us.'
                              Amen (optional)

"Thanks again Carl... Thank *you* Karl...
"Thanks comrades."

Printed in the United States
By Bookmasters